RELIGIOUS TRAINING

OF

CHILDREN

IN

THE SCHOOL, THE FAMILY,

AND

THE CHURCH.

BY

CATHARINE E. BEECHER,

AUTHOR OF

"COMMON SENSE APPLIED TO RELIGION," "LETTERS TO THE PEOPLE,"
"DOMESTIC ECONOMY," "DOMESTIC RECEIPT-BOOK,"
"PHYSIOLOGY AND CALISTHENICS," ETC.

NEW YORK:
HARPER & BROTHERS, PUBLISHERS,
FRANKLIN SQUARE.
1864.

TO THE

SELF-EDUCATED FARMER,

UNDER WHOSE EYE MOST OF THIS WORK WAS COMPOSED, AND WHOSE COMMON SENSE, COUNSELS, AND CRITICISM HAVE VERIFIED THE CLAIM THAT THE COMMON PEOPLE ARE

"AUTHORIZED INTERPRETERS OF THE BIBLE,"

This Work is Dedicated

BY HIS AFFECTIONATE NIECE.

CONTENTS.

CORRESPONDENCE.

INTRODUCTION.

For nearly forty years the writer has been educating mothers and teachers. More than a thousand of her former pupils, in almost every sect and section of our country, during that period have been rearing families, into many of which she has been received as a confidential friend to learn their difficulties and their failure or success.

As the eldest and only unmarried child of a large family, for long periods she has also witnessed the varied methods pursued with children in different homes of near relatives.

The result is a deep conviction that the *right* training of children is the most difficult of all human pursuits; that success is invariably proportioned to the wisdom and fitness of the methods pursued; that the best modes are to be obtained only by a wide experience, involving many failures, and, as yet, offering no perfect examples; that the records of experience are indispensable to future success; and that educators, like medical men, are bound to make such records for the benefit of the profession.

This little volume, therefore, is offered as one contribution to the department of *religious training.*

THE

RELIGIOUS TRAINING OF CHILDREN

IN

THE FAMILY, THE SCHOOL, AND THE CHURCH.

CHAPTER FIRST.

RELIGIOUS TRAINING—WHAT IT IS.

THE more the human mind is accustomed to reason and discrimination, the more it is perceived that the Creator of all things designed not only the *good* of his creatures, but their *best* good.

The common expression that "God orders all things for *the best*" conveys the only clear idea we can have of his perfect benevolence. When it is said that "the Judge of the whole earth will do *right*," the only intelligible meaning is that God will do that which is for the *best* good of his creatures. To do right, and to do that which is for the best, are expressions which, as the people use and understand them, signify the same thing when applied to God, and equally so when applied to man.

By the light of nature, without any revelation from God, men are led to the conviction that it is His will that all his creatures should do right; that is, that they do what is *best for all concerned.* And the various revelations from God, in different ages, now collected in the Bible, all teach the same great doctrine.

In the widest use of the term, a man is *religious* just so far as his feelings and conduct are conformed to the will or laws of his Creator, as made known either by reason and experience or by revelation.

A child is *trained* to be religious, in this use of the term, just so far as he is educated to obey the laws of God in regard to self, to others, and to his Maker.

No person can certainly know what is for the best in all the affairs of life without both experience and instruction, while these often fail to guide us correctly. But the omniscient Creator has revealed rules for our guidance, first by seers and prophets, and lastly by our Lord Jesus Christ, as recorded in the Bible.

This being so, a child may be trained to be religious, to a certain extent, without any aid from revelation; that is to say, a child may be successfully trained to obey many of the laws of God, as they are discovered by reason and experience alone. But it is only those who understand the Bible aright who are most fully qualified for the proper religious education of the young.

Religious training, then, includes *all* those modes by which children are led to understand and to obey the laws of God for securing the *best* good of all, as they are discovered by reason, by experience, and by the Bible.

The term *religious* is often used in a more limited sense, as relating only to God and his worship, while that part of religion which includes duties to self and to our fellow-beings is called *morals*.

While this limited use of the term is legitimate, none will deny that the more comprehensive sense is equally so. Nor will any maintain that the laws of God in reference to ourselves and our fellow-men are not to be included as a part of the system of true religion.

The connection in which the term religious is employed will always indicate whether it is used in the comprehensive or in the limited sense. In this work it will be used in both.

In what follows will be presented some of the modes employed in the writer's observation by those who have had the best success in training children to obey the laws of God, some contrasted methods, and other connected topics.

CHAPTER SECOND.

FAMILY RELIGIOUS TRAINING—GOOD AND EVIL—RIGHT AND WRONG.

Religious training, as previously defined, embraces *all* modes of influencing a child to obey the laws of God for securing the *best* good of all.

The infant commences life in perfect ignorance and helplessness. It knows nothing of what is good or what is evil. It knows nothing of God or of his laws, of its own wants or of the wants of others. Of course, the infant is unable, in every sense, to obey God until it is taught by the combined agency of God and man.

Its first lesson is to learn *good* and *evil*. This it can only do in the beginning by *experience*. Thus the pleasure of light to the eye and the discomfort of darkness; the enjoyment of warmth and the pain of heat; the contrasts of sweet and bitter to the taste, and of various odors to the smell; the pleasure of motion and the discomfort of confinement—these, and multitudes of other pleasures and pains that enter the mind through the senses, can only be learned by experience.

Next come the social pleasures of companionship, of sympathy, of affection, and the contrasted pains of solitude, neglect, and displeasure from those around.

All these and innumerable other modes of enjoyment and suffering can be learned not at all by instruction, but solely by "tasting the tree of knowledge of good and evil."

After a certain measure of knowledge has been gained by experience, the child is prepared to acquire the knowledge gained by *faith* in the testimony of others as to what things are good or evil. If a child could know nothing of the qualities and nature of things around, and of the consequences of its proceedings, except by its own experience, there would be no end to its dangers and mishaps. The greater portion of all useful knowledge, not only for children, but for adults, rests upon faith in the teachings of others.

The nurse and parent are daily training the child to a *practical faith* in those who have more knowledge than itself. Such and such things must not be touched; such and such must not be eaten; such and such dangerous places must be avoided, and all because some evil will ensue that the child never has experienced, and from which it can be withheld only by force or by faith in the teachings of others. Thus it is that, in regard even to this life, the child, at the very first, is trained to "walk by faith and not by sight."

After gaining the knowledge by experience and

by faith as to what good and evil are, and how they are to be gained and escaped, the next lesson taught is *the law of sacrifice.*

The child soon is led to perceive that much which is good, when taken at the right time and manner, involves evil if taken at the wrong time or place, or if taken to excess. Thus certain kinds of food are given only in very small quantities, when the little one, if left to itself, would make a whole meal of them. In such cases the child is instructed that a given quantity is good, and that more than that is evil, and that *self-denial* must be practiced in these cases, so as to take only as much as is *best.*

Again, it often occurs that two modes of enjoyment are at hand which are incompatible, so that one must be *sacrificed* to gain the other. For example, there are two tempting objects offered, only one of which will be allowed, and a choice must be made, so that the taking of one insures the sacrifice of the other. Here the child is taught that the choice must be made of that which is *best.*

And thus there is a constant training to avoid excess, and to give up the lesser to secure the greater good. This often involves *sacrifices* more or less painful, so that the little one will sometimes weep as it voluntarily relinquishes one kind of pleasure as the only means of securing another which is the *best.*

Still farther, the child is trained to *balance* and

calculate good that involves some evil, so that a given amount of enjoyment cancels or pays for a certain amount of evil. When a great degree of enjoyment is secured by a small amount of trouble, the compound result is called *a good.* If, on the contrary, the evil involved exceeds a given amount in comparison with the good, the compound result is called evil. Thus the lesson is gradually imparted that good and evil are to be regarded in two relations. In the one relation, any thing is called good which gives pleasure of any kind; but if this good can be gained only by sacrificing a greater good or inflicting a great evil, then, in this other relation, the good becomes evil. Thus a delicious fruit, in the first relation, is a good, because it gives enjoyment; but if sickness and suffering will be the result of eating it, it is an evil. This training of infancy introduces the *law of sacrifice* in reference to *self* alone.

But, as the intellect develops, the existence of other beings who suffer and enjoy is learned, and their interests become the subjects for instruction. Here the calculations as to the *balance* of good and evil become more and more complicated, and the two relations in which good and evil are to be judged become more extensive. Whatever gives pleasure to self is still called good in the first relation; but if some great suffering is involved to others, then it is called evil, and the child must make a *sacrifice* for them. At last comes forth that most difficult general law of self-sacrifice, that *the lesser good of self must always be sacrificed for the greater good of others.*

In other words, the child is trained always to choose what is best for self when others are not involved, and, when others are concerned, to choose what is best for all. Thus is established in the mind of the child the grand law of rectitude by which to decide every future act. If it is what is best for all concerned, it is right; if it is not best, it is wrong.

Thus it is seen that, in the first period of family religious training, the child gains the knowledge of good and evil by experience and by faith; and next a knowledge of what is *right* and *wrong* according to the great law of *sacrifice*, demanding the invariable choice of what is *best for all concerned.*

Here it must be noted that good and evil, right and wrong, are often used interchangeably, as meaning the same thing; while they also are used, in other cases, in the two relations indicated in the preceding pages. With these, as with all other words having several meanings, it is the connection which decides the exact sense in each case.

CHAPTER THIRD.

FAMILY RELIGIOUS TRAINING — LAW — THE OBEDIENCE OF FAITH AND HOPE.

It has been seen that in the first period of life the infant is learning what is *good* and what is *evil* chiefly by experience. Next it learns by experience, but more by faith in its teachers, what is *right* and what is *wrong*, as decided by that great law of *sacrifice*, which the infant is gradually trained to understand. This law is first applied to its own enjoyments without reference to others; but, finally, the child is trained to sacrifice the lesser good of self to the greater good of those around.

Our next inquiry is as to the *best* modes of securing obedience to this great law of rectitude, which all created beings must regard through their whole existence.

Here experience is our chief guide. We perceive that the Creator secures obedience to some of his laws by penalties that are both certain and immediate, while in other cases the penalties for violated law are remote and apparently uncertain. For example, the laws which protect the body from destruction are enforced by penalties certain and immediate. In every experiment, the child invariably finds that pain follows when the finger is put in a candle or on a hot stove. As soon as this certainty is discovered, the child obeys the law and keeps its fingers out of the danger. So a few falls teach the law of gravity and its penalties, and prompt obedience is thus secured.

But food that is injurious to health brings a penalty that is remote and uncertain, and so the fear of it has little or no influence in restraining from the indulgence, while this needful fear depends entirely on faith in those who warn from the danger.

In all cases, experience shows that, in both adults and children, the more distant and uncertain are the rewards and penalties of law, both human and divine, the more difficult it is to secure obedience.

The most effective mode of meeting this difficulty in the family is to make the *decided command* of a parent a law enforced by a penalty that is felt to be both certain and immediate. This being secured, obedience to all laws involving the future welfare of the child may be rendered not only prompt, but cheerful and uniform.

All that balancing of mind between hope and fear which induces irritation is thus avoided. A child never cries or frets because it can not play with fire or jump out of a window after it learns the certain penalties of such acts. And when an equally certain penalty follows disobedience to parental command, an equally prompt and cheerful obedience will result.

Nothing so surely saves a child from fretfulness and insubordination as the certainty that willful disobedience will be followed by a penalty such that the forbidden enjoyment will not pay for the certain pain. And the moment a child perceives that sometimes the penalty of disobedience follows and sometimes it does not, he is constantly tempted to try whether he can escape, and is doubly irritated at the uncertain penalty when it does come.

Especially is this so in the case of nervous, irritable, and sickly children, who are necessarily subjected to annoying restraints and medical inflictions. Many such have been ruined in health and temper for want of a strong and steady government, to which they would have learned to yield prompt and cheerful obedience. Such a habit of obedience once formed, the necessity for discipline ceases almost entirely. Nothing then is needed but the decided tone of authority, which the child is sure can not be disobeyed without the certain penalty. It is not the mere apprehension of the penalty that insures the obedience; it is also the blessed aid of *a good habit.*

The most perfect example of this mode of government known to the writer was that of her early life. The little flock in her own nursery no more thought of disobeying their father's decided command than they did of putting their hands in the fire. A decided "No" settled the matter, usually without complaints or repining.

One of the earliest memories of those days was the tearful outbursts of the next born child, of quick and sensitive impulses. "Stop crying, my boy!" and the command was followed by contortions of lip and brow, and heaving chest, till all was quiet. Next came, "Now look pleasant!" and, at the word, out came the smiles like sunshine through clouds. Not only prompt, but cheerful obedience was demanded until it became *a habit.*

But such decided government requires a tender love and sympathy, which in this case was never wanting from either parent. Our father was the constant playmate of his children. He rejoiced with them in all their childish joys, and his ever-ready sympathy consoled their little sorrows. The tones and looks of love were the staple of life to his little ones, while discipline was sometimes administered with tears, more effective even than the rod. Not an hour of life can the writer remember, to this very day, when the full conviction did not exist that, to her father, it was pleasant to gratify and hard to deny any wish of his child.

With this strong government and tender sympathy were combined discretion and care *not to multiply* rules whose violation demanded penalties, thus bringing the young under a kind of bondage depressing to the elasticity of childhood. But few rules for the little ones, and more added only as habit made the preceding easy, was the method pursued. The earliest years of life are now remembered, not as a period of discipline and rules, but rather as a joyous and perpetual play-spell.

In contrast to this strong and steady method, the writer has often seen what may be called the *coaxing mode.* This is adopted by parents who are either too weak to govern, or who fancy they can govern without punishing.

The first evil that results from this is irritation when the child can not be coaxed, and, finally, is forced, by violent methods, to give up his will. There are many things a child desires which it is impossible to secure, and yet no substitute can be found that will satisfy. The contests and irritations thus resulting, in the end cause far more suffering to the child than the short discipline that is needful to establish a firm and strong parental authority.

Another very great evil in this coaxing mode is the eventual loss of faith by the child in those who control. For the almost certain result is that coaxing promises are made, or hope in some way awakened, which ends in a failure. When this is done, the child is irritated, not only with fear of having his desires crossed, but with the memory of past failures of coaxing promises. Parents who govern by this mode are in perpetual parley and barter with their little ones, and in the end make more fretting, anger, and suffering in one day than the whole period of discipline experienced by a child under a strong and steady government.

Still another method is very common among parents who have a strong will, and intend to maintain parental authority by penalties. This may be called *unsteady* or *irregular* government.

Some who govern in this way have a general idea that children must be trained to obey their parents, and so they try to enforce obedience without any method or rule. They give their commands, and sometimes the child is punished for disobedience and sometimes not, and thus is always tempted to disobedience by the hope of escape. This mode is especially injurious to children of decided character and strong will. To such, submission to rule is particularly distasteful, and there is no way to secure *cheerful* obedience but by a strong and a *steady* government. Where this is wanting, there will either be frequent and stout conflicts between parent and child, or the child will avoid them by concealment and duplicity, or by absolute lying.

In repeated instances the writer has seen children, naturally inclined to be honest and truthful, thus injured by unsteadiness in government. Others of nervous temperament have become habitually irritable and ill-tempered by such irregular discipline.

Another, but less frequent evil, is *over-government.* When both parents are united in a strong and steady discipline, there needs to be great care taken not to multiply rules that make frequent liability to disobedience. If young children are obliged by penalties to be careful of their dress, careful of furniture, mindful of table proprieties, and encompassed with many other conventional rules, the result will be, either such frequent violations of authority as involves continual fear of punishment, or a hardening of the conscience and the whole nature.

To avoid this, a great part of the requirements made of children may be in the form of advice or requests, which involve no penalties if disregarded.

In observing the management of children of different families, no one thing has so strongly impressed the writer as the necessity of varying modes of discipline to diversities of character. A mode of treatment adapted to one child would often be almost ruinous to others of diverse temperament. Some children of sensitive natures suffer more from a frown or a reproof than others do from the severest discipline. Some children are born with a sensitive conscience; others seem to have this part of their nature developed only by diligent culture. Some children can be governed by love alone;

others demand the intervention of fear of penalties, and would be ruined without it. This being so, general rules must always be modified to meet peculiarities of natural character. But there are a few general principles gained by experience which will apply to all cases.

One is that, after a habit of prompt obedience is formed, it is always better to govern by hope of reward rather than by fear of punishment. Hope of good cheers, enlivens. Fear, if the predominant motive, is depressing to mind and body. This is the chief reason why the labors of slavery, extorted by fear of the lash, are so listless and so unproductive, while those of the free are so cheerful and so profitable.

This principle is of especial value in the nursery. The hope, at least of commendation for success, should always be dominant in the young; and where extra and protracted efforts are demanded to conquer any defect, the chief stimulus should always be hope of reward.

In view of this, the government of parents and teachers who chiefly notice faults, and rarely express pleasure and approval for good conduct, is very unfortunate.

Another general principle applicable to all cases is that the child should always find *sympathy* and *pity* for shortcomings in those who are training to virtue and piety.

It needs ever to be borne in mind that self-control and self-sacrifice are more difficult to a child than to one whom practice and habit have inured to this discipline. The impulsive nature of childhood revolts from rules and constraint, and these multiplying bonds should be entwined with much tenderness and sympathy. It should often be conceded that many things required *are* hard; that there is a bravery and nobleness in submitting with patience; that it is expected that there will be failures; and that, so long as there is a wish and effort to do right, these failures are causes for tender pity and sympathy. Instead of magnifying the evil done by the child, in order to prevent future repetition, as is often incautiously done, the educator needs often to palliate and excuse, and thus encourage to try again.

"Mamma," said a little boy one day, "I am tired of being good; I don't want to be good any longer." This is the frequent result of an over-stringent and unsympathizing government.

Another very important principle is what is usually called *honor*. This is a combination of self-respect and respect for the opinions of others. It is a powerful principle, and holds sway even over the most debased; so that it is said "there is honor among thieves." It is the last good principle to forsake depraved men.

The power of this good principle is often seen

among young boys, who, while disobedient to parents, truants from school, and vile in language and character, still will often suffer almost martyrdom rather than betray a companion, and thus violate the rule of honor established among their fellows.

While this principle is often abused to evil, it is not employed by Christians in the nursery, or in school and church, so often or so effectually as it often is by persons who attempt no spiritual training. Such will often succeed, by this influence, in making their offspring more honest, truthful, and honorable than many children who have been urged by the most powerful motives of the spiritual world.

The principle of honor is most valuable in cultivating habits of truthfulness, that most noble element of character. A child can not understand the importance of this virtue in early life. A strong and strict discipline tempts timid children to lie in order to escape blame or punishment, and to meet this difficulty some parents describe lying as an awful sin, and punish severely for it. Yet a child can not see the great evil of the deed, but looks rather at the benefits of thus escaping from penalties.

But if all around seem to regard falsehood as mean and cowardly—if it is called brave and noble to speak the truth—if all prevarication and deceit are pointed out as degrading and contemptible, the child is more powerfully influenced to avoid this fault than by any severer methods.

CHAPTER FOURTH.

FAMILY RELIGIOUS TRAINING—THE OBEDIENCE OF LOVE—RATIONAL OBEDIENCE.

In the previous chapters we have seen that the law of sacrifice demands that the lesser good be always sacrificed to the greater. This is the general law of rectitude, including all the laws of God which are to be enforced in the family as well as through future life.

It has also been shown that *hope of good* to self, including hope of escape from evil, is the leading influence to secure obedience to law. This hope of good is guided mainly by *faith* in the teachings of those who control the young.

But, though the first lessons of obedience are enforced by faith and hope, there is another more happifying principle which is better than either, and that is *love.* In Scripture phrase, "Now abideth these three; faith, hope, charity (or love), and the greatest of these is charity."

Love includes as its main feature *the desire to please* the one loved. The easiest and happiest way to induce obedience to law is so to secure a child's love that it will have a strong desire to please the one who controls. Some children feel such love for a parent or teacher that almost any sacrifice is a pleasure if it will *please* the one thus loved.

The relation of the parent to a child is especially fitted to call forth this happifying principle of obedience. Love is always induced toward those who are constantly bestowing good. The infant commences the discipline of life under the mother whose bosom supplies his chief joy. Her tender looks and tones of love are another unfailing source of pleasure. And, as life advances, the ceaseless ministries of parental tenderness call forth the gratitude and love which seeks expression by efforts to please those who have thus awakened affection.

Some parents make this the leading principle in the government of their children. They habitually keep before the mind of the child its obligation to please and obey in return for the love and kindness of their parents. They diligently cultivate a sense of *gratitude* for parental favors which is to be expressed by obedience.

So, also, benevolence and self-sacrifice for the good of others is cultivated. The little ones are taught that they are to do kindnesses to others as others do to them. The child is led to be generous and self-sacrificing, not only by precept and example, but these obligations are enforced by authority. Where the parents have power to control, no child is allowed to act meanly or selfishly toward others any more than he is allowed to injure himself by self-indulgence or excess. The interests of others are constantly presented as matters of care and concern to the child, and as what is due in return for benefits received.

Instead of pursuing such a course as this, how often it may be seen that even the most conscientious parents habitually train their children to be *selfish*, as much so as if they deliberately planned and intended to secure this end. The little one finds himself the chief object of attention; his wants and wishes are the great concern of all around; whatever he desires must, if possible, be secured; servants, brothers, sisters, nurse, father and mother, all bend obsequious to his wishes. He grows into a consciousness of his importance, and learns to feel that it is his right to have precedence of all others, and receives all as his due. Indifference and neglect of the feelings of others is the natural result. To make voluntary sacrifices for the comfort and convenience of others is no part of his training or experience. He is trained to a *habit* of selfishness.

While a child is being trained to the prompt obedience of faith and love, there needs also to be a *rational obedience*, induced by enlightening the mind as to the *reasons* for all the laws and rules enforced. This is especially needful in cases where self-enjoyment must be sacrificed for the greater good of others.

The gradual process by which our Creator introduces this principle of self-sacrifice is very instructive.

The infant's first experience in life is the highest illustration and example of self-sacrifice in the mother's love and care for its useless little self.

Next, a second infant appears, when this example must begin to be imitated. The first-born must give up to another its place in the mother's arms, and must become a secondary instead of the chief object in the nursery. Then it must share its toys and treasures with its baby playmate, and give up its plans and wishes, and help to protect, amuse, and aid the little one. Thus the nursery commences the first lesson of self-sacrifice for others.

Next, the school leads onward to still more difficult lessons; for it is a stranger, and not beloved parents, who controls; and it is strangers, and not brothers and sisters, for whom sacrifices must be made. There new and more extensive rules of self-government, justice, benevolence, and self-sacrifice for the general good are made known and enforced.

After this come the relations of neighborhoods and of civil society, demanding other and more comprehensive laws of self-sacrifice for the common good. Then the claims of a whole nation are to be taken into account; and, lastly, the whole world is to be admitted into the great family of man, and every individual comes under still more comprehensive rules demanding self-sacrifice for the general good.

Thus, as capacities expand and reason is matured, the obligations to sacrifice self for the good of others become more and more numerous, and, unless previous training has inured to it, the duty becomes more and more difficult.

In the first period of infancy the child can not be made to appreciate the reasons for most requirements, and obedience must rest upon faith alone. Some parents protract the obedience of faith indefinitely, and take little pains to enlist the intelligence of the child in support of law. The consequence is, that the reasoning powers and the power of self-government are both undeveloped. The child obeys without reflection or forethought, very much as a machine performs its work.

In the Chinese nation we have an illustration of this mode of training carried through the nursery, the family, the school, and the state, thus dwarfing the whole nation in the noblest features of a rational manhood.

Instead of this, the wise parent, having first secured the prompt obedience of faith, enlightens the child as to the reasons for requirements which its present capacity can comprehend, while for all others the obedience of faith is still enforced.

The child is taught that all self-control of its own appetites and passion results at last in higher enjoyment in the very respects in which self-denial is enjoined. The benefits of a good *habit* are also described, making what is at first a difficult effort easy and pleasant.

So, also, in regard to the self-denial enjoined for others, instead of the bare command, "Help your little sister," or "Share your pleasant things with your playmates," the child may be strengthened by being taught that it is noble and right to do so; that such conduct will secure love and respect; that this is the way to form habits of benevolence and self-sacrifice, which, in the end, make a hard duty a pleasure; that the contrary is base and selfish; that neglecting to do so is mean and despicable, and will tend to form a habit of selfishness which will make it more and more difficult to be generous, just, and noble.

In training a child to be truthful, the parent may simply forbid known falsehood, with a severe penalty for disobedience. But if, at the same time, the evils of deceit and lying are pointed out, and also the benefits to self and to others of a character for truth and honor, the power of motive will be greatly increased, and thus obedience be made more certain and more easy. So of all the virtues to be secured in family training.

In attempting to treat children as reasonable beings, some parents begin too early, and try to reason and persuade as the chief reliance, while authority and penalties are as much as possible relinquished. The usual result of this course is pettishness or uproarious contests whenever the parent fails to convince. The only safe mode is to insure first the prompt obedience of faith, and then teach the reasons for it afterward.

Some parents seem to put themselves on an equality with their children, coaxing and pleading as if dependent on the will of their little ones. This is the direct mode of cultivating an imperious and domineering manner, or a pettish and complaining habit. Where the parents give up habitually, the children often become ill-tempered tyrants. Where the parents retain some authority, there are incessant conflicts, complaints, and struggles, ending in ill humor at all defeats. The writer has seen some of the finest natures ruined by such training as this, and others escaping only by the force of a fine natural organization, or the intervention of others in the family or school who administered more wisely.

CHAPTER FIFTH.

SPIRITUAL RELIGIOUS TRAINING.

THE preceding is the mode of religious training to which the principles of common sense would guide all of every age and nation. It is that for which God has arranged the family state, and toward which his providence guides all men. All this would naturally result from reason and common sense, without any reference to a future state and the invisible world.

A *spiritual religion* is that for which we are dependent not so much on reason and experience as on revelations from God. It rests on faith "in things not seen," and in beings not known to the senses. In Christian nations, all instruction in this department of religious training is based on the revelations from God contained in the Bible.

At what period of life a parent should commence the communication of the existence, presence, and character of God, as the first element of spiritual religion, must vary with the character and development of each child.

In the nursery the child is under the constant care of its parents, and is preparing to know and love its Savior just in proportion as they are his true representatives. Love, patience, meekness, gentleness, sympathy, self-denying labors and cares, united with firm and steady government—these are the traits which a child can be taught to transfer in conception to his heavenly Father only as he has seen them exhibited by his earthly parents.

It is the mother who has the first lesson of spiritual training committed to her hand. If she is so happy as to find in the father of her children one who has exhibited that union of strong government with tender love and sympathy so important in life's dawn, then, when she begins her first lesson of a "Father" in heaven, the very name brings the truest conception possible to a young mind of the God and Savior to whom she would lead her child.

In the past experience of the little one, it has been his earthly father, who most of the time was absent in providing for the wants of his family, who still, when with him, loves him, cherishes him, governs him, pities him, comforts him, and sympathizes in all his pleasures. Such is that heavenly Father who, though unseen, is ever present, and who not only hears and sees all he says and does, but knows his very thoughts.

It is impossible for a child to conceive of a spirit without body. The first idea of a child must inevitably be, that God is a being with a human form, in a place called Heaven, and yet able to know our thoughts, and to see and hear all that is said and done in this world.

This being so, Jesus Christ, as "God manifest in the flesh," and "by whom all things were made," is the one especially adapted to the wants of mother and child in her first attempts to give true ideas of the existence and character of the Creator. At a very early period, Jesus Christ may be made known as he who not only made all creatures, but who made them *to be happy*. Then the lesson can commence that there are right and wrong ways of seeking to be happy, and that once Jesus Christ came into this world to teach his creatures the *true* and *best* ways of happiness—that for this end he not only instructed, but set an example. And that he might teach children, as well as men and women, by his example, he became a little child, and set a perfect example of obedience to his father and mother.

The hard duty of *sacrifice*, not alone to secure the best good for self, but to promote the best good of others, may then be illustrated by the life of our Savior. Thus, to deny self daily, and take up the cross, can be constantly referred to and illustrated by the example of the invisible yet ever-present Savior. He may be presented as the loving and tender Father in heaven, who knows how hard it is to bear the trials of childhood, because he has himself "suffered in all points" as children do. In cases of difficult duties required, the conviction may be cultivated that the kind Savior is the sympathizing witness of every infant effort to do right.

In cases of failure or wrong-doing, instead of magnifying offenses, and chastening the conscience with upbraidings, it may be conceded that for young beginners in self-denial and self-sacrifice the path is thorny and difficult, and that the tender Savior feels pity and sympathy for them, is patient and forgiving, and is pleased with every effort to do right, however many failures there may be. And every gain in self-conquest and good habits may be recognized as a matter of thankfulness, and especially pleasing to the tender and loving Savior.

Thus a child may be gradually and intelligently led to form habits of self-denying benevolence as the chief way to please an ever-present heavenly Father. And a sense of his constant inspection, love, and care may become the most protecting restraint from sin and stimulus to well-doing.

The writer has repeatedly witnessed the happy results of a mode of religious training similar to that here indicated, some of which will be more minutely described.

In one case, her residence in the family was very transient, where the eldest child was a little girl of four or five years of age. She was of feeble constitution, and highly nervous and sensitive organization, with active intellect and strong will. She was thus one who, under wrong training, would speedily have developed much of what is often called "the old Adam," which usually consists in the avoidance of self-denial and rule, or else expressions of irritability and anger at being controlled. She was just the kind of child that indulgence makes imperious, irritable, and self-willed; while a kind but strong and steady government induces uniform and cheerful obedience. In the first visit it was noticed that the little one seemed healthy, cheerful, modest, obedient, and loving.

Instead of the hot-bed training in close parlor, nursery, and school-room, which leads to irritable nerves and the ill government of a feeble child, most of little Anna's time was spent amid the woods, brooks, and fields of her summer haunts, or the sports of winter's snows. No nice dress or ornamented pantalettes to be taken care of; no racing, climbing, or noisy plays were to be shunned. To keep out of dangerous places, and to be kind and obliging to playmates, were about the only rules of out-door life. At meals, when guests were present, they saw her take her simple food without asking for any other; while, instead of absorbing the chief attention of parents, or interrupting the conversation of guests, she listened in quiet, or spoke modestly when addressed.

The chief aim of the parents at this period seemed to be to secure a happy mind in a healthy body, and a prompt obedience to the few rules required.

No attempt was made to expend the small fountain of nervous power in one so delicate by any intellectual efforts save those the Creator ordains for every child as it learns its mother tongue, and studies the properties and philosophy of the world of wonders around.

The next visit was made when this child was apparently seven or eight years of age. At this time the family was in an extensive boarding establishment, and among its inmates I frequently heard expressions of pleasure at the success of the mother in the religious training of this child. Some of them seemed to think that few mature Christians give such good evidence of the humble, obedient, and loving spirit of a true disciple as this little one; still, she was not without faults that required watchful care to repress.

It appeared that the child was not only truthful and conscientious herself, but, in the beautiful charity of rectitude, imagined all children were the same; and when, with tearful surprise, she found her mistakes in this matter, guided by the mother's discretion, she was earnestly pursuing her heavenly yet childish mission of striving to reform those who had been deprived of the blessings she had enjoyed in her early religious training.

It was at this period she heard persons spoken of as Christians, and others as not so, while, at sacramental occasions, the Christians remained and the others left the church. One day, after such an occasion, she said, "Mother, I love Jesus Christ; I try to obey him all day; when I do wrong I am sorry, and pray to him to forgive me and help me to do better. Mother, do you think I am a Christian?"

Having decided that a true Christian is one who habitually strives to obey Christ in all things, the mother felt no hesitation in answering the little one that she was one of the lambs of Christ's flock, such as he, on earth, took in his arms and blessed as heirs of the kingdom of heaven.

She was early taught a common form of infant prayer. One day she said, "Mother, I want to *pray myself*, because when I *say my prayers* it does not seem to me as if I was talking to my dear Savior." The mother encouraged this, and ever after the child was heard to tell all her little wants, and express her love, and gratitude, and happiness in the simple language of infant life.

At a sacramental occasion she once heard the minister give this invitation to the congregation: "All those who love our Lord Jesus Christ, and who intend to obey him in all things, are invited to come to his table."

On hearing this, the child whispered, "Mother, I love the Lord Jesus, and intend to obey him in all things; may I eat of the bread?"

This may serve for the present to illustrate one

of several cases in which Christian life commenced in the nursery with little or no use of any other doctrine of revelation than the character, teachings, and history of Jesus Christ, as "God manifest in the flesh," together with an appropriate use of the influences thus secured.

There is no period in the training of the young where the diverse constitutions of children are so obvious as when spiritual religion first is introduced.

Some have a nature peculiarly adapted to such influences. Others, diversely, but equally well endowed, seem to have little receptivity for such ideas till a mature period of life.

In the same nursery will be found one child who is imaginative, sensitive, reflective, and possessing strong susceptibilities of emotion. Such can be led by the influences of spiritual religion to an early experience, dangerous and almost miraculous. Another child, with vigorous body and strong nerves, seems to have nothing but the animal nature first developed. The same sort of training as makes his delicate little sister a precocious saint, passes over his mind as the idle wind. The outer world fills all his eye and thoughts. Play, and nothing but play, has any attraction or can fasten his attention. He listens with a momentary wonder at pictured realities of a future life, and in a few moments the impression is all gone. And yet a day is coming when conscience, and reason, and the spiritual element will be developed as strongly as is now the animal.

Children are not only differently constituted, but the development of the various faculties varies as greatly; and every parent needs to take this into account in judging of the diverse success of religious culture in their different children. A healthy, robust child, with fine animal developments and a strong will, may be as well developed morally, when he has become perfectly obedient to parental rule, as another child in whom the spiritual element is more largely developed.

The Apostle Paul teaches that "milk is for babes" in reference to the discretion needed in selecting the truths to be used for beginners in Christian life. In the preceding example of successful training, it will be noticed that no reference was made to the invisible world, or to the rewards and penalties of the future state.

The Old Testament training of our race exhibits God's example in this very thing. The patriarchs and Israelites were visited by God and angels in human form. The ritual had a visible Shekinah. Prophets and seers received direct instructions from God; and all that was attempted was to bring this nation to obey the laws of God relating to this life only, while all the sanctions were exclusively temporal rewards and penalties. Though a future state was recognized, no use was made of it as a motive to secure obedience.

The attempt to influence children by fears of hell, of the devil, and of the day of judgment, ordinarily results in false conceptions, that agitate without any compensating healthful results. These are topics which should be reserved for the investigations and influences of more mature life.

The great difficulty in regard to the use of motives of fear in respect to the future state is that they affect most vividly those who least need them, while those who most demand such influences are unaffected by them.

Some children who have a highly sensitive and nervous organization, combined with great conscientiousness and a lively imagination, are greatly excited by such appeals, and, if timid as well as sensitive, are often overwhelmed with terrors. Many times the writer has heard her pupils describe the fear and distress that darkened the whole period of childhood by representations which still are very common both in the family, in children's books, and from the pulpit.

In one case a friend stated that such was the state of her mind thus induced in early life, that she repeatedly had meditated killing an infant brother whom she passionately loved, because she was told that infants escaped all such dangers; and when disease blasted the beautiful flower, the poor child, in spite of her poignant grief, was glad that death had ended for the babe the risks of such dreadful horrors as in her forebodings might be her own doom. And yet this child had far less said to awaken such fears than is often done by parents and teachers.

In the writer's family history this point is well illustrated.

A little book, called "*Hymns for Infant Minds,*" written by the lovely and gentle Jane Taylor, was the nursery favorite both with parents and children.

One of these hymns, which the writer probably always skipped in reading, or contrived to forget after hearing, fastened the most painful and abiding impressions on a younger sister of vivid imagination, strong feelings, and timid nature. She was so affected by this hymn that for years it haunted her in hours of darkness, often banishing sleep, while sometimes, covering her head, she lay sweating with distress and dread. And yet, bashful and sensitive, she never ventured to reveal her sufferings. It read as follows:

How dreadful, Lord, the day will be
  When all the tribes of earth shall rise,
And those who dared to disobey
  Be dragged before thine angry eyes.

The wicked child, that often heard
  His pious parents speak of Thee,
And fled from every serious word,
  Shall not be able then to flee.

No; he shall see them burst the tomb,
  And rise, and leave him trembling there,
To hear his everlasting doom
  With shame, and terror, and despair.

While they appear at Thy right hand,
  With saints and angels round the throne,
He, a poor trembling wretch, shall stand,
  And bear Thy dreadful wrath alone.

No parent then shall bid him pray
  To Him who now the sinner hears,
For Christ himself will turn away,
  And not regard his sighs and tears.

CHAPTER SIXTH.

SCHOOL RELIGIOUS TRAINING.

THE period when a child most needs the motives of the spiritual world is when it passes from the nursery to the school-room. There temptations become more numerous, new and more difficult duties are imposed, while parental inspection and authority cease for a while.

The child must now obey a stranger whom it has not learned to love and trust, and who can show no special interest in one pupil more than in another; one who must stand in the same relation to a child, in enforcing law, as does the Great Teacher and Ruler of all in regard to his creatures.

Its associates are strangers of various ages, tastes,

and tempers, all placed on an equality as to rights and privileges, fitly representing the great world for which the child is to be trained to still more difficult and complicated rules and duties.

Here it is that a sense of the presence and inspection of a heavenly Parent, whom the child regards as the ceaseless observer not only of acts, but of feelings and thoughts—a tender Father whom it has learned to love and to desire to please, may become the most powerful of all influences to stimulate to well-doing and to protect from sin.

It is at the head of a school from diverse families, whose children have experienced diverse modes of training, that a teacher is enabled to retrieve parental neglect or mistakes, and add new power to parental influence. This is especially the case in reference to the employment of the motives of the spiritual world. A large portion of every school comes from families where spiritual religious training is entirely neglected, or where it is administered with great mistakes and deficiencies.

For this reason, the teacher needs to begin with explaining to his flock that the great end of school education is *to train them to a loving and prompt obedience to the laws of God*, as the best and only sure way of being happy.

Our Father in heaven should be described as one who loves little children even more tenderly than any earthly parent can do; who sees what is *best* for them to make them truly happy, both in this life and forever. The Bible should be appealed to as the book in which this loving Parent has given all needful rules for right feeling and action in order to attain the best and highest happiness; and in administering school rules and government, it should often be appealed to as the standard of truth and duty.

Before the rules of punctuality, order, and silence are enforced, the reason and conscience should be enlisted by explaining how the enforcement of such rules promotes the comfort and happiness of all concerned, teachers, children, and parents. It should be shown how *selfish* it is to break over rules which are made for the best comfort and enjoyment of all. It should be shown how those who thus sacrifice the good of the many for the gratification of one, in the end lose more than is gained by this course.

The duty of *self-sacrifice* for the common good should be continually held up as a noble and generous aim, and one in which we are imitating Christ, our great exemplar, who came as our Savior from selfishness and its consequent miseries.

The children may be trained to self-sacrifice not only in cheerful obedience to rules for the common good, but by personal efforts to aid those who are younger, or who are subject to any infirmities. As an illustration of this, the following experience of the writer in a little school which for a few days came under her care, is offered.

One of the pupils was a remarkably fine child both in disposition and intellect; but an accident in early infancy had interrupted her education, so that, while in size she was apparently the eldest, she was, in point of acquirement, the youngest in the school. She was anxious to learn, and very docile to any attempts for her improvement. Nothing was needed but constant and persevering efforts to bring her mind to its appropriate development.

But, unfortunately, her very social and affectionate nature was accompanied with peculiarities somewhat annoying, so that, while she was constantly seeking to join in the groups and sports of the children, they thoughtlessly endeavored to exclude and avoid her.

It was a real trial not only to the young, who had formed no habits of self-sacrificing benevolence, but to her teacher, who felt annoyed by the noisy and impulsive intrusions of the child, and troubled by her desire for society and sympathy.

After some attempts to modify some disagreeable habits, and also some experiments on her capacity, the attempt was made to use religious motives with some of her companions to meet the difficulty. A bright and amiable child was selected, who shall here be named Fannie. After some chat with her on other topics of childish interest, this conversation ensued:

"Fannie, do you think you are a Christian?"

"No, ma'am," was the reply, and an expression of sadness passed over the ingenuous young face.

"Do you wish to be a Christian?"

"Yes, ma'am;" and the tears began to start.

"Do you know what it is to be a Christian?"

"No, ma'am," with a look of uncertainty.

"Does your mother teach you to pray to Jesus Christ?"

"Yes, ma'am."

"And do you pray to him every day?"

"Yes, ma'am."

"And do you say prayers that are taught you, or do you make your own prayers?"

"I make my own prayers."

Both the parents of this child were trained to believe that all children come into this life with such depraved natures that they never feel or do any thing that is truly Christian, and acceptable to God, till he regenerates their ruined nature.

This point was not referred to, from uncertainty as to how far the child had been so instructed.

"Fannie, Jesus Christ came into this world to teach us how to be good and happy, and also to *help* us to become so; and one way in which he helps us is by his own blessed character and example. He was living in his glorious and beautiful home, in heaven, with his Father and the blessed angels; but he gave it all up, and came to this world to teach poor ignorant and sinful creatures the way to be happy. It was not pleasant to live with them. It was painful to toil and suffer for such ungrateful, ignorant, and sinful beings. But he spent thirty-three long years in such wearisome and painful labors. And now his example and teachings are written in the Bible for our guidance, while he watches over us in heaven, and he sees and loves all those who try to follow him. Moreover, he saw how difficult it is to do all that he teaches, and so he promised to send his good Spirit to help all who try to follow his commands.

"Whenever, therefore, you do not like to do any thing which you ought to do, then say to yourself, 'Now I will be like Christ, and *deny myself*, and take up my cross, as he did.' And when you thus are trying to follow him, his good Spirit, in some way not explained to us, will help you. And then you are a follower of Christ, and so are *beginning* a Christian life. And the more you go on trying to be like Christ, the better Christian you are.

"Now, here at school, you have a great opportunity to follow Christ, such as children seldom have. Here is poor Bessie, who by a great misfortune has been kept from school, so that, though she is so large, she is behind all the other children, and she can not be made to catch up with them in knowledge without a great deal more labor and attention than any teacher can give who has so many scholars.

"Then the poor little girl has some disagreeable tricks that make the children shun her, and yet she is affectionate, and social, and wants to be with them all the time, and she feels grieved and mortified to see them run away from her.

"Now every day you can say to yourself, 'I will deny myself for poor Bessie, as Christ did for me and for us all. I will help teach her to read; I will play with her, and try to make her happy; and so I shall please our dear Savior, and he will send his good Spirit to help me.' Dear child, do you now understand how you may become a Christian?"*

"Yes, ma'am;" and the tears glistened amid smiles.

"And will you try to-morrow how much you can do for Bessie, and thus do for your kind Savior? He loves and cares for the poor child even more than your tender mother cares for you, so that every thing you do for her he receives as done for himself."

Tears fell abundantly, and watered the good seed thus sown.

The next day Bessie came to me with a joyous smile. "Please hear me say another lesson; Fannie has been teaching me." In the afternoon she

* See Note A.

came again. "Only see! I have read all these pages to Fannie, and she is going to hear me read some every day."

Fannie came herself to tell of other things she was going to do for Bessie, and seemed elated with her success.

This is a case where the seed was sown on remarkably fine soil, and yet, even in this case, after the novelty and first enthusiasm had ended, the young Christian would falter, just as older ones do, without the constant line upon line of instruction, and the constant personal influence of a religious teacher and friend. The head of a school enjoys the combined advantages of both parent and clergyman; and the school is that great transition period when the child is passing from the limited field of action in which the interests of our family are concerned, to the higher plane where the whole world, and its relations to eternity, are to be included.

In the New Testament this new relation is recognized where the Jewish dispensation (or law) is spoken of as "a schoolmaster to bring us to Christ." The Jewish dispensation was the transition period of the *race* to a higher plane of action, as the school is to the child.

In pursuing this elevated plan, the teacher can habitually assume that the school is a commonwealth, in which each individual has a common interest as much as the teacher.

Some of the most successful teachers, in carrying out this idea, commit a great part of the school responsibilities usually borne by the teacher to the pupils. Thus a committee takes charge of the school-room and premises, to secure neatness and order in every part. Another committee is instructed to devise and enforce modes of securing quiet and punctuality. Still another supervises the recitations and scholarship, and devises methods of improvement. Rewards are offered to the *whole school* for the success of these committees in elevating and improving its general interests, thus engaging every pupil to lend aid.

The writer has seen a very large school in the highest state of order and improvement, where the teacher, by this method, was relieved of almost every care but that of supervising his committees, hearing his classes, and giving general instructions to the whole school. At the same time, the motives of spiritual religion were brought to bear on practical daily life in a way more effective than either parent or clergyman could command, in preparing children for the duties of mature life.

CHAPTER SEVENTH.

CHURCH RELIGIOUS TRAINING — WHAT IS THE CHURCH?

RELIGIOUS training in the family, as has been shown, teaches first what is *good* and *evil*, and next what is *right* and *wrong;* as best or not best for the child itself. Next is taught what is right or *best for the whole* in relation mainly to the family, a small community who love each other, and whose interests are one.

Next is taught what is best for the whole in the school, where strangers are brought together whose opinions and interests are diverse.

Thus far the laws of God, and the motives for enforcing them, may be taught simply with reference to this life; and many parents and teachers have great success in cultivating the social and moral virtues, without any reference to dangers and duties connected with a future life, and without employing any motives of the spiritual world.

In the Old Testament we find a similar mode of training. All the duties required related to this life, and were enforced by temporal rewards and penalties. Although a future state was recognized and the immortality of the soul was believed, no recorded revelations were made of dangers and duties in reference to the eternal state, nor were the Jewish nation required to interest themselves in the temporal or spiritual welfare of any out of the bounds of their own nation.

To believe in Jehovah as the only true God, and to *profess* this belief by the rite of circumcision, were all that was required, even of aliens, to make any person a member of the Jewish congregation, and entitled him to all its privileges. Infants were circumcised, as born into this congregation, to be trained to this faith in Jehovah. The whole congregation, including infants and all circumcised believers in Jehovah, constituted "the Church of God" of the Old Testament.—Acts, vii., 38.

The standards of the Presbyterian Church thus define the *visible Church:*

"The *visible Church* is a society made up of all such as, in all ages and places of the world, do *profess* the true religion, and of *their children.*"

This definition includes both the Jewish and Christian Church. The latter differed from the Jewish in substituting baptism in place of circumcision, and in taking Christ's teachings in place of those of Moses. All persons who *professed faith* in Christ, together with their children, were, according to this definition, members of the visible Church.

Now *faith*, or *belief*, is used by all men in all ages to signify sometimes mere intellectual conviction or belief, and nothing more. At other times it signifies this belief, together with the *feelings* and *conduct* that result appropriately from this belief. The first is called a dead faith, as it does not produce its appropriate fruits. The last is called a living or saving faith.

In regard to the Church of God in the Old Testament, no one ever claimed that the qualification demanded for membership was any thing more than the intellectual belief that Jehovah was the true God, and the *professing* this belief by circumcision.

All adults who were circumcised professed to believe in Jehovah, and thus in their obligations to obey his laws as revealed by Moses. But as there were all degrees of obedience, no attempt was ever made to divide the Jewish congregation into two portions—one, as those having only a dead faith, and the other as those having the living faith. All were together, as one church, to be *trained* by the ministries of that church into obedience to God's laws.

When Jesus Christ came, he first clearly revealed the danger of our race in reference to a future life, and the obligations resulting not only in reference to self and one nation, but in reference to *the whole world*. He taught, for the first time, that the dangers of the future life are so great, that the chief object of this life should be to escape them ourselves, and to aid our fellow-men to escape them.

It was in reference to these new dangers and new duties that Jesus Christ instituted his *Church.*

The greatest perplexity and confusion have arisen from the fact that the expression *the Church of Christ* has been used in diverse senses without such clear definitions as alone can prevent this confusion.

The New Testament speaks of all Christ's obedient followers in all times and places as "Christ's body, the Church." The Episcopal communion-service defines Christ's Church as "the mystical body of the Son, which is the blessed company of all faithful people."

This is also called the *invisible Church.*

Thus it is seen that there are two uses of the word *Church*, viz., the *invisible Church universal*, including all that have a true and living faith in God and Christ, and the *visible Church universal*, including all who *profess* faith in God and Christ, *with their children.* These are both *unorganized.*

But all matters in dispute on this subject relate to the *organized Church* in distinction from one that is unorganized. A congregation or company of people are organized only when they have officers to represent and act for the whole, rules to be enforced, and the power of receiving and excluding members.

The Roman Catholics and some called High-Church in the Episcopal denomination claim that the visible Church universal was *organized* by the apostles, the ministry ordained in direct succession from the apostles being constituted the officers to act for the whole body.

Thus, on this view, all baptized persons all over the world constitute one great *organized* body, of which all ministers, so ordained, are the officers, while each local church is only a *part* of this one great body, and not a distinct organization by itself.

But this is simply a *theory*, to which facts do not correspond; for the Roman Catholic Church, and the Episcopal Church, and the Greek and Armenian Churches, all claim to have their ministry ordained in direct succession from the apostles, and yet no one of them recognizes either of the others as belonging to their body, nor their ministers as officers acting for and representing their own Church. The visible Church universal certainly, at this day, is not *organized* as *one* body by having officers to represent the whole body, and the same rules to be enforced.

There are now but two modes of organizing the Church of Christ, viz., the *local* and the *denominational.*

The *local Church* consists of individuals organized as one body, with officers to act for the whole.

The *denominational Church* consists of a number of local churches united as one body, with officers to act for the whole.

Thus, in various towns, we find a local Episcopal Church and a local Presbyterian Church, each consisting of individuals united as one body, with officers to act for the whole.

Again, we find a denominational Episcopal Church meeting in General Convention, consisting of the clergy and lay delegates representing local churches of that denomination. These are organized as one body by having officers, constitution, and rules.

So the denominational Presbyterian Church, consisting of ministers and delegates of local churches meeting in General Assembly, is organized with officers, constitution, and rules as one body.

The only way to join a denominational Church is to become a member of a local Church of that denomination.

We do not find in the New Testament or in history that any *denominational churches* existed in the first Christian age.

The question then is, What was the *local Church* as *organized* under the apostles of Christ?

The English word *church* came from the Greek, through the Goths, to our Saxon ancestors. It is formed by certain changes from the Greek word **κυριακός,** signifying *belonging to the Lord.*

In the Greek Testament *ecclesia* is the word which in our Bible is translated by the now English word *church.* This word *ecclesia* is used 114 times in the Greek New Testament, and it always signifies *a con-*

gregation or assembly of people, without indicating the kind of persons.

Thus, in Acts, xix., 32, the *ecclesia* or "*assembly*" were heathens; in Acts, vii., 38, the *ecclesia* were Jews; in Philemon, the *ecclesia* is one family; in Romans, i., it is the congregation of Christians in one city; in 2 Thessalonians, i., 1, it is the congregation of Christians in one province; in Acts, ii., 47, it is the congregation of Christians generally, without regard to place; in Colossians, i., 18, it is the great congregation of all saints in all places and all ages, or the *invisible Church universal.*

This being so, the word *ecclesia*, or *church*, in the New Testament signifies simply a congregation of people, and we are to find out by other means than this word alone what *kind* of persons constituted the organized Church of Christ.

All agree that, in order to be an *organized* Church of Christ, there must be officers to act for the whole body, rules to be enforced, and power to admit and to exclude members.

The points of difference are as to what class of persons constitute the Church of Christ, and *how* this Church is organized.

In regard to these points there are these diverse views:

The first is the Roman Catholic view before mentioned, viz.: the organized visible Church of Christ consists of all who have received Christian baptism.

The apostles organized it by instituting a ministry, ordained in direct succession from the apostles, as officers to represent and act for this one indivisible Church in all ages.

The ministry, thus ordained, are authoritatively to interpret Christ's teachings for the laity; baptism admits to this Church, and also confers a partial or an entire remedy of the injury done to the mind of the baptized person by Adam's fall. The clergy also receive, by ordination, the power of communicating the Holy Spirit at confirmation, and of imparting certain spiritual influences in the Eucharist.

On this view, there are no *local* visible churches as distinct organizations, but only *parishes*, in which all the baptized are members of the one *organized* visible Church of Christ on earth.

Now, as there is no way to *unbaptize*, and as most of the scoundrels of Christendom have been baptized, while the debased priests of the Romish, Greek, and Armenian churches, as much as the Episcopal, have been ordained in apostolic succession as officers, this view of the organized visible Church of Christ is a painful one; especially so, inasmuch as it is claimed that it is the clergy of these debased churches who have the right of deciding the true interpretation of the Bible.

As to administering the discipline of this vast Church, including all baptized persons, nothing of the kind is, at the present day, either taught or attempted.

The only Scripture texts used to establish the Roman Catholic view are Matthew, xvi., 18, 19, and Matthew, xviii., 15–21.

The "power of the keys" given to Peter and to "the Church" in these two passages all agree signifies the power of discipline and expulsion from the Church on earth, which Christ here promises to confirm in heaven.

All agree, also, that the Church is to exercise this power by its *officers*. The only question in dispute is this: Are the officers of the Church who are to exercise this power diocesan bishops, ordained by the apostles for this purpose, who transmitted this power only to other diocesan bishops ordained in direct succession from themselves? The Roman Catholic and High-Church affirm it. Others hold that this power of discipline is given to any local Church, to be exercised by officers whom it appoints for the purpose.

The New Testament evidence that there were *local* churches organized with officers, having rules to enforce, and the power of receiving and expelling members, is abundant. The single expression "the *seven* churches of Asia" seems alone sufficient to settle the matter. There are thirty-five different churches named in the New Testament.

As to any *historic* evidence that there was *only*

one organized Church of Christ, Lord Chancellor King, a distinguished writer of the English Episcopal Church, says:

"I find the word *ecclesia* once used by Cyprian for a *collection* of churches, as the *ecclesia* of Numidia *and* Africa, otherwise I can not remember that I ever met with it, in this sense, in any writings of this or the rest of the fathers; but whenever they speak of the Christians in any kingdom or province, they always said—in the plural—the churches; never in the singular."

Passing the Roman Catholic view as a mere unpractical theory unsupported by evidence, we find that, as a matter of fact, there have been only two modes of organizing the *local* Christian Church.

The first is properly called the *primitive Church of Christ*, consisting of any number of Christian people, with their children, statedly meeting as a congregation, having officers to sustain the worship and ordinances of Christ.

The second may properly be termed the *Puritan Church*, as first instituted by the Puritans. It consists of a *portion* of a Christian congregation, who unite by profession and covenant as *regenerated* persons, believing a certain creed, and admitting by majority vote only such as, on examination, give evidence of such regeneration and belief.

This kind of Church has no constitution, creed, or laws, except such as are imposed by a majority vote.

In defense of the Puritan Church, its advocates

bring those passages of the New Testament which show that the first *local* churches of Christ were organized with ministers to preach, and with other officers, also, for temporalities; and that they exercised discipline by casting out unworthy members from their communion. But they do not seem to perceive that these texts do not show that the ecclesia that exercised this discipline was *regenerated persons*, holding a given creed, and organized *within* the ecclesia that met for worship.

What needs to be proved is that each local ecclesia of the New Testament consisted of two *organized* bodies—one, the whole congregation of worshipers, and the other that portion of it which constituted themselves judges of their brethren, to decide when regeneration existed, and how far doctrinal and practical errors should exclude from baptism and the sacrament. This is never attempted.

The defenders of the Puritan Church never have offered even *one* text from the Bible to prove that each local ecclesia, or congregation of stated worshipers, had an inner ecclesia *organized* with officers—the two corresponding to the New England *parish* and *church*—nor do they quote from history in its defense.*

* The writer is justified in this statement by the fact that this work, before printing, was submitted to some of the most learned defenders of the Puritan Church, and neither from them, nor from the Bible, nor from any other book, has there been *any* evidence

In the primitive Church, faith in Jesus Christ is assumed to be complex in nature, involving diverse particulars and many degrees of advancement in each. The first step is a knowledge of Jesus Christ, and the intellectual conviction that he is authoritative Lord of faith and practice; then follows the desire or purpose to obey him; then a seeking to understand his teachings; and then more or less obedience. In this view, the Church is a congregation organized to *train* men, women, and children to faith in Jesus Christ, and thus to prepare them for heaven.

On the Puritan theory of a Church, faith in Christ is the result of a new creating act of God, changing *the nature* of the mind, and the Church is an organized collection of persons who, being regenerate, have already attained the faith that secures heaven.

The Congregationalists and Baptists, in this country, have carried out this theory of the Puritan Church more consistently than any other sects; for, by these, all children are excluded from the Church till Church officers examine and find evidence of a regenerated nature.

The Presbyterians, both Old School and New, are required by their standards to organize only *one* ecclesia, which includes the *whole parish*. It is

obtained to establish the Puritan mode of organizing the local Church of Christ, as sanctioned either by the teachings or example of the apostles.

the whole congregation or parish who choose the elders and the minister to act for and represent them, and every man of the parish is entitled to a vote who will agree to be guided by the officers they elect.

Of the children it is said

"they are to be taught to read and repeat the Catechism, the Apostles' Creed, and the Lord's Prayer. They are to be taught to pray, to abhor sin, to fear God, and to obey the Lord Jesus Christ.

"And when they come to years of discretion, *if they be free from scandal, appear sober and steady*, and have *sufficient knowledge* to discern the Lord's body, they ought to be informed it is their duty and their privilege to come to the Lord's table."

Thus, by the standards of both portions of the Presbyterian Church, the children are "born within the pale of the visible Church;" there is no *organized* inner ecclesia, but the whole congregation and the Church are one and the same.

But, under the influence of the Puritan element, a large portion of the Presbyterian churches have adopted the inner ecclesia, which shuts out the children from the Church.

The Methodist denomination, also, organize the Church to consist, not of the congregation, but only of the regenerate, thus excluding the children.

The Episcopal Church is the only large denomination in this country which, in theory and practice, has retained the local primitive Church organization.

According to the *Thirty-nine Articles*, the "*visible Church of Christ* is a congregation of faithful people" in which the pure Word of God is preached, and the sacraments of Christ duly administered.

Here "faithful people" is used in the generic sense, including men, women, and children; and "faithful" signifies having faith in Christ, without deciding how much or how little.

The Episcopal *local* Church is a congregation of believers in Christ, organized with a minister and church-wardens as officers, "in which the pure Word of God is preached, and the sacraments of Christ be duly ministered." This is what constitutes them a *visible Church of Christ*. In addition to this, the congregation adopt the liturgy and constitution of the Episcopal denominational Church, and this constitutes them a *local Episcopal Church*. The children are born into the Church as were the Jewish children, and baptism is the seal or sign of their membership, as was circumcision in the more ancient Church.

We are now prepared to answer the question what is the *organized local* Church of Christ as established by the apostles according to the New Testament, and also according to other history.

This will be the subject of the next chapter.

CHAPTER EIGHTH.

THE PRIMITIVE CHURCH OF CHRIST.

It is claimed that the only *organized* Church of Christ in the New Testament was the *local* Church, and that this church consisted of the whole, and not of a portion of a congregation statedly assembling to worship. The following presents evidence of this from standard historians. In Mosheim [Book I., Chap. ii.] are the following statements:

"In those primitive times, each Christian Church was composed of *the people*, the *presiding officers*, and the *assistants* or *deacons*. These *must be* the component parts of every [organized] society. The principal voice was that of *the people*, or the whole body of Christians; for even the apostles themselves inculcated by their example that nothing of any moment was to be done or determined on but with the knowledge or consent of the brotherhood: Acts, i., 15; vi., 3; xv., 6; xxi., 22.

"The assembled people therefore elected their own rulers and teachers, or by their free consent received such as were nominated to them. They also, by their suffrages, rejected or confirmed the laws that were proposed by their rulers in their assemblies; they excluded profligate or lapsed brethren, and restored them; they decided the controversies and disputes that arose; they heard and determined the causes of presbyters and deacons; in a word, the people did every thing that is proper for those in whom the *supreme power* of the community is vested.

"Nor in this first age of the Church was there any distinction between the initiated and the candidates for initiation; for whoever *professed* to regard Jesus Christ as the Savior of the world, and to depend on him alone for salvation, was immediately baptized and admitted into the Church. But, in process of time, as the churches became enlarged, it was deemed advisable and necessary to distribute the people into two classes, the *faithful* and the *catechumens*. The former were such as had been solemnly admitted into the Church by baptism, and who might be present at all the parts of religious worship, and enjoy the right of voting in the meetings of the Church. The latter, not having yet received baptism, were not admitted to the common prayers, nor to the sacred supper, nor to the meetings of the Church.

"The *rulers* of the Church were denominated sometimes *presbyters* or *elders*, and sometimes also *bishops;* for it is most manifest that *both terms* are promiscuously used in the New Testament for one and the same class of persons: Acts, xx., 17, 28; Philemon, i., 1; Titus, i., 5, 7; 1 Timothy, iii., 1.

"That the Church had its public servants or *deacons* from its first foundation there can be no doubt, since no association can exist without its servants: 1 Timothy, iii., 8, 9.

"There were also in many churches female public servants, or *deaconesses*, who were respectable matrons or widows appointed to take care of the poor, and to perform several other offices.

"In this manner Christians managed ecclesiastical affairs so long as their congregations were small and not very numerous. But when the churches became larger, and the number of presbyters and deacons, as well as the amount of duties to be performed, was increased, it became necessary that the council of presbyters should have a *president*, a man of distinguished gravity and prudence, who should distribute among his colleagues their several tasks, and be, as it were, the central point of the whole society. He was at first denominated *the angel* (Revelation, ii. and iii.), but afterward *the bishop*, a title of Greek derivation, indicative of his principal business. It would seem that the Church at Jerusalem, when grown very numerous after the dispersion of the apostles among foreign nations, was the *first* to elect such a president, and that other churches, in process of time, followed the example.

"But whoever supposes that the bishops of this first and golden age of the Church corresponded with the bishops of the following centuries must blend and confound characters that are very different. For in this century and the next, a bishop had charge of a *single* church, which might ordinarily be contained in a private house; nor was he its *lord*, but was, in reality, its minister and servant: he instructed the people, conducted all parts of public worship, and attended to the sick and necessitous in person; and what he was unable thus to perform he committed to the care of the presbyters; but without power to ordain or determine any thing, except with the concurrence of the presbyters and the brotherhood.*

"It was not long, however, before the extent of episcopal jurisdiction and power was enlarged; for the bishops who lived in the cities, either by their own labors or by those of their presbyters, gathered new churches in the neighboring villages and hamlets; and these churches, continuing under the protection and care of the bishops by whose ministry or procurement they had received Christianity, ecclesiastical provinces were gradually formed, which the Greeks afterward denominated *dioceses.* The persons to whom the city bishops committed the government and instruction of these villages and rural

* In a note it is added, All that is here stated may be clearly proved from the records of the first centuries, and has been proved by Joseph Bingham, *Origines Ecclesiast.;* W. Beverege, *Codex Canon. primit. ecclesiæ;* and others.

churches were called *rural bishops*, or *chorepiscopi*, (i. e.) bishops of the suburbs and fields.

"All Christian churches had *equal rights;* nor does there appear in this first century any vestige of that consociation of the churches of the same province which gave rise to *ecclesiastical councils* and to *metropolitans*."

The following, containing more minute details, is taken from the work of an Episcopal writer, entitled *Primitive Christianity, or the Religion of the Ancient Christians in the first Ages of the Gospel. By Wm. Cave, D.D.* Book I., Chap. viii.:

"As Christianity gained admission into great towns and cities, so all the believers of that place usually assembled and met together, the Christians of the neighboring villages resorting thither at times of public worship. But religion increasing apace, the public assembly, especially in the great cities, quickly became too vast and numerous to be managed with any order and convenience, and therefore they were forced to divide the body into particular congregations, who had their pastors and spiritual guides set over them, but still were under the superintendence and care of him that was their president or bishop of the place."

The following is somewhat abridged from the same work:

"The people of each congregation were divided into classes, which had distinct seats in the church, and *gradual* admission into the several parts of public worship. The lowest class were the *imperfect catechumens*, who were not allowed to stay to the public worship, but were to depart as soon as certain lessons were read. Such were privately instructed at home by persons appointed by the bishop, till prepared to be admitted to hear the sermons, but not allowed to be present at the more solemn rites.

"The next class were the *more perfect catechumens.* These might stay, not only to the reading of the Scriptures, but even to the very last part of the service.

"The candidates for baptism, after completing their instructions as catechumens, were called the *competentes,* as sueing for the grace of baptism.

"The highest class, called the *faithful,* were those who were baptized and confirmed, and approved by the long train and course of a virtuous life, and were then admitted to the Lord's Table.

"Besides these three classes there were five classes called *penitents,* consisting of those who, either among catechumens or the higher class of the faithful, had been guilty of misdemeanors.

"The lowest of these were not allowed to enter the church, but stood in the porch, clad in squalid dress, with tears beseeching the prayers of the faithful.

"Next were the penitents who were allowed to enter the church with the lower class of catechumens, to hear the lessons and depart with them.

"Next were those penitents, seated near the reading-pew, for whom the congregation and elders, kneeling, prayed, the elders laying hands on their head; these also departing with the catechumens.

"The fourth class were those allowed to join in prayers and singing, but not in the sacrament.

"The last class were those allowed to come to the Lord's Table."

Discipline of the Primitive Church. Dr. Cave, Book III., Chap. v.:

"The Christian Church, being founded and established by Christ as a society, is, by its very nature, invested with the inherent power of censuring and punishing its members who offend against the laws of it.

"The usual crimes and offenses which came under the discipline of the ancient Church, in the general, was any *vice* or *immorality;* for the holy and good Christians of those times were infinitely careful to keep the honor of their faith unspotted, to stifle every sin in its birth, and, by bringing offenders to public shame and penalty, to keep them from propagating the malignant influence of their bad example. For this reason they watched over one another, told them *privately* their faults and failures, and, when that would not do, brought them before the cognizance of the Church. In those days, by reason of the violent heats of persecution, the great temptation which the weaker and most unsettled Christians were exposed to, was to deny their profession ["denying the Lord that bought them"], and to offer sacrifices to false gods, *it being that which for some ages mainly exercised the discipline of the Church.*

"As to the penalties inflicted in the first age, especially, the apostles had power to inflict bodily punishment upon offenders, which they sometimes made use of upon great occasions, as St. Peter did toward Ananias and Sapphira; and St. Paul punished Elymas the sorcerer with blindness; and this doubtless he primarily intends by his '*delivering over persons unto Satan;*' for no sooner were they cut off from the body of the faithful but Satan seized upon them, and either by actual possession, or some other sign upon their bodies, made it appear that they were delivered over into his power. This could not but strike mighty terrors into men, and make them stand in awe of the censures of the Church; and, questionless, the main design of Divine Providence in affording this extraordinary gift was to supply the defect of civil and coercive power.

"In administering discipline, the first thing in this solemn action was to make *reproofs* and *exhortations*, thereby to bring the offender to the sight and acknowledgment of his fault.

"Then the sentence or censure was passed upon him, whereby he was suspended not only from the communion of the Holy Eucharist, but from all commerce in any way, especially in the *public* duty of religion. During this space of penance, the penitents appeared in all the formalities of sorrow and mourning, in a sordid and squalid habit, with a sad countenance and head hung down, with tears in their eyes, standing without the church doors, for they were not suffered to enter in.

"All beyond the apostles' age, the common, standing penalty they made use of was excommunication, or suspension from communion with the Church; the cutting off and casting out an offending person as a rotten and infected member, till by repentance and wholesome discipline he was cured and restored; and then he was re-admitted into Church society, and to a participation of the ordinances and privileges of Christianity."

Religion and Morals of the Primitive Church. Dr. Cave, Book I., Chap. iv.:

"Their religion and way of life was approved of all. 'Who,' says St. Clement to the Corinthians, 'did ever dwell among you that did not approve your excellent and unshaken faith? that did not wonder at your sober and moderate piety in Christ? You were forward to every good work, adorned with a most virtuous and venerable conversation, doing all things in the fear of God, and having his laws and commandments written upon the tables of your hearts.' They placed religion, not in *talking*, but in *living* well.

"'Among us,' says Athenagoras, 'the meanest and most mechanic persons, and old women, although not able to discourse and dispute for the usefulness of their profession, do yet demonstrate it in their lives and actions. They don't, indeed, critically weigh their words, but they manifest virtuous action; while being buffeted they strike not again, nor sue them at law that spoil and plunder them, but liberally give to them that ask, and love their neighbors as themselves.'

"Clement of Alexandria says, 'Certainly none were ever greater enemies to a naked profession and the covering of a bad life under the title of Christianity. Do any live otherwise than as Christ commanded, 'tis a most certain argument they are no Christians.'

"Pliny the Younger, being commanded by the Emperor Trajan to give him an account of the Christians, tells him that, after the best estimate he could take, and the strictest inquisition by tortures, he found no worse of them than this, that they were wont to meet early for the performance of their solemn devotions, and to bind themselves, under the most sacred obligations, to commit no vice or wickedness.

"Serranus, proconsul of Asia, writes the Emperor Adrian to represent how unjust it was to put to death Christians, when no crime was duly laid to their charge, merely to gratify the tumultuous clamors of the people.

"Origen tells Celsus that the churches of God, which had taken on them the discipline of Christ, if compared to the common societies of men, were among them like lights in the world. 'For who,' says he, 'but must confess that the worser part of our Church is much better than the popular assemblies? as, for instance, the Church of God at Athens is meek and quiet, as endeavoring to approve itself to the great God.'

"So Minutius Felix: 'Should we Christians be compared with you (heathens), we should be found infinitely to transcend you. You forbid adultery, and then practice it; we keep entirely to our own wives. You punish wickedness when *committed;* with us even a wicked thought is sin. And, last of all, 'tis with your party that the prison is filled and crowded, and no Christian is there unless such a one as is either a shame to his religion or an apostate from it.'

"A little while after he tells how much they exceeded the best philosophers, who were filthy and tyrannical, and only eloquent to declaim against vices of which themselves were most guilty.

"Lactantius having discoursed of the prodigious debaucheries and wickednesses of the heathen, 'but of which of these,' says he, 'can be objected to our people, *whose whole religion is to live without spot or blemish?*'

"Tertullian openly declares that when men depart from the discipline of the Gospel, they so far cease among us to be accounted Christians; and that they shunned the company of such, and did not meet or partake with them in the offices of religion, and that therefore the heathens did very ill to call them Christians whom the Christians did disown."

Mosheim gives this statement on this point:

"Most authors represent the lives and morals of Christians in this early age as patterns of purity and holiness, worthy of imitation in all subsequent ages. This representation, if it be understood of the *greater part* of the professed Christians and not of *all*, is undoubtedly true. The visible purity of the churches was much promoted by that law which deprived of ordinances and *excluded from the community* persons of vile character, or who were *known to be vicious*, provided they would not reform on being admonished. Such a law we know was established by the apostles (1 Corinthians, v.) soon after the churches began to be formed. In the application and enforcement of this law the teachers and rulers generally pointed out the persons who seemed to merit exclusion from the Church, and the people sanctioned or rejected the proposal."

Children Members of the Primitive Church.

That the children of Christians were members of the primitive Church is thus stated by Dr. Cave, Part I., Chap. x.:

"If the constant *practice* of the Church, and those who immediately succeeded the apostles, be (as no man can deny it is) the best interpreter of the laws of Christ, the dispute, one would think, would be at an end. For that it always was the custom *to receive the children of Christian parents into the Church by baptism* we have sufficient evidence from the greatest part of the most early writers, Irenæus, Tertullian, Origen, Cyprian, etc., whose testimonies I do not produce because I find them collected by others; and the argument is so forcible and conclusive that the most zealous opposers of infant baptism know not how to evade it; the testimonies being so clear, and not the least shadow that I know of, in those times, to make against it. There was, indeed, in Cyprian's time, a controversy about the baptizing of infants, not whether they ought to be baptized (for of that there was no doubt), but concerning the *time* when it was to be administered.

The following is a condensed view of the various uses of the word *Church.*

Visible Church universal: all who profess to believe in Christ. This is unorganized.

Invisible Church universal: all who so believe as to *obey* in heart and life. This also is unorganized.

Of the *Church* as *organized* there are three uses:

1. The *local Primitive Church,* consisting of individual believers in Christ statedly meeting in one place for worship, and organized as one body with officers.

2. The *local Puritan Church,* a portion of a *local primitive church* united by covenant, and profession of regeneration, and a given creed, also organized with officers.

3. *Denominational Church,* any number of local churches organized as one body, with officers, as the Greek, Roman, Episcopal, or Presbyterian Church.

CHAPTER NINTH.

THE PURITAN CHURCH—ITS HISTORY.

IT has been shown that, in the beginning, the *unorganized* visible Church consisted of all who *professed* to believe in Christ; and that the only *organized* church known at that time was the *local Church*, consisting of *any* congregation of professed believers in Christ organized to sustain his worship and ordinances, the chief officers being the elders (called, also, bishops or presbyters) and the deacons.

All the elders or bishops, at first, had the care only of a single local Church.

But as, in large cities, a Church extended not only in the city, but around in the country, the elders divided these large congregations into smaller ones, and appointed *rural* bishops, who in some sort became subordinate to the metropolitan bishops.

The final result was the *diocesan* bishops, and the name *bishop* was then relinquished by the inferior clergy, and was confined to the diocesan order.

As Christianity increased in power and honor, the ranks of the clergy, and their claims to authority in faith and practice, multiplied. Councils were called, and decrees passed as to what the laity must and must not believe, and the power more and more passed from the people to the clergy.

In what follows, it is needful to mark the distinction to be made as to the *facts* revealed by God, and *the philosophy* which men have contrived to account for these facts.

A *fact* is a thing done: the *philosophy* of it is the mode of explaining the cause or reason of this fact, or explaining the *how* and the *why* it is so.

Christ and his apostles began their teachings among the poor and unlearned. Such received the facts of the Gospel without seeking to discover the philosophy of them. They knew by experience that they were sinners; they were instructed in the danger of eternal ruin by sin in the life to come; they were taught that, on condition of faith in Christ, pardon for past sin, and redemption from its penalties, were secured to them through the atoning sacrifice of Jesus Christ; they understood that faith in Christ included believing on him intellectually as Lord of faith and practice, receiving his words and *practically obeying them;* they received Christ's instructions as intelligible to all, and set themselves to obey as a practical and rational service, while he was deemed the best Christian who most faithfully obeyed.

After a while the wise and learned of this world were gathered into the Christian Church, and then commenced the agitations consequent on philosophizing questions and theories such as these: *Why* do all men sin? *How* did all men become sinners? What is *the cause* of the universal sinfulness of man? *How* was Christ God and *how* was he man? *How* do his sufferings and death avail to save man?

From such questions as these as to the *philosophy* of things revealed arose most of the early contentions and sects of the first centuries of Christianity. The first controversies respected the *nature* of Christ as God and man. In the fifth century, the controversy became fierce as to the *cause*, or *origin of evil*, or the *why* and the *how* men came to be sinners; and the leaders were Augustine and Pelagius.

Augustine maintained that this is the cause why men sin. God ordained that Adam should act for the whole human race, so that, if he ate the forbidden fruit, his own nature should become depraved, and that this depravity should be shared by, or transmitted to, all his posterity. Adam sinned, ruined his own nature, begat children with his own ruined nature, and this depraved nature thus engendered is the *cause* or *the why* that all infants suffer and become sinners.

But Pelagius [see Dr. Walsh, as abridged by Schlegel] taught that men come into life *with the same powers and abilities, and in the same state*, as Adam was created; that human nature was not changed nor depraved by the fall of Adam; that his sin is not *imputed* to his posterity; that men have sinful propensities, but these are not sin; that man has power to discover, to devise, and to *perform* virtuous deeds; that the *grace* of God consists in his giving man a good constitution of mind, the revelation of his will, light to the understanding by the aid of the Holy Spirit, the teachings and example of Christ, and forgiveness of past sins through his atoning sacrifice.

Previous to this period this matter had not been a subject of ecclesiastical decisions, but only of individual speculation. The first council called on this subject was at Jerusalem, which decided on the side of Pelagius, 415. The second was at Diospolis, 415, consisting of fourteen bishops, who also decided for Pelagius. Pope Zosimus, at Rome, also pronounced in favor of Pelagius; but, after a long and fierce controversy, the African bishops, led by Augustine, succeeded in turning the tide against Pelagius. Finally, the councils of the Church and the edicts of the emperor, by cruel persecutions, put an end to this doctrine in the churches. The Augustinian dogma was decreed to be taught in the Bible, and from the Papal Church it has descended into the creeds of the chief Protestant sects.

This doctrine of man's depraved nature, incapacitating him at once from understanding and interpreting the Bible for himself, and from any true obedience till remedied by supernatural interference, became the chief foundation of ecclesiastical power. The priesthood claimed to be ordained, at once to interpret the Bible for the people, and to administer, by Church rites, the only remedy for this depravity of nature engendered from Adam.

The final result culminated in the papal hierarchy, in which the people became as nothing, and *the Church*, which decided all questions of faith and practice, was exclusively the *pope* and *councils* of the clergy.

But in all periods of the papacy there were *Protestant reformers* who resisted this dominion of the clergy over the laity. In 1160 the Waldenses were the most conspicuous. They denied the supremacy of the pope, and claimed that every Christian, in a certain measure, had a right to exhort, instruct, and confirm. After them came the Albigenses, who also opposed the papal claims.

In 1324 Wickliff appeared in England. He denied that bishops were a different order from priests in the primitive Church, and claimed that there were only priests and deacons; that heresy was error, not against clerical decisions, but against Holy Writ; and maintained the right of the laity to interpret the Bible for themselves. He held that infants dying without baptism could be saved; that baptism did not confer grace, but was a sign of grace already given.

In 1376 Huss appeared in Bohemia, teaching liberty of conscience, and the right of the laity to oppose the decisions of the clergy.

In 1483 Luther appeared, and fought the great battle for the rights of the laity against the claims of the Romish hierarchy.

The Reformation spread rapidly in England, where Wickliff and his Bible had prepared the way. Henry the Eighth then separated from the Romish Church, and declared himself the head of the English Church, and was accepted as such by the reforming clergy of his kingdom. A Bible was put in every church, with the implied admission that the laity were at liberty to interpret it for themselves. Every decision in the Church was settled by appeals to the Bible, and not to past Church decisions or practices.

The first English reformers held to only two orders of the clergy—priests and deacons. This appears in what is called *the Bishops' Book*, issued in 1535, subscribed and recommended by two archbishops and nineteen bishops. It says there are "but two orders of the clergy," and "no one bishop has authority over another, according to the Word of God.'

In 1543 came the "King's Book," which says, "There is no real distinction between bishops and priests;" also it says, "Of these two orders only—that is to say, priests and deacons—Scripture maketh express mention." This was drawn up by a committee of bishops and divines. Of *deacons* it says, "Their office in the primitive Church was partly to minister meat and drink, and other necessaries, to the poor, and partly to minister to the bishops and priests."

As to the *people* being the controlling power, the English reformers held these views, as expressed by the Archbishop of Canterbury [see *Bishop Burnet*, vol. ii., p. 326–329]:

"Sometimes the apostles and others, unto whom God had given abundantly his Spirit, sent or appointed ministers of God's Word; sometimes the people did choose such as they thought meet thereto; and when any were appointed or sent by the apostles or others, the people, of their own voluntary will, with thanks, did accept them; not for the supremity, empire, or dominion that the apostles had over them, to command, as their princes and masters, but as good people ready to obey the advice of good counselors, and to accept any thing that was necessary for their edification and benefit."

In the reign of Edward VI., the present English Prayer-book was compiled by Archbishop Cranmer chiefly from ancient books of devotion.

In the reign of Mary, the claims of the papal clergy were renewed amid the fires of persecution.

Elizabeth patronized the reformation from popery, but demanded conformity to the English Established Church. The *Non-conformists* were called *Puritans*, as those who favored the *entire* purification of the national Church from Romish rites and ceremonies. They opposed the bishops as a superior order, and their exclusive right to ordain; and especially the power of the *bishop's courts*, which inflicted civil pains and penalties for not conforming to their decisions. Persecution followed; the Non-conforming clergy were expelled from their pulpits, suspended from the ministry, and otherwise impeded. In 1566, those thus persecuted met and decided to withdraw from the Church of England.

The Puritans were divided into the two classes of *Non-conformists* remaining in the Established Church, and the *Separatists*, who withdrew and established independent churches. Of this last class was the noble and venerated John Robinson, who may be properly named the father of the *Puritan Church.*

He first was a Non-conformist in the English Establishment; then he became a Separatist, and fled with many of his people to Holland to escape persecution. Here he became a leader and a distinguished writer, and first drew up in detail the principles on which the Congregational churches of New England were afterward established.

John Robinson's definition of the "Church visible" is this:

> "The word *ecclesia, church,* translated to religious use, denoteth an assembly of persons *called out of the state of corrupt nature into that of supernatural grace* by the publishing of the Gospel."

Another definition is this:

"The Church is a company of faithful and holy people, *with their seed*, called by the Word of God *into public covenant with Christ and among themselves* for mutual fellowship in the use of all the means of God's glory and their salvation."

Again:

"And, for the gathering of a Church, I do tell you that, in what place soever, by what means soever, whether by preaching the Gospel by a true minister, by a false minister, by no minister, or by reading, conference, or other means of publishing it, two or three faithful people do arise, *separating themselves* from the fellowship of the world into the fellowship of the Gospel and *covenant* of Abraham, they are *a Church* truly gathered."

In regard to infants, he says:

"The infants of the faithful are within the limits of the new covenant."

In replying to opponents, he says:

"Since all children coming naturally from Adam are conceived and born in sin, and by nature children of wrath, if these men believe, as they do of all, that their children so dying shall be saved by Christ, then must they have part in his testament, or in this *new covenant.* There are not two new covenants or testaments established in the blood of Christ, but one. And since Christ is propounded unto us as the Savior of 'the body,' which is 'his Church,' it is more than strange that these men will have all infants to be saved, and yet none of them to be of his body, or *the Church.*"

From these quotations it appears that Robinson had formed a theory of Church organization which involved an irretrievable difficulty. It was a Church to be composed (as by his first definition) "of persons called out of the state of corrupt nature by supernatural grace;" according to his second definition, they are "to separate themselves from the fellowship of the world into the fellowship of the Gospel and *the covenant* of Abraham." This covenant includes the *seed* or *children.* But, according to Robinson, children are at birth unregenerate, and there is no *sure* and *certain* way to secure their regeneration. Some children of a family, all trained alike, become regenerate, and some do not, and only the regenerate are members of the Church. So there is no covenant possible like that of Abraham, which included *all* circumcised children in the Jewish Church without respect to character.

Robinson did not seem to see the difficulty of his Church theory as some of his associates did; for one Smyth took the ground that if the Church is to be a separated body of *regenerated* persons, infants can not belong to it. So he became the originator of the Baptist denomination, which consistently excludes all but persons supposed to be regenerated.

The Cambridge Platform, which expresses the views of the New England clergy in 1648, defines the visible Church of Christ thus:

"The whole body of men throughout the world *professing* the faith of the Gospel and obedience unto God according unto it, not destroying their own profession by any errors everting the foundations, or unholiness of conversation, they, and *their children* with them, are and may be called the *visible catholic Church of Christ;* although, as such, it is not intrusted with any officers to rule and govern *the whole.*"

Here it appears that it is not all who *profess* to believe in Christ, with their seed, that constitutes the visible Church, but those only who profess actual *obedience* to it, not destroying their profession by *errors* in *doctrine* or *unholy living*, together with their children.

The first Pilgrim fathers all joined the Church by covenant and profession as regenerated persons, and regarded their children as made members by baptism.

But when the next generation became parents, many of them could not belong to the Church as persons professing to be regenerate, and so did not bring their children to be baptized. And thus Cotton Mather describes the first working of this new mode:

"The good old generation could not, without uncomfortable apprehensions, behold their offspring excluded from the baptism of Christianity and from the ecclesiastical inspection which is to accompany baptism." "It was the study of these prudent men that the children of the faithful may be kept, as far as may be, under Church watch, in *expectation* that they may be *in a fairer way* to receive the grace of God" (i. e., regeneration of a depraved nature).

Moreover, he adds, "there was a numerous appearance of sober persons who professed themselves desirous to renew their baptismal covenant [made by parents] and submit to Church discipline, and so have their houses also marked for the Lord's; but yet they could not come up to that experimental account of *their own regeneration* which would sufficiently embolden their access to the *other* sacrament."

In consequence, it was decided by a convocation of ministers that, "in case they understand the grounds of religion," and are not scandalous, and solemnly own the covenant (baptismal) in their own persons, wherein they give both themselves and their children unto the Lord, and desire baptism for them, we see not sufficient cause to deny baptism unto them. Thus arose "*the half-way covenant*," to enable parents to secure the baptism and admission of their children to *Church watching* without professing *regeneration* or *going to the sacrament* themselves.

This added to the complication. Were these children of parents not professing regeneration made members of the Church by this half-way covenant and baptism? and, if so, could they have their children baptized and under the watch of the Church? If allowed to do so, in process of time nearly every body would come to be Church members by baptism and the half-way covenant, and the Church would cease to consist of "persons called out of the corrupt state of nature by supernatural grace, and their children," as Robinson's plan demanded.

After this half-way covenant had been tried a

while, President Edwards met the matter with his stern logic; and, by his influence, it came to pass that the New England churches became close corporations, taking in by majority vote only such as, on examination, gave evidence of regeneration and belief in a given creed. Still, the children were by many considered in some sort members of the Church, but not so as to be allowed any of its peculiar privileges, and not so but that they were ordinarily spoken of as out of the Church, and to be taken into it by majority vote when they gave evidence of regeneration.

The Baptists never baptized infants, nor regarded them as in any sense members of the Church. A large portion of the Presbyterian Church, in defiance of their standards, and also the Methodists, practically took the same course. Thus a majority of the children of this nation have been shut out of the Church of Christ.

Dr. Bushnell, in his last work on Christian nurture, endeavors to meet the difficulty on this subject by what he terms an "*organic unity*" of the family, which he claims makes children members of the Puritan Church with their parents.

But he does not discriminate between organized bodies founded on individual covenant and promise, such as free-masons or temperance societies, and those which are constituted of *families* without individual covenant, such as towns and states.

The Puritan Church exists by the promise and covenant of individuals with each other, together with the profession of regeneration and the belief of a creed. A child, therefore, no more belongs to this corporation by a parent's joining it than it enters a free-masons' lodge when its father joins it.

Dr. Bushnell also attempts to meet another difficulty. If the baptized children of the Church are members of the corporation, then it ceases to be an organization of *regenerated* persons, and becomes what the *primitive Church* is claimed to be, (i. e.) a mixture of persons in all stages of advancement in Christian knowledge and experience, without any organization dividing the regenerate and unregenerate.

To meet this, Dr. Bushnell takes the ground that regeneration *may* exist in embryo, as it were, in children who have been consecrated by baptism and trained by pious parents, so that the baptized children of the Church may thus be, in a certain sense, classed as the regenerate. This is very similar to the High-Church notion of baptismal regeneration, and, to be consistent, all baptized persons should be recognized as the regenerate, and members of the Church.

In defiance of these explaining theories, when persons baptized in infancy come to officers of the Puritan Church wishing to be received as members, they are met as those *out* of the Church, and are admitted by *vote* only on giving satisfactory evidence of regeneration and belief of a creed.

Dr. Bushnell's claim that these persons are already members of the Church, either by organic unity with their parents or as regenerated, is thus practically contradicted.

The same contradiction is to be met in the Presbyterian Church; for in their standards the Church is defined to be a congregation of Christians "with their children," and yet these children are afterward *taken into* the Church by a formal vote of Church officers, as those who are *out* of it till thus received. Nor has a baptized child any more advantages or privileges as a member of that Church than one who is not baptized.

Still another difficulty arose from this new mode of organizing the local Church of Christ.

The contest of the Puritans with the Church of England was not so much for individual liberty as for the freedom of the laity from the authority of the clergy. Instead of taking the true ground that no man, or body of men, is to be *rabbi* or master of our faith, they formed close corporations of regenerated laity, in which the majority of male members admitted by vote, and assumed exactly the authority which the bishops had maintained. The bishops demanded, "Believe and practice as *we* prescribe, or we cut you off from *our* Church and its privileges." The Puritan Church majority said,

"Believe and practice as *we* prescribe, or we cut you off from the privileges of *our* Church."

Both parties certainly had a *legal* right to form an association on any terms they pleased, and to admit or exclude on these terms. The question which both had to settle was, Do the teachings or example of Christ and the apostles warrant such claims? Is this the New Testament mode of organizing the local Church?

If the preceding history of the primitive Church is correct, we must say that the Puritan local Church is liable to the same objections as the Papal Church. The chief difference is, that in one case the power to enforce conformity to doctrines in faith and practice is held by the clergy, and in the other by the majority of male members of a local Church.

CHAPTER TENTH.

PRIMITIVE CHURCH TRAINING.

In regard to the training of children in the primitive churches, the whole question turns on the meaning of the expression "faith in Christ," and its equivalent term, "believing in Christ."

It is conceded that these terms mean what mankind intend and understand by these expressions when they use them in common life. For the Bible was written in the language of common life, and not in the language of philosophers and metaphysicians.

What, then, do men mean when they say a man "believes in" or "has faith in" a person?

A man has faith and believes in Mohammed when he intellectually is convinced that he is the authoritative teacher of the true religion. He openly acknowledges or *professes* this belief when he publicly attends the forms of worship prescribed by Mohammed; and the degree of his faith is measured by the strictness with which he obeys the lord of his faith.

So a man "believes in" physicians, and "has faith" in them, when he is intellectually convinced that their prescriptions will cure diseases, and his degree of faith is measured by the extent and strictness of his obedience to their directions.

Faith or *belief* in Jesus Christ, then, involves these particulars: intellectual conviction that he is Lord of faith and practice; receiving his teachings; a purpose to obey them; and the carrying out this purpose in feelings and conduct.

Now there are all degrees of advance in each of these particulars which constitute true faith in Christ. Some have a strong and some a feeble conviction that Jesus Christ is Lord of faith and practice; some have a correct knowledge of his teachings, and some have very imperfect understanding of their true meaning. Some have a strong purpose of universal obedience, and some have a very feeble one; and some carry out this purpose in feelings and conduct very extensively, and others very imperfectly. Nor do we find in the New Testament how much of each ingredient is indispensable, nor how low one may fall in any one, and yet have saving faith.

We find, in common life, that men use the word *faith* sometimes as including the mere intellectual conviction. At other times the word is used to include also the appropriate feelings, purpose, and conduct. In the New Testament the same uses of the word occur.

Thus one apostle, in the first use, says, "Faith without works is dead;" meaning the intellectual part alone. Another apostle teaches that faith saves us; meaning the faith that includes not only belief, but appropriate feelings and conduct.

Thus it appears that there are various ingredients of true saving faith, each being capable of different degrees, and all also being matters which educational training can secure. The first ingredient every parent can *promise* that a child shall possess, and that is, the intellectual belief that Jesus Christ is Lord of faith and practice. For the distinctive trait of young children is confiding belief in what their parents tell them; so that a pagan, a Mohammedan, and a Christian child are sure to believe in the first point of their parents' creed, viz., who is the Lord to be obeyed. The intellectual faith of childhood can be increased by culture as years go on, or it may pass away.

The second step, receiving the teachings of Christ, is also a slow and gradual process. So a purpose to obey, while it may be, and often is, an instantaneous act, is also frequently a matter of slow development and culture, and of various degrees of strength.

Finally, the actual *obedience* in heart and life to *all* Christ's teachings is also a slow and gradual matter, resulting from appropriate culture, and never perfected in this life.

These things being so, the primitive churches regarded their children as prospective Christians in *name* and *intellectual belief*, and in reference to this they baptized them, and thus made them members of the *visible Church universal.*

And as each local Church was a *portion* of the Church universal, *organized* to sustain the worship and ordinances of Christ, the children became members of it when their parents did, just as in a New England town or *parish* the children become members when their parents do.

And there is not a sentence or line to be found, either in the Bible or in primitive history, to show that the primitive Christians ever attempted, as the Puritans have done, to *organize* the *invisible Church*, as consisting of persons who have the full amount of faith which secures eternal life, and of which Church officers shall be the judges.

The first Christian churches commenced at a time when there were no persons trained from childhood to believe in Jesus Christ as Lord of faith and practice. Converts, at first, were made entirely from adults. The first step was to convince them that Jesus Christ was the rightful Lord. This frequently was secured by *miracles.* After this was done, then followed instruction in Christ's teachings, which was a slow and gradual process. The purpose to obey, and the carrying out this purpose in daily life, were also a gradual process.

It often happened, as in the case of Paul and of many who witnessed miracles, that the intellectual conviction of Christ's authority, and the purpose to obey him, were almost simultaneous. In other cases the process was a gradual one. The local churches consisted of persons in all stages of advancement, and of young children of all ages and all degrees of training.

We can not have a true idea of the training of children in the first Christian churches without bearing in mind that the talents, cultivation, riches, honors, and civil powers of this world were sustaining pagan temples and worship. At that time, in the proud Roman empire, including all civilized nations, it was even more disgraceful to be a Christian, than it now is, in this country, to be a Mormon. Christians were a poor, despised sect of the Jews, a nation universally hated; their leader was a man who suffered a death as disgraceful as hanging now is; their numbers were small, and chiefly of the ignorant lower orders; while the rulers and rich of their own nation hated and despised them even more than did the heathen.

Meantime, this despised sect, "every where spoken against," and regarded as the "filth and offscouring of the earth," set up the claim, not that their religion was as good as that upheld by the noble and wise, but that it was the *only* true one, to which all others must bow, and that a crucified criminal is the Creator and Lord of all in heaven and on earth, whom all must love and obey, or perish forever.

It was as monstrous a claim, to the great and wise, as it would be to us, at this day, if some negro, escaped from a gallows, should make the same claim, and be sustained by a few poor and ignorant persons of his own class.

The Jews, also, when this new sect arose, were required to give up their proud claims as the favored nation, and receive the Gentiles as their equals; while Abraham and Moses, their pride and boast, were to be placed below the crucified Galilean, and even worship him as God.

It is not possible to imagine a religion which could start under more appalling difficulties.

Amid all this hatred and obloquy, the Christians were required not only to believe in Christ and to train their children to do so, but to *profess* this religion publicly by baptism and by uniting with a Christian community. They were not to save self by a secret faith, but to *profess* Christ at the risk or sacrifice of reputation, property, and life itself. And the reason of this was, that Christ's religion might be spread abroad through the whole world by its glorious truths, and by the harmonious love, pure lives, and sacrificing suffering of its professors.

And as purity of life was indispensable as the chief mode of extending the true faith, not only all who denied Christ's authority as Lord, but all who were openly immoral, so as to disgrace a Christian community, were to be not only cast out of it, but openly shunned; none were to "receive them into their houses or bid them God speed."

On the contrary, every person, however ignorant or sinful, who believed that Christ was the Lord of faith and practice, and wished to be taught his religion, was received into the Christian churches for training and help. Nothing was required but a willingness to come and be taught, and to behave decently and peacefully as a member of a Christian community. A desire to be a Christian sufficient to bring into regular attendance at a Christian church, and decent behavior, constituted membership; and openly denying Christ as Lord, disgraceful vices, and refusing to submit to the counsel of the Church in personal quarrels, were the only grounds of expulsion.

The children were trained from infancy to understand that they were to stand ready to suffer and die for the salvation of their fellow-men, just as Christ did. And they were continually witnessing or hearing of their neighbors, or friends, or fellow-Christians in other places suffering the loss of all things for this end.

St. Paul's vivid description was to them not a tale of imagination, but a daily reality: "We are troubled on every side, yet not distressed; perplexed, but not in despair; persecuted, but not forsaken; cast down, but not destroyed. For we which live are always delivered unto death for Jesus' sake.

Others had trial of cruel mockings and scourgings; yea, moreover, of bonds and imprisonment. They were stoned; they were sawn asunder; were tempted; were slain with the sword. They wandered about in sheepskins and goatskins; being destitute, afflicted, tormented; of whom the world was not worthy."

To live lives of purity and harmony—to be examples of every Christian virtue, as the way to extend the faith to which they devoted their reputation, their property, and their lives—this was the constant training to which all of every age and station were subjected in the congregation and in the family. In short, *to save their fellow-men* from the dangers of the future life was the *chief end and aim* of Church and family training in the primitive times. The churches were *communities*, and every child was born into the Church, just as children now are born into the communities in which their parents reside.

These communities knew that in all places they must be persecuted for professing to be Christ's followers, and by persecutions they "were scattered abroad, preaching the word." They did not expect to live to enjoy this life; for the apostle wrote, "If only in this life we have hope in Christ, we are of all men most miserable."

Therefore they educated their children to be *martyrs.* They did not expect nor aim at a portion for

them in this life, but rather that they should be prepared to "endure hardness as good soldiers." *All* were to stand ready, some in places of comparative ease, but all prepared to march themselves, or to send their children, to the *forlorn hope*, whenever the command came.

The world now has more darkened and miserable idolaters than it had in the primitive age. It is far easier now than it was then for the churches to be "scattered abroad preaching the word." There is no reason why children now should not be trained "to endure hardness as good soldiers," and to live, not to enjoy this life, but to save their fellowmen from ignorance and sin, as their great Master did.

In what follows we may find some reasons why the churches of Christ at the present day are not equal to those of the primitive age in these respects.

CHAPTER ELEVENTH.

PURITAN CHURCH TRAINING.

In the preceding pages it has been seen that the Puritans, who separated from the Church of England, were the first who attempted to organize portions of the *invisible Church* into local churches; that at first their organizations included the children of these churches; that the Baptist sect commenced by being consistent in excluding infant children; and that, under the influence of President Edwards, the Congregational churches of the country have finally come to the same result in reference to excluding children, as have also the Methodists and a large portion of the Presbyterian churches.

All this has been the logical result of the doctrine of a depraved nature transmitted from Adam to all infants descended from him.

On this theory of a depraved nature, saving faith in Jesus Christ is never the result of educational training, but it is the result of an instantaneous new creation of the *nature* of a child, without which preliminary act of God no degree of saving faith is ever attained.

In this chapter will be exhibited the mode of religious training of a young child, conducted strictly according to the Puritan Church theory, as held and practiced by the Congregational, Baptist, and a large portion of the Presbyterian churches of this country.

The author of the work to be quoted was the daughter of the celebrated Dr. Payson.

She states that "the book is not a fictitious narrative. It is *substantially* a record of conversations and incidents which really occurred. Though it is not pretended that the precise words of the dialogue or the very circumstances of the narrative are always preserved, it is sufficient to its essential truth that similar incidents and conversations occurred, and that the general progress and results are correctly described."

That this is a correct exhibition of the usual mode of religious training pursued in the Congregational, Baptist, and Presbyterian denominations in this country, and to a great extent in other denominations, can not well be denied. It certainly is the exact reproduction of the methods which were adopted with young persons by the leading clergy of New England, as the writer has heard them, year after year, from her father and from his personal friends, such as Dr. Taylor, Dr. Nettleton, Dr. Hewit, Dr. Tyler, Dr. Payson, Dr. Finney, and many others, who, both in private and in public, have taught the young, both in conversation and in the pulpit, in her hearing.

Moreover, the little work from which extracts are to follow has been widely circulated, introduced into Sunday-schools, and extensively recommended by the religious press, while no intimations have ever been made that it in any way deviated from the established theological system of the above-mentioned denominations.

It probably was rarely the case that children were thus instructed *at so early an age.* It is therefore put under the head of *Church* training rather than that of the family.

The following extract indicates some of the earliest methods pursued in this case:

"When Maria was between two and three years old, she would sit on a little stool at her father's feet, with tears rolling down her cheeks, while he talked to her of the sinfulness of her heart, and the impossibility of her ever being happy till it was changed.

"Before Maria was three years old, she was very unwilling to be convinced that she did not love God, and often wept because her father seemed to doubt this affection. She observed one day that she 'wished she could die, and then her father would see her fly right up to Heaven like a little angel, and he would know that she loved God.'"

One day, not long after the preceding,

"Maria suddenly asked, 'Ma, how can I be good?'

"Her mother told her she must have a new heart.

"'How can I have a good heart? I will take out my naughty heart, and stamp on it, and beat it—will that make it good?'

"Her father heard the question. 'No, my daughter,

said he, 'you can not make your heart good—nobody but God can make new hearts, and if you want one you must ask him.'"

The following occurred in her fifth year:

"'Pa,' said Maria, suddenly, one day after she had been thinking some time, 'what does *heart* mean? When you talk about my heart, I can not think of any thing but those gingerbread hearts that we eat.'

"The father replied: 'You know there is something within you which loves and hates; this something is your heart. So, when God says give me your heart, he means 'Love me.'

"'Pa, it seems as if I wanted to love God, but don't know how.'"

The father proceeded to describe how we actually love persons whom we never saw, and in beautiful language portrayed the benevolent character of God, and the multitude of blessings he had bestowed on the child, when she impulsively exclaims,

"'Oh, pa, I will, I do love him!'"

But her father then strives to convince her that she *does not*, because she often does what God forbids. But the child was unconvinced. Then follows an account of her efforts to be good and struggles to avoid sin; but at length she grew tired of such constant watchfulness, and relapsed into former habits of childish thoughtlessness.

Soon after, on hearing her father describe the cruel treatment of Christ by the Jews, all her sympathies were called out, and especially her indignation against this cruelty. Whereupon her father took the occasion to teach her that her heart was like the Jews, and if she had been there she probably would have done the same.

"'Papa, you don't think that I should have helped to crucify Christ?'

"'How can I disbelieve the Bible, Maria? and this tells us all hearts are alike.'

"'Oh, papa, I never—never—' but her sobs would not allow her to go on.

"'My dear, you have had no opportunity to show your hatred and contempt of Christ as the Jews did, but you have done it just as plainly in other ways.'"

These ways which the father pointed out were the common faults and failings of most little children. Then follows this:

"Maria was much distressed, and wept violently. She could not think her heart so bad as her father represented it, and yet she dared not say so when her conduct was no better. However, she resolved to 'try again.'"

This chapter ends thus:

"We can not describe each of Maria's efforts and its result, for, as in the former case, they were gradually relinquished and forgotten. They were not, however, useless, for she began, after a time, reluctantly to admit the conviction that there was no love to God in her heart. As her feelings were ardent and easily excited, she was generally much affected, and wept abundantly when listening to her father's conversation, and it was easy to mistake these natural emotions for love and gratitude. And if she found it difficult to believe that she did not love God, much less would she be convinced that she hated him. Her father labored much to convince her of the enmity of her heart and the necessity of regeneration."

In the next chapter the child says she thinks it strange that her father should be so anxious to convince her of what would make her so unhappy, without doing her any good, so far as she could see. Her father states the reason thus:

"'Before you can be happy, before you can go to Heaven, you must have a new heart; and before you have a new heart, you must be convinced that you need it, and that your present heart is unreconciled to God.'

"'I am sure, papa, I am willing to be convinced, if it is the truth; but I don't see how I could hate a person without knowing it.'"

The following is the father's exposition of the matter:

"'You think of God, I suppose, as a Being who loves you, and remember some of the blessings you have received from him. Now Christ says that *sinners* love those that love them. Every person feels a sort of selfish love or gratitude toward those who confer favors on them, and this is what you feel toward God. The God whom you love is not the God of the Bible, but a false deity, a creature of your own imagination. You leave out the holiness, justice, and truth of God. You think of a being who is kind and merciful, and who is, moreover, good to you, and such a being you find it easy to love. Instead of this, we must not only take into view God's holiness and hatred of sin, but we must love him *on account* of these very perfections, and feel that we could not love him without them.'"

The next states that

"Maria did not take as much pleasure as she had done

in thinking of God. After all, she could not see why the holiness and justice of his character were so essential to his glory, or why a being whose requirements were less strict and difficult would not be entitled to as much reverence and love. But, though she felt that God did not appear amiable in the light in which he had been now presented to her, she was far from perceiving that this implied guilt in herself. It seemed to her that God had become less lovely instead of her having just learned that she did not love him. Of the desperate wickedness of her heart she as yet knew nothing, but was to learn it by painful experience."

Then follows an account of a succession of trials "to be good," in which, like all children, she often failed. After an ebullition of quick temper, her father said,

"'You promised me to make an effort to govern yourself.'

"'Yes, papa,' sobbed Maria, 'and I meant to try; and I thought, when you talked so kindly to me, that I never should be angry again in my life; and, papa, I did try a little while, but I forgot it again; and—and—'

"'But, my dear child, how can I place any confidence in your promises or resolutions, you have so often broken them.'

"'I know it, papa; I can not tell what is the reason. If I am ever so sure of not doing wrong again, the very next day I forget all, and I do the same things.'

"'I can tell you the reason, Maria; it is that wicked heart of yours. As long as you have this heart you will sin.'

"'I don't see as I can help myself, then, papa.'

"'You must first feel that you are to blame, that it is your own fault, that you can not do better, and then seek the assistance of the Holy Spirit.'"

After various trials to be good, the child said to herself,

"'Papa was right in saying I could not be good without God's help; but, now that I am convinced of this, I will pray to him every day.'

"It is not intended that Maria had never been taught to pray, but she had never, at least since her father's assertion of her inability to do right, *sought the assistance of the Holy Spirit.*

"Several days she prayed for this help, and yet she often failed. She could not conceal her disappointment and vexation. Bursting into tears, she began:

"'Papa, you said the reason I did not succeed in trying to be good was that I depended on myself; so to-day and yesterday I prayed to God to help me, and I have been worse than I was before.'

"Her father could with difficulty repress a smile at this bitter complaint, that a single prayer, *proceeding too from a selfish and unhumbled heart,* had not effected a conquest which would probably require months of prayerful effort."

The father then instructed her that

"even when prayer is offered aright, and when God intends to answer it, he seldom does so immediately and at once. He bestows a little grace at a time, and often not until many weeks or months of prayer.

"Maria was surprised, but not discouraged. She thought it would not be difficult to pray for ever so long a time, if she might receive an answer at last."

But, in the next chapter, the father teaches thus:

"'Now I must tell you that God is not only not obliged to answer you, but that he has reason to be displeased with you on account of your prayers.'

"Maria was surprised, and looked at her father to see if she had understood him aright.

" 'Suppose, Maria, a poor person should come to you for food or clothing, would you expect him to demand it as a right or to entreat it as a favor?'

" 'As a favor, papa, of course.'

" 'Well, now, suppose, farther, that this beggar was a person who had injured you very much; suppose you had frequently assisted him before, that he had abused all your benefits, and then endeavored to prejudice others against you, what should you think?'

" 'I should think he was very impudent to come again, and should send him away fast enough.'

" 'At least, you see you would be under no *obligation* to relieve him.'

" 'No, indeed, papa.'

" 'Well, my dear, your case with regard to God is just that of this poor beggar. He has been bestowing blessings upon you all your life long, which you have abused, and for which you have felt no gratitude. Even if you had had any claim to his favor, you would have forfeited it by this conduct.'

" 'Papa, I believe I see why God is not obliged to hear me, but I do not see why he should be displeased with me for praying.'

" 'You thought, it seems, that you should find reason enough to be displeased with the beggar in the case I supposed. Suppose you possessed the power of reading the heart, and that all the time he was talking you could see that his heart was full of enmity to you; that he was prompted by mere selfishness to come and ask favors, for which he felt no gratitude; if, in short, you saw he was not sincere in one word that he uttered, you would be displeased and disgusted.'

" 'Yes, papa; but I do not see how this applies to my prayers. I am sure I am sincere in them.'

" 'In one sense you are sincere. You sincerely wish to be saved from punishment, but this is mere selfishness. You do not sincerely love God and repent of your sins.' "

The narrative states that the child was mortified and distressed by such reflections, and retired to bed with a half determination "not to try any longer."

Thus far the leading aim of religious training has seemed to be, to convince the child that she was born with a heart so depraved that she not only did not love God, but that she hated him; that she could not be good nor go to Heaven till this bad heart was changed; that she was dependent on the Spirit of God to change it, and yet that her prayers for this aid were as displeasing and disgusting to God as those of the hypocritical beggar; because, so long as she had this bad heart, her prayers must all be selfish and hypocritical.

It was not strange that the child felt mortified and distressed, and half determined not to try any longer.

CHAPTER TWELFTH.

PURITAN CHURCH TRAINING, SECOND PART.

SOON after the conversations in the preceding chapter, the child comes to the root of the whole difficulty.

"'Papa,' said she, 'I don't see how I can help being wicked. I didn't make my own heart.'

After some preliminaries, the father thus instructs:

"'The faculty of *choosing* is called *the will*, and the will of every human being is *depraved* or *inclined to sin*, and therefore chooses sin instead of holiness.'

"'Well, then, papa, God must have created my will depraved.'

"'My dear child, I do not suppose it is possible to explain this subject in such a way that you will be satisfied, for no sinner was ever satisfied. It is true that' *in some way*, we have *sinful natures in consequence of our connection with Adam.* Our hearts are, from the beginning, disposed to sin, and our wills are opposed to God. We do not understand how this is; it is enough for us to know that it forms no excuse for us.'

"'I am sure I should think it was an excuse.'

"'Well, let us see how it would apply in all cases. Here is a man to be tried for murder. He confesses the crime, but says to the judge, "You certainly will not condemn me for what I could not help. It was my wicked heart which made me do this." Should we not tell him that this was the very thing he was punished for, because he had a heart which disposed him to commit this crime?' "

The child was puzzled. The father adds:

" 'Well, Maria, on this point I have one condition to make with you. Whenever you are ready to admit this excuse, in cases of injury offered to yourself, I will allow that it is a good one in your favor. So, if George should pull down your baby-house, or break your doll, I shall expect that, instead of being angry with him, you will say, "Oh, poor fellow! he couldn't help it; he has such a bad heart." ' "

The child was not convinced. The father says,

" 'Only begin to love God, and the difficulty will vanish.'

" 'I wish I could; but my heart won't let me.'

" 'The same excuse again! Why, my dear, your heart is *yourself*. To say that your heart won't love God is just the same as to say *I* won't love him, which is your guilt, not your excuse.'

"Maria sighed; her father sighed too. *She* thought the conditions of salvation were so hard that they could not be complied with; *he* sighed to see how powerless is argument where the heart is concerned."

In all this argument the child was defeated by false and imperfect analogies. She might justly have replied to her father's illustration of the murderer and the judge, that, if the judge had caused the mind of the criminal to be so depraved on account of some sin of his father, and also had power both to prevent and to rectify the bad disposition, it was the judge more than the murderer who was to blame. The criminal might justly say to his judge, "It is what you caused me to do by entailing the bad disposition, and what you could have prevented by removing it, and so you are more guilty than I."

This was what the child *felt*, though she knew not how to express herself. That God had made such a state of things that Adam's "bad heart," consequent on his sin, should be transmitted to her, and that, when God had the power to change it, he would not do it, *this* was the distressful and awful infliction that made it seem so impossible to love and trust her Creator. This is shown still farther in the next extract:

"'Papa, when you talk about *going to Christ*, how can I tell what it means, because it is not literally going to him.'

"'When we use this expression, my dear, we mean the same act as when we say *loving* Christ, or *believing* in him, or *trusting* him. They all mean the same thing. Have you not felt, when you were thinking of some person whom you loved, and who was away from you, as if your heart *went out* to that person?'

"'Oh yes, I know what sort of feelings you mean very well. When you and mamma were gone last summer, I used to think of you till it almost seemed as if you were here, and then my heart would almost jump out to meet you, and the tears came into my eyes when I remembered how far you were away.'

"'On the other hand, when you think of a person whom you do not like, your heart draws back, as it were, and retires into itself. Now just tell me, in which of these ways is it affected when you think of Christ?'

"Maria was silent.

"'Does your heart ever go out to him in love and confidence?'

"'I—I— No, papa, I never felt toward him as I did to you. But how can I make my heart love him?'

"'*Make* your heart *love*, Maria? You can not.'

"'That is what I have said a hundred times, papa, and you always tell me it is no excuse.'

"'And I have told you a hundred times *why* it is no excuse. Suppose you had come to me, when I returned, and said, "Pa, I am not glad to see you at all, and I do not love you, but I suppose I ought to; and I wish you would teach me how to *make* my heart love you." Do you think I ought to be satisfied?'

"'No, papa.'"

Next he explains "*faith*" to be implicit confidence in Christ's power and willingness to save her, and continues thus:

"'And has not Christ given you the fullest proof of his ability and willingness to save you? Has he not saved all who trusted in him? You can not offer him a greater insult than to doubt either his power or his love.'

"'Why doesn't he save me, then?' said she, in a petulant tone, though she felt ashamed and frightened the moment the words escaped her. Her father paused and looked at her solemnly, almost sternly, as he said,

"'Because *you will not let him*, Maria,' and left the room."

After similar instructions, showing the inability of man,

"'Father,' Maria exclaims, 'I see there is no hope for me!'

"Then hard thoughts of God and his law began to rise in her mind. *Why had he created her with such a heart?* Why did he require what her utmost efforts would not enable her to perform? She hardly dared again propose these objections to her father, but at length she ventured to say that, if sinners were so unable to change their hearts, she could not see why they were to blame.

"Her father sighed: 'They are to blame, because their very inability, consisting simply in *unwillingness*, constitutes their guilt. They have all the powers necessary to doing their duty; there is nothing wanting but a *disposition;* and, if a want of a disposition constitutes an excuse, there is no such thing as guilt in the universe, but, the more a man sins, the less guilty he is. Why will you offer to your Creator an excuse which you would blush to present to a fellow-creature?'

"It was now Maria's turn to sigh.

"'I know what you think, my dear,' resumed her father; 'you think that you are a poor unfortunate creature, who are to be punished for having a wicked heart, which you can not help, and for not obeying a law which it is impossible that you should obey. It seems to you that you have been doing every thing you possibly could to obtain salvation, and as if it would be very unjust and cruel in God to leave you to perish, after all your prayers, and tears, and efforts. Is it not so?'

"Maria hesitated.

"'I do not mean that you have those thoughts distinctly arranged, but you have such feelings.'

"'Yes, papa, it does seem as if I am trying all I can to be saved.'

"'Well, my dear, all I can say to you is, that, before you will ever be saved, you must feel that you have *never done any thing toward your salvation, but every thing to prevent it;* that it would be perfectly just in God to leave you to perish; and, in short, that God is all right and you all wrong; for

"'Christ would sooner abdicate his own,
Than stoop from heaven to give *the proud* a throne.'"

In order to understand clearly the mistaken method of this good man, we need to notice how mankind use and understand the word *love.*

In its widest sense, we say we love any thing when it gives us pleasure by gratifying some desire. Thus we love fruits, and flowers, and agreeable perfumes.

But when we love *persons*, we have a complex experience. We not only find pleasure in their agreeable qualities, but we desire to please them in return, while this desire leads to purposes and acts that show our affection.

The simple *emotion* of love, which does not result in a desire and purpose to please, by action, is of small value. It is the desire and purpose to please, by *conforming to the will and wishes* of the one loved, that is the chief ingredient of true love. A child who simply was pleased with a mother's agreeable qualities, and yet constantly neglected to conform to her wishes, would never be said truly to love her; while another child, who made it his chief aim to find out what his mother wished and then to do it, would be said to love his mother truly.

Christ uses the word in this last sense when he declares, "He that hath my words and *keepeth* them, he it is that loveth me." So the apostle defines true love toward God: "This is the love of God, that ye *keep his commandments.*"

It has been shown in the previous pages that true *faith in Christ*, also, has for its main ingredient the purpose of obedience carried out in feeling and action. If this be so, the father's preceding explanation of faith is very incomplete.

So *repentance* toward God, which often in the Bible is made the indispensable requisite to salvation, has as its main feature not the *emotion* of sorrow for sin, which may exist without ceasing from it; but the distinctive ingredient of *true* repentance is *ceasing from sin*, or purposing to obey God, and carrying out this purpose in feelings and conduct.

But while, in all these three "*terms of salvation*," it is *obedience* in purpose and conduct that is the chief and indispensable thing, it is of the utmost importance that *emotions* of love toward God be awakened, as the *means* of leading to easy and cheerful obedience.

In the chapter on the *obedience of love* it is shown that there is no so easy and sure way to secure the obedience of children to law as to gain their grateful and admiring love. When a child is moved by an ardent affection, what would otherwise be a hard duty becomes a pleasure if it will please the beloved parent. So in regard to the heavenly Parent: the more we understand his lovely character, and realize his love and kindness toward us, the easier it is to try to please him by *obedience* to his laws. Thus it is that the lovely character of God exhibited in Christ, and all he did and suffered for us, tends to make it easy to obey him.

In the case of this child the father made two great mistakes: the first was in representing the *emotive* part of love as the chief duty required, and the second was so representing God and Christ as to make it almost impossible to feel any other emotions than those of terror and aversion.

In the course of his religious training, the father gives the common view of this class of theologians as to the use of the "means of grace" as follows:

"'Papa, do you suppose a person who reads the Bible and prays every day is more likely to be converted than one who does not?'

"'The Bible, Maria, gives *no* encouragement to those who read and pray *with an impenitent heart.*'

"'Then I don't see any use in praying at all.'

"'Of praying *insincerely*, I suppose you mean. There is a great deal of use in praying *from the heart*, though there is none in praying without it.'

"'Then, papa, I may as well give up at once.'

"'See how unreasonable you are, Maria. Because *heartless* prayers are of no avail, you will not pray at all; and you think hardly of God because he will not accept hypocritical and selfish services.'

"'But, if I can not do any better, papa, what *must* I do?'

"'*If* you can not do any better, why, then, there is no help for you. God has said that those who do not repent must perish; and, if you can not repent, why, you must suffer the consequences.'

"Maria, at these dreadful words, burst into a flood of tears, and sobbed for some time without being able to speak. Her heart rose against the demands of God. She wanted to say, 'Then he is unjust to require what can not be done;' but her father had answered this objection so often that she was afraid to advance it again. At last her father said,

"'Do you not see, Maria, that it is to accuse God of injustice to say you can not repent? He has *commanded* you to do it, and threatened to punish you if you do not; of course, to say that you can not do what he requires is to say he is cruel and unjust.'

"'But, papa, if I really *feel* that I can not? There is no arguing against consciousness; and, so long as I am conscious of being unable, I can not be convinced that I am able.'

"'If we could not be *deceived in our consciousness*, this would be unanswerable. What you are conscious of is that *very strong unwillingness*, which, while it exists, amounts to inability, and which is sometimes called *moral*, in distinction from natural inability.

"'It would be impossible that an affectionate mother should kill her child while that affection continues—*as* impossible as if it *could not* be done. The disposition might be changed, and then the impossibility would be removed. In this sense, I acknowledge that it would be impossible for you to repent, or, what amounts to the same thing, it is absolutely *certain* you never will repent of yourself.'

"Maria sighed deeply.

"'You see that it depends on the *sovereign grace of God* whether you are ever saved or not. Dr. Doddridge has remarked that a person who diligently uses the means of grace is *more likely* to be favored with the renewing influences of the Spirit of God than one who neglects them; not because there is any merit in such services, but because the fact that a person is inclined to offer them shows that the Holy Spirit is already striving with him. This remark, however, is merely the result of his own observation, and has *no warrant in the Bible.*'

"'Is there nothing I can do, then?' said Maria, in a tone of despair.

"'Nothing—if you *will* not do what God requires. My dear daughter, I would willingly help you if I could, but I dare not pretend to be more merciful than God. I *must* leave you where his word leaves you, shut up between these truths. You never can be saved without repentance; you can repent if you choose; but it is *absolutely certain* that you *never will* choose unless God makes you.'

"Maria's distress was terrible. She went up stairs and threw herself on the floor.

"'Oh, I wish I had never been born! I wish I had never been born!' burst from her lips.

"To feel that she was to blame for not repenting, and yet never would repent of herself—in short, that she was in the hands of the Almighty, to be dealt with according to his sovereign will and pleasure, this was distressing indeed.

"While these inward conflicts lasted, Maria could take no pleasure in any thing; she felt like an outcast, often envying the beasts and birds their happiness, or wishing she had never existed. At other times she was generally obliging and good-tempered, having overcome some of her childish faults; but when under the influence of these feelings she appeared unkind and morose. One reflection which increased her distress was that her guilt was aggravated by the very privileges which she enjoyed; and next to the wish that she had never been born was this—that she had been born a heathen.

"After this, Maria's distress continued for several weeks with scarcely any abatement. She felt as if the wrath of God pursued her wherever she went, and gave her no rest day nor night. When she lay down at night this reflection would present itself to her mind with irresistible force: God knows whether I shall ever be saved or not. He looks forward through the ages of eternity, and *perhaps* he sees that I shall spend them *in hell!* This perhaps had all the force of certainty, and her anguish hardly could have been deeper had she been assured of perdition.

CHAPTER THIRTEENTH.

PURITAN CHURCH TRAINING, THIRD PART.

In the following chapter will be found the continuation of the preliminary training, and finally the time and mode in which the *regeneration* of the child took place.

"One day, while Maria stood behind her father's chair, combing his head, with an expression of hopeless misery, and tears rolling down her cheeks, 'Papa,' said she, 'I do not see why Christians are ever unhappy. Oh, it seems to me that, if I were only sure of being saved, I should be perfectly happy all the rest of my life.'"

After narrating various reasons for the gloom experienced by Christians, he adds:

"'Still, it ought to make them happy that all things are in the hands of such a God—a God who is their Father and Friend.'

"Maria's tears flowed faster. 'He is not *my* Father and Friend,' thought she.

"'My dear child,' said her father, tenderly, 'if you really wish to be a Christian, what is there to hinder you? You can not doubt God is willing; if not, why has he given his only Son to die for you? Why does he allow the Bible and the Sabbath? Why is he sending his Spirit even now to draw you, if possible, to himself?'

"'I know it, papa,' said Maria, as soon as her tears would allow her to speak; 'but then, what *can* be the reason that I am not a Christian? I am sure if I were required to go a pilgrimage, or to submit to any of the penances which the Hindoos impose on themselves, I would not hesitate a moment—no, not a moment.'

"'I believe it, Maria. I believe you would do any thing to *purchase* heaven; but I believe too that, at this moment, you are refusing to accept it as a free gift, *for the sake of Christ.* This is the great stumbling-block in the way of every sinner's conversion. At first he would fain owe his salvation *entirely* to his own merits; and when he finds, by repeated trials, that this can not be done, he still tries to patch up a miserable righteousness of his own, which shall *almost* entitle him to heaven, and then the merits of Christ may do the rest.'

"He paused, but, as Maria did not reply, he went on:

"'My dear child, why will you not give up every thing of this sort, leave off all dependence on every fancied goodness of your own, and *trust simply in Christ.* Can you not fall down at his feet and say, "Lord, I am a poor, miserable sinner; I do not deserve any favor, but I pray thee to pardon me for Christ's sake?" Only say this *sincerely*, and the work is done.'"

Here the child is again driven on to the thorns; for the father had taught that it is impossible to pray to God *sincerely* with an unrenewed heart, and when God has renewed the heart there is no need of praying to have it done.

Still farther on we have the following, in reply to a remark of his child that she "should not think the Jews would have dared to talk as they did to God." The father attempts to show that she does the same sort of thing, thus:

"'You accuse God of placing you in such a situation as renders obedience impossible, and then of threatening to punish you for disobedience. I should like to know when the Jews said any thing worse than this.

"'Another of your excuses is, that you did not make your own heart. Now what is the meaning of this, if fully expressed? Why, it is this: "What an unfortunate creature I am! God has given me a depraved heart, and then blames me for having it. He has implanted propensities which he blames me for indulging; and, after making it impossible that I should love him, threatens me with eternal misery if I do not."

"'Of course, on this ground, all the sin and misery of the universe must be ascribed to God, and it is his fault that all mankind are not virtuous and happy.'

"'Papa, I am sure I should not have thought of saying such horrible things.'

"'No, I dare say, not in words; but to God, who looks at the heart, and sees all the feelings there, it is the same. Besides, you can not deny that you have brought forward all these excuses I have mentioned, and many others. When you complain of God for not answering your prayers, and assert that "it is of no use to pray or to do any thing," what is this but saying it is vain to serve God?'

"Maria could not deny this; she therefore remained silent.

"'The fact is, Maria,' resumed her father, 'that God and the sinner can not both be right. They are directly at variance, and one or the other must be wrong. If God be in the wrong, then he is infinitely wrong, for an infinite being must be infinite in all his attributes. He is infinitely unjust, cruel, and tyrannical; a being deserving no love, reverence, or obedience. Then you must give up saying that you are right. You must acknowledge that it is your fault, and not God's, that you do not love him, and it will be your fault, and not his, if you perish.'

"Maria sighed. She was unwilling to take the blame upon herself, and she was afraid to throw it on God.

"At last she said, 'Papa, perhaps we might have been able to obey the laws of God once, but have lost the ability on account of Adam's sin.'

"'That will not help the case at all; for, if you have iost the ability to obey God, even though you lost it by your own fault, yet, if it is lost, God has no right to command you to use it. God absolutely commands you *now* to repent; and, if you can not do it, the command is a tyrannical and unjust one, whether you ever had the ability to obey it or not. No, Maria, there is no other alternative. Either you are wrong, or God is so; which will you say?'

"Maria did not reply.

"'Did you ever think,' said her father, 'that you may, sometime or other, become an infidel?'

"'An infidel! Oh, papa!' said she, with a mixture of grief and reproach.

"'Just what I say, my dear. I think it extremely probable that if you should not be converted before many years, you will be an infidel. And I will tell you why. A man can never be happy so long as his conscience and his conduct are at variance. While he believes that endless misery awaits those who reject the Gospel, and yet he continues to reject it, he can not be at ease. If, therefore, he is determined not to alter his conduct, he tries to get rid of this belief; to persuade himself that he is not in so much danger as he supposed; that all men will be saved, or that there is no God. When God sees a man is bent on destruction, and wishes to be deceived, he gives him up to strong delusions, to believe a lie, and the wretched victim goes on blindfolded to ruin.'

"This conversation alarmed Maria exceedingly. She was almost distracted at times with doubts and apprehensions, and her mind was, indeed, 'like the troubled sea when it can not rest.' But let it be remembered all this was her own fault. *She would not submit.*"

The following conversation soon occurred:

"'Papa, if the hearts of all men are alike, and one no more deserves to be saved than another, why does God choose to convert some and not others?'

"'For no reason that we know of, Maria, but his own good pleasure. Creation gives the Creator an absolute sovereignty over his creatures. "Hath not the potter power over the clay, to make one vessel to honor and another to dishonor?" It would have been consistent with justice *if God had left us all to perish in consequence of the sin of Adam;* much more, then, is it just to leave those to perish now who reject the offered merits of a Savior, trample his blood under their feet, and do despite to the spirit of grace.'

"'Yes, papa, it would be just if he treated us all so; but if he saves some—'

"'That does not alter the case at all in regard to others. The case is just this: God has provided salvation for all; he offers it to all, but all reject it. He invites and entreats them to be saved, but they will not. Then, by the secret constraining influence of his Spirit, he obliges some to accept his offers, or rather *makes them willing* in the day of his power. But why should you object to others being saved, Maria, even if you should not be? Do you not see that only a feeling of envy could prompt such a wish? Are you not content with refusing the offers of mercy yourself, but do you wish all the world to refuse them too? What sort of disposition is that which could be consoled under suffering by the sufferings of others?'

"Maria burst into tears. 'I see papa hates and despises me,' thought she; 'and I do not wonder, if he supposed I had such feelings.' This idea put the finishing touch to her misery. I am indeed forsaken of God and man, was the feeling with which she rose to go to her own room, there to give vent to her sorrows in tears and groans. But her father detained her. 'My dear child,' said he, 'I know you do not love to hear these things, but if they are true, ought you not to hear them? If you are in the hands of God, is it not better that you should know it now, when by timely submission you can make him your friend, than to learn it for the first time when he becomes your irreconcilable enemy? I *must* tell you, then, my child—my duty to God and to your soul requires me to tell you—that the power of a giant over an infant is nothing compared with the entire and absolute control which God has over you. Escape you can not. Submit you must. Will you submit voluntarily and be happy, or by constraint and be miserable?' "

The next account of this poor child is this:

"The tumult of her mind increased to such a degree that she could no longer maintain her resolution (of silence). 'Oh, how I wish that I had never been born!' was the exclamation that broke from her lips after one of these struggles.

"'That is a very foolish as well as very sinful wish,' said her father, gravely. 'You ought, rather, to be grateful for the blessing of existence.'

"'I am sure I should not think it a blessing,' said Maria; 'we are created without our own choice, and then we don't know but we shall be eternally miserable, and we have no way of helping ourselves.'

"'Is that true, Maria?'

"'I don't see, papa, but it is. If God has declared that I shall be saved, I shall be; and if not, I shall perish; I can not alter his decrees.'"

Then follows an argument by her father to show that she has power to love and obey God, although she feels that she has not. It concludes thus:

"'Then, papa, I do not see what I am to do. It is very plain that love to God does not spring up in my heart spontaneously; and if [as her father had told her] it can not be excited by effort, how can I obtain it?'

"'Take care, in the first place, not to feel that, because love can not be awakened by *direct* effort, you are therefore not to blame for not exercising it. Recollect that it *ought* to be the spontaneous growth of your heart; and that it is not only proves your depravity. If you can be brought to feel and acknowledge this, one obstacle in the way of your loving God will be removed. You are *unwilliug* to see that he is lovely, because, if he is, you are unlovely. But only give up the pride of your heart, be willing to see that you are in the wrong, and you will be prepared to acknowledge that God is in the right, and to love him.'

"'But even this, papa, I can not do.'

"'No, not of yourself; and I was going on to tell you *how* you might do it. God says, "Let him (that is, the sinner) take hold of my strength, that he may be at peace with me." You will not be punished for not repenting by your own strength, but for rejecting the offered aid of the Holy Spirit. Go and fall down at the feet of the Savior, and tell him you know he deserves your love and gratitude; that it is *the fault of your own sinful heart* that you do not love him; yet acknowledge that you do not, and that you never shall of yourself, and beg him to send his Spirit to aid you. Do this *sincerely*, and I can promise you that you shall not come away unblessed, for the Savior saith, "Him that cometh to me I will in no wise cast out."'

"Maria sobbed out a request that her father would pray with her, and as he uttered in his prayer the sentiments he had just recommended her to adopt, her heart seemed *almost* ready to join; yet still it hung back."

The grand difficulty still remained—she must ask *sincerely*. She had been taught that she certainly never would do this until *her heart* was renewed by the Spirit of God: to pray with an unrenewed heart was to insult God with insincere professions. If God renewed her heart, the boon of regeneration was already given, and she could not pray for that already bestowed. So, on either alternative, no available prayer was possible.

The narrative states that

"for *many years* Maria's history would be only a repetition of similar circumstances and conversations. All this time she was engaged in constant efforts to recommend herself to the favor of God, and purchase Heaven by her own good works. There were, however, weeks, and even months, when she appeared totally regardless of the subject. After such intervals of carelessness her impressions would return with renewed force. At such times she was exceedingly distressed at her situation, and began to attend to religious duties, and read the Bible, and prayed every day with great zeal so long as her impressions lasted. By degrees, however, they were effaced, her devotions were neglected, and her goodness was as the morinng cloud and early dew.

"Her external conduct was such as might be expected from such a state of heart. Sometimes, for a few days, all went on smoothly; nothing occurred to call forth the corruptions of her heart, and she fancied they were subdued. But some unexpected temptation sufficed to put to flight all her good resolutions, and ruin all her self-righteous projects. Then her distress and mortification equaled her previous security. She was irritated, impatient, desponding, and this led to new faults in conduct. On the whole, the principal benefit she derived from all these years of trial and disappointment was increased knowledge of the desperate wickedness of her heart, and a deeper conviction that, *of herself, she never could perform one holy act.*"

After having secured this paralyzing conviction, there succeeded a course of constant appeals to induce her to do what she was convinced she *never should* do, of which the following is a specimen:

"'My dear, you have a work to perform—a work which must be done. The longer you delay, the greater will be the difficulty and the less your strength.'

"To escape from this, which she knew not how to answer, Maria proposed another question.

"'But, papa, why will it be harder to repent by-and-by than now?'

"'Even if it should not be so, you are not the better off, for you say you *can not possibly* repent now. But the truth is, you do not believe this.'

"'Do not believe it, papa?'

"'No. If you believed it, would you be sitting here so quietly?'

"'Why, if I could not do any thing to help myself, I might as well be quiet as not.'

"'Might as well be quiet! yet you would not be, any more than you would be quiet in a burning building, and knew all efforts to escape would be useless. No, no, it is not the nature of men who know *they are to be forever miserable* to be quiet about it. Is there not a secret feeling that, after all, if you were dying you *could* repent.'

"'Why, yes, papa; although I think sometimes I have tried as hard as I possibly could, yet it seems as if I might do a little more, perhaps, if it should come to the worst.'

"'Yes, that is the way with all sinners. In regard to you, Maria, it is absolutely certain that the present moment is the most favorable you will ever have; and if you do not repent now, there is no reason to hope, so far as your efforts are concerned, that you ever will. I pray God my child may never have occasion to say, "The harvest is past, the summer is ended, and I am not saved."'"

The following is a part of a chapter, the aim of which is to convince Maria that

"'the law of God requires *perfect* obedience *always;* it requires you to love God with *all* your heart, and your fellow-men as yourself, *every moment of your life.* It is as impossible that a man who has committed but *one* sin in his *whole life* should be saved by his *good works,* as if he committed a million.'

"It would be impossible to describe the emotions of grief, despondency, and anger which filled Maria's heart as she listened and became convinced that all her goodness was thrown away; that it did not give her the least claim to the favor of God, and that, in spite of all she could do, it would be just in him to punish her forever. The law of God seemed to her unreasonably strict and impossible to be observed; his character appeared hateful to her, and, *since her goodness was of no use, she would not try to be good any longer.* But then came the dreadful thought of eternal misery—of dwelling with everlasting burnings. With a heart full of enmity, hatred, and despair, she retired to bed."

The preceding is the history of Maria's experience till she was about thirteen, when the period of her regeneration arrived.

Immediately previous the following experiences are recorded:

"In compliance with her father's advice, she wrote a formal resolution to make it her first object to secure the salvation of her soul.

"In pursuance of this resolution, Maria immediately commenced a series of religious duties to which she strictly adhered. She prayed night and morning with much apparent fervor and many tears, read the Bible and other religious books, prayed with her little brothers and sister, and, in short, performed all the external duties of religion. The watchful care of her parents had before corrected many faults of her childhood, others were naturally abandoned as she grew older, and others still she was able to subdue under the influence of the powerful motives now operating. At the end of a short time her interest began to decline gradually, devotional duties became wearisome, were imperceptibly shortened, and finally omitted. She began to attend a day-school, where her attention was engrossed by her studies and companions, and her resolutions and hopes forgotten. Still, they had not been wholly useless. Maria gained by it *new experience of the deceitfulness of her heart, of its inconceivable depravity, of her utter inability to do any thing right of herself.* She became more distrustful of herself, and, in conversation with her father, did not, as usual, attempt self-justification.

"The next summer she read Doddridge's 'Rise and Progress' every Sunday, and, as regularly as the Sabbath returned, Maria would be full of the most pungent distress, and during the week as careless as if she had no soul. The Sabbath was spent in weeping, praying, and forming resolutions; and on Monday morning she rose, remembered she had lessons to prepare for school, learned them, went to school, and thus spent the day and week until the next Sabbath renewed her distress.

"The following winter a new change took place in her feelings. Her distress gave way to a conviction that she never should be saved—a conviction which was attended with a quiet, almost sullen despair. She supposed that the Spirit of God had forsaken her, but the thought did not occasion distress. She listened with silence, and without shedding tears, to all that was said to her, acknowledged its truth, at least, by her silence, but still seemed to be without feeling.

"She saw her past services did not entitle her to the favor of God; that they had been prompted by self-love, and that she should never be able in any way to entitle herself to his favor. She wondered she had never seen this before; but it excited no tumult in her mind, no enmity against God, no desires of self-justification. By degrees, the sort of sullenness which had at first accompanied the conviction that she was lost, gave place to a feeling not less desponding, but more tender. She was not distressed, but disconsolate, as if nothing on earth could make her happy.

"She went thus to a meeting. The love of Christ

was the theme of her father's remarks; it was one on which he always delighted to expatiate; but on that afternoon he was more than usually eloquent. Maria forgot herself and her despondency; she thought only of the Savior who was thus presented to her; admiration, love, gratitude, and penitence filled her heart.

"As soon as her father spoke to her, on going from the house, her tears burst forth again, and she could only tell him she was thinking of the love of Christ. This subject occupied her thoughts continually. Instead of complaining that she could not 'make her heart love God,' she wondered how she could help loving him. Instead of thinking herself unfortunate in not being able to obey the commands of God, she perceived that it was entirely her own fault that she had not done so sooner.

"Maria could not but be aware of this change in her feelings; she could not but see that they were different at present from any she had ever experienced before; and she began, though at first with trembling, to cherish the delightful hope that her sins were forgiven. This hope was gradually strengthened, and, three months after, she publicly acknowledged the Lord to be her God, and Jesus Christ her Savior."

This change was, as the father supposed, the re-creation of a new heart or a new nature. Without this remedy of the nature inflicted on this child for Adam's sin, no prayer could be sincere, and no act right and acceptable to God. After this change, though the child still had faults and sins, they did not, as before, prove, in her father's view, the utter depravity of heart and moral inability to please and obey God, but only her imperfect sanctification.

CHAPTER FOURTEENTH.

THEOLOGICAL TRAINING RESTRAINED BY COMMON SENSE.

In the preceding chapters we have seen a child trained from three to thirteen in the New England theological system, which is based on a dogma originated by theologians nearly four hundred years after the apostles.

According to this system, the child is taught that it has a "nature" or "heart" so dreadfully depraved that, until it is regenerated, all feelings and actions are sinful and offensive to God, so that even prayers to have this heart changed are hypocritical and insulting; next, that all the blame for this rests on the child, and not on God; next, that nothing that the child can do has any promise or encouragement from God to secure a remedy, but that he regenerates some and does not others, without any reasons that man can discover; that, though this depravity is so great that no human being ever will love and serve God acceptably till God re-creates this depraved nature, yet the longer the child delays to do so the more hardened in sins he becomes, and the less likely God is to bestow this mercy.

Finally, it is taught that eternal misery in hell is the certain consequence of living and dying without this change of nature, while acceptable prayers for this boon are impossible, and every kind of effort from unrenewed children has no tendency to propitiate God to bestow this gift.

At the same time, though the child is taught that God formed Adam with a perfect nature, and has power to give perfect minds to every infant, *he will not do it*, nor will he regenerate the whole, but only a portion of our race, all the rest being condemned to the unutterable, hopeless miseries of an eternal hell. Nor will he give any reasons for this dreadful state of things.

The question must arise in every mind how it is possible that children trained under this system can grow up light-hearted and virtuous, as is the case where it most extensively prevails.

One reason is, that this system is so contrary both to common sense and the Bible that it never is *fully believed.* Especially is this the case in reference to innocent and helpless infants. It therefore is rarely the case that parents ever attempt to instruct quite young children in the manner pursued by the father in this case of an unusually precocious child, as exhibited in the previous pages.

Moreover, all parents, even the most consistent in their theological training, are forced alike by their feelings, their common sense, and the Bible, to *contradict* their own system. Even in this work in hand we shall find examples to illustrate this. The one selected will show at once the amiable disposition of the child and the common-sense training of the father, and how it led him to *contradict* the theological system he had enforced on his child in the preceding chapters.

"'Well, Maria, how much is the world better for you to-day?'

"Maria blushed, but did not reply.

"'Have you added any thing to the "heap of happiness?"'

"'I don't know, papa; I—'

"'Do you mean that you have tried to?'

"'Yes, papa; or, at least, I meant to in the morning, but—'

"'But you found it harder than you expected?'

"'Yes, papa.'

"'But I suppose you have done *something* to-day for other people. You have done some things for me; you know you bathed my head because it ached, and read me to sleep, and dusted my books.'

"'Oh! but, papa, I love to do any thing for you.'

"'Well, don't you love to do things for other people?'

"'Yes, papa, sometimes; but, papa, I have done some good to-day, I believe, in helping mamma to take care of the baby and such things, but I thought I ought not to count them, because—'

"'Because what, my dear?'

"'Because I am obliged to do them. I mean, I should have to do them if I did not want to, and, therefore, there is no goodness in doing them.'

"'Very true; that is, there is not *necessarily* any goodness in them; but should you not *like* to help your mother, even if you were not obliged to?'

"'Sometimes I like it, papa, and sometimes I do not—when I am tired, or the baby is cross, or I want to read.'

"'Well, at these times you have an opportunity to exercise *self-denial.* Instead of performing your work reluctantly and impatiently, wishing you were not obliged to do it, think with yourself, "Now I have an opportunity of doing some good. I can make my mother happy by assisting her cheerfully; I can make the baby happy by amusing him, and can *please my heavenly Father* by quietly and cheerfully performing the duties which he has allotted me."'

"'Yes, papa,' said Maria, her eyes filling with tears. She longed to throw her arms around her father's neck and tell him how much she loved him, and wanted to do all that would give him pleasure. But she never found it easy to express her feelings of affection either by words or caresses, and she sat perfectly still, looking into the fire, and trying to keep the tears from her eyes."

In this whole passage the father directly *contradicts* his theory that an unregenerated heart vitiates every moral act. He speaks of making happiness for others, practicing self-denial, and *pleasing her heavenly Father* "by quietly and cheerfully performing the duties which he has allotted," as what the child may do just *as she is* without a preceding regenerating process.

The first lessons of religious training to little children, even among the sternest theologians, usually present God as *a father;* one who loves them, and is pleased when they try to do right. These ideas are taken with the perfect faith of childhood, while the conflicting theological system does not attract their notice till the period when they begin to reason and inquire as few children in the nursery ever do. It has been only at a more mature period that this theological mode has been adopted and vigorously enforced. Especially has this been the case in "revival" periods, when the great aim was to force the mind to an immediate decision. At such times, the preceding course with this young child was exactly the method which that class of ministers has pursued who were deemed most successful as *revival preachers.*

It is interesting to trace the struggle of humanity against this fearful dogma of a depraved nature inflicted on infants for Adam's sin.

This can be noticed chiefly in the history of the Christian Church. Ever since the introduction of this dogma, there has been a ceaseless conflict in regard to it; the *common sense* of humanity on one side, and theological theories on the other.

Here we need to notice the meaning of the word *common sense.* There are some *truths* which men believe from testimony, others from a course of reasoning, and others from the evidence of the senses. But there is a class of truths, called the *principles of reason* or *common sense,* which all men believe, not from testimony, or reasoning, or the evidence of the senses, but because the Creator has implanted the belief of them as a constitutional part of the mental organization.

For example, a man believes he exists, not because he is told so, nor does he reason it out, but he believes it because his mind is so made he can not help thus believing. So also he believes that he is the same person to-day that he was yesterday, and that the world around him is a reality and not a dream. These, and many other truths, are intuitively or necessarily believed by all men who are not insane.

This feature in the constitution of mind is sometimes called *reason*, as it is the foundation of all *reasoning*. It is, also, often called *common sense*, because it is common to all intelligent and sane minds.

The *test* for distinguishing these truths from all others is, that all sane persons talk and act as if they believed them; and whenever they cease to do so, are regarded as having "lost their reason."

The history of the Christian Church presents a ceaseless *conflict* as to the character, condition, and prospects of young children, resulting from a theory as to "the origin of evil," and a theological system founded on this theory which contradicts common sense, and thus forces theologians to contradict themselves.

The first Christians were the common people, who received the *facts* of Christ's religion without attempting any philosophizing as to the mode or reasons of these facts. That all men are sinful and in danger of eternal misery from sinning; that the only way of escape is by faith in Jesus Christ, which includes not only intellectual conviction, but a controlling purpose of obedience to his teachings; that this faith secures pardon for past sin and the aid of the Holy Spirit, these *facts* were accepted without speculations as to the *how* and the *why*.

But when philosophers became Christians they introduced their theories as to the "origin of evil." The Gnostics taught that *matter* is the cause of all evil; that Christ came to deliver us from it; and that, as a pure and perfect being, he was not connected with a natural body, but only appeared to have one. This introduced long conflicts as to the *nature of God and Christ.*

Then came another theory as to the origin of evil, resulting in long conflicts as to the *nature of young children.* One party, led by Augustine, taught that the origin of all the evil and sin of this world is the *fallen nature of infants* consequent on Adam's sin. The other party, led by Pelagius, denied that the souls of infants were in any way injured in nature by Adam's sin, and that this was not the origin of evil.

After a long and fierce controversy, the Pope and Emperor decided against Pelagius, and his doctrine was driven out of the Romish Church by severe persecution. The doctrine of the Romish Church on this matter is set forth in the decrees of the

Council of Trent. In giving a short statement of Catholic doctrines, the writer has consulted these decrees in the original Latin and in Percival's translation; also the *Star of Bethlehem*, authorized by Archbishop Hughes. But in her intercourse with intelligent Catholics, both at the East and West, she has discovered that their theologians differ as essentially as to the true meaning of "the Church" and "the Councils" as Protestants do as to the true meaning of the Bible.

According to the Council of Trent, Adam was created with a righteous and holy nature, and, by sinning, lost it for himself and for all infants, who thus incur not only temporal death and suffering, "but sin, which is the death of the soul."

In consequence of this, "no one can be righteous unless the merits of Christ are communicated." This is done by "baptism, which restores the righteousness lost by Adam"—faith, hope, and charity being thus infused into the soul.

This is called "grace," or "the grace of justification." It can not be secured except by baptism, so that all infants not baptized lose eternal life. The soul being dead before baptism, no one has power to do works of righteousness except when "grace" is infused.

When an adult is baptized, all his past sins are removed, the righteousness lost by Adam is restored—faith, hope, and charity, flowing from Christ, being infused into his soul.

There are two kinds of sin, *venial* and *mortal*, but the writer has not been able to find a clear definition of the distinction between the two classes.

If a baptized person commits a mortal sin, all is lost that was gained by baptism, and his soul is dead again, so that he can do no works of merit that are acceptable to God. Repentance, confession to a priest, and absolution secures God's forgiveness and escape from hell, but he is still liable to church penalties and to punishment in Purgatory until God's justice is satisfied.

When any person, in a state of grace, performs more good works than are needful for his own salvation, or inflicts on himself some suffering not required as a punishment for his own sins, it is *merit* or *righteousness*, which is laid up, and can be transferred to the account of sinners, to lessen church penalties or the pains of Purgatory. The sufferings of Christ were very much more than were needful to save the whole world from hell, as the least drop of his blood was sufficient for this. These superabounding merits of Christ's sufferings also avail to save from Purgatory and church penalties, and this treasury is given to the Pope to dispense at his discretion. An *indulgence* is the Pope's remission of some punishment of the church or of Purgatory.

If a person, after committing a mortal sin, dies before he is restored to grace, he goes to hell without any chance of escape. All persons, however good, at death go to Purgatory. The time of their detention depends on the number and kind of sins committed, and also on the indulgences received from the Pope through the merits of Christ and the saints, or on *masses* offered for their relief.

Catholic theologians hold that the above is the system taught by Christ and his apostles, and transmitted in the New Testament or by tradition.

But in the Roman Catholic Church there have been fierce controversies, embittered by persecution, on the main points of man's ruined nature and preventing grace. One party has been led by the Dominicans and Jansenists, and the other by the Jesuits, and both claimed to agree with Augustine and with the Catholic Church.

The Popes have been much perplexed in deciding the case. Clement VIII. called an assembly of learned theologians, which met *seventy-eight* times without settling the conflict. Paul V. suppressed the discussion, and decreed liberty of opinion on these subjects. In 1640 the work of Jansenius renewed the controversy, and a large party adopted his views on these points. Urban VIII. condemned them, and upheld the Jesuit side, which ever since has prevailed, though many Jansenists have held to their distinctive views, and still remained in the Catholic Church.

Thus it appears from history that the theory of infant punishment for Adam's sin was first established *by church authority* in the Romish Church amid a severe conflict, which has been perpetuated, more or less, ever since.

Before noticing farther conflicts on this subject in the Protestant churches, we will point out several particulars in which the Roman Catholic system conflicts with the principles of common sense.

In the first place, this system contradicts the common-sense principle of *free agency*. All men prove by words and actions that they believe they have power to choose *either* that which seems best as most agreeable to self, or that which seems best as conformed to the rule of rectitude, demanding the *best* good of all concerned. An irrational animal has power to choose only what is most agreeable to itself, without any reference to the rule of right; but rational beings have the power to choose either what is *most agreeable* to self or what is *right*. And this is what is meant by *free agency*.

But the Catholic system teaches that children have no power to choose right till grace is infused at baptism. The Council of Trent distinctly decrees that, without the preventing grace communicated in baptism, "they are not able, *by their own free will*, to move themselves unto righteousness." Also, that it is "not possible for them to believe, to love, and to repent as they ought to do, so as to receive the grace of justification, without the *preventing* (i. e., preceding) aid and inspiration of the Holy

Spirit." Also, that without this preventing grace "their good works would in *no* wise be grateful to God and meritorious."

Another principle of common sense in conflict with the Catholic system is, that it is the *motive* or *intention* which decides an act as meritorious, and deserving reward, or as sinful, and deserving punishment. If a child chooses what it likes best without regard to rule, all men feel that there is no merit or desert of reward; but if the motive or intention is to do what is *right*, at whatever sacrifice, all men feel that there is merit and desert of reward.

Here one other distinction must be recognized. A child may choose right as it respects *motive* or intention, and be mistaken as to the *rule;* for, in many cases, God alone can judge what is right as *best for all concerned.* An act, to be right in both relations, must be in agreement with the rule of rectitude, and the motive or intention must also be to act right.

It is the motives and purposes also which decide the *character* of men as virtuous or wicked. If a man's *habitual purpose* and *aim* is to act right, he is believed to be a righteous and virtuous man; but if he has an habitual purpose to gratify self without regard to the rule of right, he is believed to be an unrighteous man. This principle of common sense is found in all men, in all ages and nations.

The Catholic system contradicts this principle in

making merit or righteousness a physical thing, which can be poured from one mind into another, and which can be accumulated in a treasury, so as to be divided and measured out by the Pope. So, also, *religious character* on this system is decided, not by the voluntary aims and purposes, but by the nature or condition of the mind as transmitted from Adam in a fallen state, or as rectified by grace.

Another principle of common sense in conflict with Catholic theology is, that reward and punishment are *just* only for *voluntary* deeds and character.

Here we must notice that men sometimes use the words *reward* and *punish* to signify the natural consequences of right and wrong acts; as when a child is said to be punished by sickness for eating green fruit, or rewarded by good health for abstaining. But more frequently these words are used to signify *voluntary* penalties and rewards in addition to the natural ones, as when a child is whipped for eating green fruit, or caressed for abstaining. This distinction between *natural* and *voluntary* penalties is very important.

Of the laws of nature established at creation, we, with our present knowledge, can not decide whether they were instituted by God's will, or were inherent in the eternal nature of things independently of his will.

All must concede that there are some things independent of God's will and power. For example,

God exists, not by his own volition, but by an eternal necessity in the nature of things. God has not power to begin to be, nor to change his past experience. All theologians grant that God can not love selfishness and malignity, nor hate self-denying mercy and love. In regard to the laws of the material world, how far they are inherent in the eternal nature of things, and how far dependent on God's will, man can not judge.

But this distinction is clear, even to the humblest capacity. The natural laws of both matter and mind are fixed and unchangeable, so far as we can see or reason. Nor do we judge of them as we do of the voluntary laws of God and man, which are designed to influence the character and conduct of free agents. Instead of this, they seem to us not only as fixed principles to which all must conform, but as what exist by a *necessity* of things that *no* power can change.

The voluntary penalties of the laws of God and man have this distinctive peculiarity, that their express aim is to induce free agents to act in agreement with law, either natural or statute. And they are deemed *wise* and *just* only so far as they tend to secure obedience to the laws of nature or to the voluntary laws of society.

With this distinction in view, we find it a principle of common sense that *voluntary* penalties are just only when inflicted for *voluntary* acts. If a child eats green fruit and sickness follows, men say it is punished for violating a natural law. Whether this punishment is just or not is put out of the reach of human decision. But if a child is punished for blind eyes by additional voluntary penalties, all men feel that it is unjust.

Catholic theology contradicts this principle of common sense in teaching that infants are punished with "a fallen nature," or original sin, for an act of our first parents in which they had no voluntary agency. God, it is said, made a voluntary rule. Adam and Eve disobeyed, not a law of nature, but a voluntary precept, and for this all infants are punished by a ruined nature, from which results their sin and suffering.

Theologians teach that if Adam and Eve had not eaten the forbidden fruit, a holy nature would have been transmitted to all infants; so that the ruined nature of infants was a *voluntary* penalty, originating in the will of the Creator, and not a fixed necessity in the nature of things.

This all men feel to be unjust. Yet Catholic theology teaches that it is just, and that God can do such things, and yet be a perfectly just being.

That the constitutional traits of parents, both mental and bodily, are transmitted to their children, and that the vices of parents often deteriorate these traits, both for themselves and their offspring, is seen to be a law of nature, either established by God, or existing by a necessity in the nature of things. But this is a diverse case from that of Adam and Eve; for the command not to eat the fruit was not a law of nature fixed for all, but a voluntary law for a single case, and its penalty was a voluntary penalty.

Another principle of common sense in conflict with Catholic theology is, that voluntary penalties, in order to be just, must be inflicted on the wrong-doer, and not on the innocent.

If a parent should make it a family rule that whenever a lie was told, or an article stolen or destroyed, some one of the family should be punished who was innocent, all men would say such punishment was unjust; or if, in the state, laws were enacted with penalties to be inflicted on the innocent instead of the guilty, all men would say such penalties were unjust and absurd.

The Catholic theory conflicts with this principle in supposing a treasury of righteousness or merit gained by penalties inflicted, not on the guilty, but on the generous and good, thus enabling the wicked to sin and escape punishment. The principle thus assumed is that every sin must be followed by some *voluntary* penalty in addition to the natural penalties of wrong-doing, and that it is *just* that this punishment should be inflicted on the innocent and benevolent instead of the selfish and guilty.

This system of physical righteousness, which can be accumulated by the penances and self-inflictions of the good, and then employed to remit the penalties due to the wicked, resulted in various excesses of asceticism and penance among the generous and conscientious, and in the abuse of papal indulgences by the selfish and wicked. From these excesses arose the first Protestant contest led by Luther.

This great conflict all centred around the question of *justification.* The question was, How is the infant, born with a fallen nature, to become righteous or *just*, and how are sinful men to become righteous? The Catholic theory is that baptism restores the child to the condition from which Adam fell by infusing Christ's righteousness into its soul, after which works of righteousness can be performed. In the case of adults, repentance and faith in the teachings of the Catholic Church are required, and then baptism makes a sinner *just* or righteous, as Adam was at first.

But Luther and his followers, rejecting this, went to another extreme, and taught that children and adults are so ruined and corrupt in nature that they can do no good works at all, or have any merit of their own. The only remedy possible is to have Christ's righteousness *imputed* instead of being *infused.*

Thus the doctrine is expressed by Luther. Speaking of the purity and righteousness of a christian, he says, "This purity is not ours, but extraneous purity; for the Lord Jesus Christ clothes us with his purity and righteousness. If you regard a christian aside from the purity and righteousness of Jesus Christ, as he is in himself, you would simply see, however holy he might be, no purity at all in him; you would see him as black and ugly as the Devil himself almost." "God can see no sins in us, even though we were nothing but sin. He sees only the dear costly blood of our Lord Jesus Christ with which we are sprinkled. Wherefore he can not and will not see us other than were we his beloved Son himself, full of justice, holiness, and innocence."

Thus commenced the theory still found in the creeds of most of the Protestant sects, by which all men are represented as utterly incapable of any righteousness of their own. All children can sin, be guilty, and be justly punished for sinning. But all are utterly unable to have any righteousness of their own.

On this Protestant theory, *justification* consists in God's "accounting and accepting their persons as righteous, not for any thing wrought in them or done by them, but by *imputing* the obedience and satisfaction of Christ unto them, they receiving and resting on him and his righteousness by *faith*, which faith they have, not of themselves, it is the gift of God." This *faith* consists in "receiving and resting on Christ and his righteousness," which none can or will do till God re-creates the depraved nature transmitted from Adam. [See Presbyterian Confession of Faith and Catechisms.]

It thus appears that the Protestant theory of the ruin wrought by Adam's sin and its remedy is as much in conflict with common sense as the Catholic.

Common sense says that *righteousness* is the *voluntary* obedience to God's laws by rational beings; and whoever has a *controlling* purpose thus to obey is a righteous person in *character*, although there will always be shortcomings by the rule of perfect obedience.

But the Catholic says that righteousness is something infused from Christ at baptism, while the Protestant says we can have no righteousness at all of our own, only Christ's imputed to us.

Common sense teaches that *faith* is believing in Christ as Lord of faith and practice, with a controlling purpose to obey him.

But the Catholic says faith is belief in the teachings of the Romish popes and councils, while the Protestant says it is resting on Christ's righteousness, as having none of our own.

Common sense teaches that we are *justified*—that is, made righteous, and treated as such, when we believe in Christ as Lord, and maintain a controlling purpose to obey him.

But the Catholic says we are justified or made righteous by having Christ's righteousness *infused* at baptism, while the Protestant says we have none at all, but only have Christ's righteousness *imputed* when we trust to his righteousness, as having none of our own.

Common sense teaches that the infant must be *trained* to believe in Christ and obey his word in order to be saved.

But the Catholic says infants must have their nature new created by baptism in order to salvation, while the Protestant says infants must be regenerated by faith imparted only to "the elect."

Thus the whole system, both of Catholic and Protestant theology, turns on the theory of infant depravity.

The Protestants, after forsaking the Romish Church, soon came into conflict among themselves over this same theory of transmitted infant depravity. Having given up the doctrine of justification by the infused righteousness of Christ imparted at baptism, every parental heart yearned over each new-born infant with anxious questionings, especially at the approach of death. For this reason it was impossible entirely to root out the hope of some mysterious efficacy in baptism. This accounts for the language used in the baptismal form of the Episcopal Liturgy, which was arranged by Archbishop Cranmer, with the aim of violating popular feelings as little as possible in breaking from the Romish Church.

Soon after, commenced the Arminian theory.

The Episcopalians and Methodists, who are the chief Arminian sects, in their Articles of Religion, both of them hold that a child, owing to its fallen nature received from Adam, "can not turn and prepare himself, by his own *natural* strength and good works, to faith and calling upon God;" yet both sects teach, also, that Christ's death has purchased a remedy for this, so that all children have some power or a "gracious ability" to turn to God and work righteousness. That is to say, God creates them without *any* power to work righteousness, and at birth, for Christ's sake, gives them *some* power to do so.*

The Calvinists, in opposition, maintained that children are born without any kind of power to work righteousness, and that God bestows some power on "the elect," and that all the rest perish. It is this which ever has been the point of conflict between the Calvinists and Arminians.

* The following passages were sent to the writer as a correct statement of the Arminian doctrine by a learned professor in the chief Methodist Theological Seminary:

"In regard to the moral nature of children, the Arminian theory recognizes the fact of their fall in Adam, and their *not partial, but ample* restoration in Christ."

"It would be correct to say that Arminians teach that God, owing to the sin of Adam, creates infants without natural ability to serve him acceptably, but that, through Christ, he gives them *ample* gracious ability thus to serve him."

"The atonement is not available to any *till after birth.*"

But the Calvinists, again, have had a conflict among themselves on this same doctrine. The High Calvinists, or Old School, maintain that the child has no power of *any* kind to work righteousness, or even to prepare to do so, until its depraved nature is re-created. The New School Calvinist, on the contrary, teaches that the child, before regeneration, has full power to obey God's laws, but, owing to this transmitted depravity, *never will use this power* till regenerated. This last system is illustrated in the foregoing narrative of Dr. Payson's child. This conflict between the Old and New School Calvinists has greatly agitated the Congregational churches, and divided the Presbyterian Church into two distinct denominations.

The New Haven Calvinistic School is another division, whose main peculiarity is, that there is no sin except the *voluntary* act of an intelligent being. This is regarded by all other Calvinists as the entire relinquishment of the doctrine of transmitted infant depravity, and a return to the doctrine of Pelagius, that infants are born free from any sin or sinful nature.

As an illustration of these theories, a father sets an enticing but dangerous mixture before his wife, and tells her if she drinks of it all her children will be blind. She takes it, and all her infants are blind.

They are then placed in a dangerous morass, full

of pitfalls, and their only chance of escape to their home is by an intricate path that none can find without sight.

The Catholic theory restores sight by baptism, which is lost again at any great mistake in the way home.

The Arminian theory restores *some* sight, but imperfect.

The Old School Calvinist restores some sight to elect infants.

The New School Calvinist supposes a power to open the eyes, when the child would see; but such a baleful stupor has been caused by the deadly potion as makes it *certain* that no child ever will open its eyes.

Common sense rejects the whole thing, and says children are born with perfect eyes, and all they need is light and guidance from educators, and the aid Christ affords to all who seek it.

Still farther divisions and conflicts of Protestants may all be traced to this same dogma of transmitted infant depravity.

Thus the Baptists separated from other Calvinists on the ground that infants, being depraved in nature and unregenerate, are not to be baptized or admitted to Christ's church as lambs of his fold.

The Methodists separated from the Episcopal Church when, as a state religion, it was prostituted to irreligious ends. To avoid these evils, they established a church of regenerated persons, from which children and all unregenerate persons are excluded, till church officers are satisfied that regeneration has taken place.

The conflict between Unitarians and other sects has resulted mainly from the doctrine of transmitted infant depravity. They deny any such depravity, and consequently they deny any necessity of the atoning sacrifice of Christ to purchase a remedy. The denial of the Trinity not improbably resulted from denying any need of Christ's intervention to purchase the regeneration of a depraved nature.

The conflict of the Universalists with the other sects also resulted from this same doctrine of infant depravity; for they hold that God, as a perfectly benevolent being, having inflicted such a dreadful evil on innocent infants, insuring their sin and misery, and having full power to remedy it, will do so; and, to prove it, they use the very passages employed to prove infant depravity. "As by one man's disobedience many were made sinners, so by the obedience of one shall many be made righteous." "As, by the offense of one, judgment came upon *all* men to condemnation, even so, by the righteousness of one, the free gift came upon *all* men unto justification of life."

These passages affirm that the evil done to all men by Adam is remedied to all men by Christ;

and if this evil is not the death of the body alone (as the first Christians understood it), but the additional infliction of a fallen nature and all the sin and suffering caused by it, then Christ will remedy this evil done by Adam to *all* whom Adam has injured. Thus comes the doctrine of universal salvation to the whole race.

This brief outline of Church History shows that the conflict which separated the Catholics and Protestants, and then the subsequent conflicts and divisions of the Protestants, resulted mainly from this doctrine of transmitted infant depravity. It has been the CONFLICT OF AGES, in which common sense has been struggling against this theological dogma and the systems resulting from it.

In studying the conflict of the various Christian sects in regard to transmitted infant depravity, it will be found that they all have done just what Dr. Payson did in administering the New England Calvinistic system to his child. They all contradict their own system just where this system contradicts common sense. And the reason is clear. Every theologian necessarily believes the principles of common sense by the very nature or structure of his mind; and when his theological system contradicts them, he either argues *on both sides*, or he *reasons* in defense of his system, and *acts* in all practical matters so as to contradict it.

Moreover, each sect, while blind to its own contradictions of common sense, perceives them in its opponents. Thus the Catholic theologian will deny that his system contradicts free agency, but charges it on the Protestant. The Arminian Protestant denies it as to his own theology, and charges it on the Calvinist. The Calvinist denies that his system contradicts free agency, but the New School charges it on the Old School. And all are correct thus far; they all hold to free agency in practical matters and in certain portions of their creeds, and the *systems* they uphold, all of them, contradict free agency. And then the mistiness and perplexity thus caused they call "a mystery" revealed by God, to which our *reason* must submit in silence. This will be farther illustrated in succeeding pages.

We will next notice the advances that have been made in this long struggle of theology with common sense.

In the beginning we find Augustine writing thus: "We are obliged to confess that the souls of the little ones are condemned if they die unbaptized." And his antagonist Julian says to Augustine, "God himself, say you, *consigns to eternal fire* for an evil will the children who, as he knows, can have neither a good nor an evil will."

It was the monstrous cruelty of thus punishing infants for Adam's sin through all eternity in hell fire which probably led to the theory of baptismal regeneration, and also to the decree of the Romish

Church that this rite is valid, so as to save the dying child, if administered by man, woman, or child when no priest can be obtained. This was to soften the rigor of the infliction by making it possible, at least to every christian parent, to deliver an infant from inherited sin and its awful penalty by a rite so easily administered in all possible circumstances.

But at this day, in most of our largest Protestant sects, no infants are baptized except those whose parents profess to be regenerated; so that, in these sects, probably a majority of infants who die are unbaptized. What, then, are the teachings of theologians in the different sects as to the character and future state of infants?

In the Roman Catholic sect, where the doctrine of the transmitted ruin of infants first was established, there still is taught a penalty for Adam's sin on all unbaptized infants in the eternal world. Thus we find in the *Star of Bethlehem*, published with the sanction of Archbishop Hughes, of New York, the following: "Baptism is *so necessary to salvation* that any person may administer it. Take care, then, to be instructed in the manner of doing it." "What becomes of children who die unbaptized? It has not been revealed where they go, but they *certainly are excluded from heaven.*" This is some advance on the doctrine of Augustine, that unbaptized infants are "consigned to eternal fire" for Adam's sin.

In addition to this, we find that the Romish clergy, although they are bound to believe the decree of the Council of Trent that all infants receive from Adam, as a penalty for his sin, not only natural death and temporal sufferings, but "sin which is the death of the soul," and, if unbaptized, exclusion from heaven, yet feel at liberty to explain this last as only being deprived of the "beatific vision," which "consists in gazing upon God's essence," and as consistent with their being happy. Thus, though the principle remains of a voluntary penalty inflicted on infants for a sin they never committed, they lessen the worst part of the penalty by an unintelligible expression; for most parents will not conceive of it as any great loss to an infant not to "gaze upon God's essence."

Still more, we find some of the most learned and popular ministers of that Church teaching in their quarterlies* that the *nature* of infants is good, and only good; that when Adam sinned his nature was changed, not to an evil one, but only to a lower grade of being, perfect of its kind and good only. This lower nature was transmitted to infants; but, if they are baptized, they recover the nature which Adam lost for himself and his race.

Unbaptized infants lose the "beatific vision," and, though sent to a hell, are made to suffer there but very little, if at all.

* See Bronson's Quarterly for July, 1863.

Moreover, hell is not a place of penal torment, but only a world of undeveloped creatures of a lower scale of being, but perfect in kind, and tending to endless progress in goodness and happiness.

In the Episcopal Church, many teach a mysterious spiritual influence imparted by God at baptism, by which the fallen nature of an infant is in some degree remedied, or a "seed" of grace implanted, which confirmation and the Eucharist nourish till it is developed into true piety and virtue. Yet those who are most earnest in this doctrine never teach that infants will lose heaven for want of these church ordinances.

Another class, who reject the above view as involving a physical kind of virtue like that taught by the Romish Church, hold that baptism is the rite of admission to the Church of Christ, in which are secured ordinances and instruction that are attended by some *special* influence of God's Spirit, not bestowed except in connection with this rite.

Still, these, also, never teach that an infant will be excluded from heaven because it is not baptized. Such regard baptism as the seal of a covenant between the parents and God. On the part of the parents, it is a promise to train the child in the belief and practice of Christ's religion. On God's part, it supposes a promise of the influences of the Holy Spirit to aid both parent and child in exact proportion to their fidelity. In this view, the religious education of a child is a gradual process of government, training, and prayer for Divine aid, with the assurance that such aid will thus be bestowed.

But there is still another class, who hold that Christ's death availed to purchase restoring grace for *all* the race, so that infants come into life as lambs of Christ's fold, entitled to all the privileges of his flock, and, even when unbaptized, have power to do works pleasing and acceptable to God.

Such regard baptism as the outward sign of the child's relationship to Christ as his child, just as matriculation is the outward sign of membership in a college, or as coronation is a sign or rite that does not *make* a sovereign, but gives outward expression to the fact of actual sovereignty.

It is probable that the larger portion of the clergy of the Episcopal denomination would regard *all* infants as lambs of Christ's fold, even if many parents so little regard the rite as never to have their children baptized.

But the most marked point of advance in the Episcopal Church is the agreement of the wisest and best of their clergy and laity to cease contention as to the *theory* of transmitted infant depravity and the remedy, and unite practically in training *all* children on the assumption that they are lambs of Christ's fold, and that the "grace" needful to their successful training for heaven will be bestowed in exact proportion to the faithfulness of parents and children in striving to understand and obey the teachings of Christ.

The Episcopal local church embraces the whole parish; for it is assumed that *all* the children of the parish will be baptized, and thus recognized as members of Christ's Church.

Every Episcopal Church offers its baptismal font to *every* parent who desires for a child this sacrament. There is no division in the Episcopal Church into parish and church, each having its own officers. Nor does the Sunday-school consist of "the children of the church," who have been baptized, and the children not of the church, who are unbaptized. All children who belong to the parish or the Sunday-school are received and treated as lambs of Christ's fold.

In the Methodist denomination will be found a recent and very remarkable development in throwing off the doctrine of infant depravity.

According to their creed, children *by nature* have no power to "do good works pleasant and acceptable to God without preventing grace." Children also, by their rules and practice, are excluded from the local church until they give satisfactory evidence of regeneration.

But, recently, their leading theologians and periodicals are teaching thus: "Children belong to the kingdom of God as legitimate heirs and subjects, and if so, according to the universal law of that kingdom, it is because they are *made fit for it;* and both the fitness and the consequent membership are the free gift and fruit of redeeming love. That children are *in a state of grace*, in favor with God through the atonement, is incontestibly taught in Scripture.

"That the fruit of the atonement, as conveyed to them, is not a mere negative justification, not a mere acquittal from liability to punishment, but *a positive moral good*, *a principle of spiritual life*, is equally clear.

"This is not the fruit of baptism by any order of God, as the Church of England authors have erroneously assumed, but is by the direct grace of God in Christ. It is prior to baptism and the moral ground of fitness on which the baptism of children rests. And this grace, emanating directly from Christ to the infant, is not conditioned on its dying in infancy (this is a mere invention of theologians), but comes to *all*, without distinction, *who are involved in the consequences of Adam's fall.*"

"The idea that the Church is made up only of believers is as rational and scriptural as that a family or commonwealth is made up only of adults. It is not the personal act of faith, apart and by itself, that is to be considered, but the spiritual relation to Christ. If an infant without faith can belong to Christ, who is the Head, an infant *without faith* can belong to the Church, which is the body or community."

According to this view, *all* infants have "a principle of spiritual life," that is, "the fruit of the atonement," which makes them "legitimate heirs and subjects of the kingdom of heaven." This is "the moral ground of fitness on which baptism rests."

This being so, the whole human race, when infants, are fitted for the kingdom of heaven, and entitled to be members of Christ's Church; and the present Puritan mode of organizing the local Methodist Church, which shuts out all children till they give evidence of regeneration, can not long be maintained. Soon, in that large and useful denomination, the lambs of Christ will be taken into his fold, and never turned out till they prove the loss of their "moral fitness."

The great advance of these Arminian theologians on former opinions will be still more evident by comparing the preceding extracts with the following, taken from the writings of Arminius himself:

> "Adam, by sinning, corrupted himself and all his posterity, and so made them obnoxious to God's wrath. Infants have rejected the grace of the Gospel *in their parents*, by which act they deserve to be deserted by God; for there is a permanent principle in the covenant of God that children should be comprehended and adjudged in their parents." "For I would like to have proof adduced how all posterity could *sin in Adam* against law, and yet infants, to whom the Gospel is offered *in their parents* and rejected, have not sinned against the grace of the Gospel."

It is probable that there is now not a minister or

layman in those denominations that bear the name of Arminian who would not reject the above as false and absurd.

In the Congregational and Presbyterian denominations, in which the Calvinistic system prevails, the advance on this subject can be discerned in private conversation with individuals who stand high as leaders of opinion, rather than in theological schools and periodicals.

The Confessions of Faith in both these large sects still allow the implication that, on account of Adam's sin, none but the "elect infants" escape a miserable eternity in hell. But the writer has never seen or heard of an individual in either of those denominations who believed so monstrous a doctrine.

About ten years ago was published "*The Conflict of Ages*,"* which had a large sale, and was read by more laymen than any other strictly theological work ever issued from the American press.

In this work, the author, while still maintaining the *depraved nature* of the infant soul, insisted that there are implanted principles of *honor* and *right* in all mankind; and that, according to these principles, all attempts of theologians to justify God for causing a depraved nature to be transmitted to infants for Adam's sin are failures.

The chief aim of the work is to show that, infant

* "The Conflict of Ages, by Edward Beecher, D.D." Crosby & Nichols, Boston.

depravity being true, the doctrine of *a pre-existent state*, in which, after God had created every human soul perfect, each one *ruined his own nature* by sinning, and that this world is a place of probation designed to restore ruined minds to their original perfection of nature, is the *only* theory ever invented which does not implicate the Creator as violating the principles of honor and right.

The same author also maintains that the doctrine of *transmitted* infant depravity *for Adam's sin* is not taught in Romans v., the chief passage used to prove it, and that during the first three centuries it was never so interpreted in the Christian churches.

He also maintains that there is *no other* passage in the Bible which teaches transmitted infant depravity for Adam's sin.

This work was criticised in the leading religious periodicals of all the largest denominations, and in not a single instance was the fact questioned that Romans v. was never interpreted during the first three centuries to teach transmitted infant depravity as the penalty for Adam's sin. Nor was the author's argument to prove that the only penalty for Adam's sin taught in that chapter is *natural* death, and *not* a *transmitted, ruined nature*, ever controverted.

It was this work of her brother, and its treatment by theologians, which first settled the conviction in the mind of the writer that the doctrine of *any* infant depravity, either transmitted by God's constitutional arrangement, or originated in a pre-existent state, is not taught either by reason or in the Bible.

With this also came the conviction that the existence of a universal depravity of all infant minds, as the cause of all sin and suffering, would destroy all possibility of proving a benevolent Creator, or of *reliable* revelations from him.

Under this conviction, the writer published a volume entitled *Common Sense applied to Religion; or, The Bible and the People.* In this work the principles of common sense were defined and illustrated, and also the *test* by which they can be identified. These principles were then employed to prove that all infant minds are perfect in constitutional powers, and enter this life as God made them, and not depraved in nature.

A second volume followed, entitled *An Appeal to the People,** in which these same principles of common sense were employed to educe the system of *natural religion,* hereafter to be shown coincident with that of the Bible as interpreted by the same principles of common sense.

The argument of the APPEAL TO THE PEOPLE is based entirely on the perfect *constitution* or *nature* of the infant mind; and in it, it is asserted that the

* "An Appeal to the People in behalf of their Rights as the authorized Interpreters of the Bible." Harper & Brothers, New York.

existence of universal infant depravity as the cause of sin and suffering, would destroy all possibility of proving a *benevolent* Creator, or of any *reliable* revelations from him.

For the grand difficulty on all theological theories is this: Whatever the supposed depravity of nature is, all theologians who teach it agree that it is the cause of human sin and misery, and that God has power to prevent and to remedy it.

Now our only idea of a malignant being is that, having power to will virtue and happiness, he does not, but allows sin and misery instead.

The mode of doing this is not the difficulty, but the fact; all infants, on this theory, come into this life with a depraved nature, when their Creator has power to create them perfect, and thus to save them from the sin and misery consequent on a ruined nature. On their theory, God proves himself by his works to be a malevolent being, from whom no reliable revelation is possible.

This is the fatal difficulty of every system having the depravity of infants as a part.

The theory of a pre-existent state, in the *Conflict of Ages*, does not escape, for it starts with an assumption without proof, that God can create minds with a nature tending to holiness and not to sin, and that, having power to do this, and also to re-create every infant mind, thus preventing resulting sin and misery, he wills *not* to do so. This proves him a malignant being, from whom no reliable revelation is possible.

No attempt has yet been made by any theologian, of any sect or school, to meet the arguments of these two volumes; not because, as some editors claim, these arguments have already been met, for this attempt of the writer is entirely original, no other of the kind being extant in the English language, nor in any other, so far as the writer can discover. Neither was it because these works were not extensively known and read, for they were noticed in most of the leading periodicals, both secular and religious; while the one paper most extensively read commended the first work as "a remarkable specimen of intellectual masonry," and great curiosity was expressed by this and other periodicals as to how theologians would treat the argument.

The result has been that every theologian, in regard to *the argument*, has yielded a respectful silence. Some minor matters have been criticised, but to controvert the argument has never been attempted in a single case known to the writer.

It is this implied acknowledgment that has convinced others besides the writer that the doctrine of transmitted infant depravity is not taught either by reason or by the Bible.

The character of the persons to whose notice these volumes have been presented, in public and in private, forbids the idea that, either as gentlemen or as Christians, they would leave such arguments unanswered if it were in their power to point out fallacies in a course of reasoning which removes the very foundation of the theological system they are upholding.

But great changes in *systems*, and in habits of thought and reasoning connected with them, are always slow; nor does silence, in such a case as this, in any way implicate the intelligence or motives of the persons to whom reference is made. It is often the case that men perceive great difficulties in the system they are defending, and yet do not publicly relinquish it, because they have not yet found another which they are ready to offer in its place.

Add to this many practical embarrassments that interfere with any sudden or open changes in theological systems long imbedded in the public mind and connected with established church organizations.

On the other hand, the slow but steadily upward progress of humanity, the strong instincts of personal interests and of parental tenderness, all combining with common sense and the Bible, are slowly but surely driving away the cruel dogmas of past ages, which have shrouded the teachings of Christ in mystery and gloom.

The grand question, now to be settled as a *practical* one by every educator, minister, and parent, is briefly this:

When our Lord and Savior took infants in his arms, blessed them, and said, "Suffer the little children to come unto me, for *of such is the kingdom of heaven*," did he intend us to understand that all children have such fallen and ruined minds that they never do good works pleasing and acceptable to God till their *nature* is changed by baptism, or by a supernatural new creation wrought only on elect infants? Or did he intend to teach us that *every* infant can be *trained*, by right instruction, example, prayers, and the aid of his ever-ready Spirit, to christian life and eternal safety? And did he intend us to understand that *all* children are to be taken into his church as lambs of his fold, or are they to be kept out till they can prove to church officers that their *nature* is changed from that of a young wolf to that of a lamb?

CHAPTER FIFTEENTH.

THE BIBLE ON INFANT CHARACTER AND PROSPECTS.

THE grand difficulty in relieving parents and teachers from the system of theological training which has been exhibited in previous chapters is, that there are a few passages in the Bible which have been so long employed as proof-texts to establish it, and thus incorporated into religious literature and the popular mind, that to question the theological system *seems* like disputing the Bible.

This difficulty is relieved by noticing again the distinction between *facts* revealed in the Bible and the *theories* contrived by men to explain these facts. We may give up these theories, and have none at all, or we may adopt other theories, and still hold the revealed facts.

In attempting to gain the teachings of the Bible on infant character, these preliminaries will be assumed as conceded.

Firstly, that our English version is sufficiently correct for all the practical wants of the common people, and that this is the standard to settle the question.

Secondly, that the words used are to have the common ordinary meaning.

The whole question turns on the words *death*, *justify*, and *faith*, each of these words having two meanings. Thus the word death signifies the death of the body only, and also "to be carnally minded," which is death to the soul, or spiritual death. The word justify, in its literal sense, means to *make* righteous; in its secondary sense it signifies *to regard or treat as righteous.* The expression *having faith*, in its primary sense, means believing in or trusting in the claims of any person; in its wider sense it means not only intellectual conviction, but practical obedience to the teachings of that person. The first is a "dead," and the second a "living faith."

All men know by experience that breaking just rules in the family causes anger and a desire to punish. All men perceive that a just ruler is angry when his laws are broken, and that punishment is the only way to sustain human laws.

As soon, then, as men are led to believe in a God who is both good and just, comes the anxious inquiries, "How shall man be just [righteous] with God? How can a good and just God love sinners, and how can he pardon for *past* sin without destroying law? And how can man, with all his bad habits, his ignorance, and his guilt, ever be made righteous in character and conduct?"

In the Bible we are taught that Jesus Christ, by his example, his teachings, his death, and his resurrection, has overcome all difficulties, so that now God can be just, and yet love such sinful beings as we are, even as a tender parent loves an erring child. His heart and home are still open, just as much as if we had not sinned; and, owing to what Christ has done and suffered, nothing is needful for acceptance as righteous but to repent of the past and begin a life of obedience. In respect to God's feelings toward our whole race, his tender love for us, and his readiness to receive us without punishment, we are *just as if we had not sinned at all.* In this respect the whole race is justified.

This is illustrated in the parable where an earthly parent, when he saw the repentant prodigal a great way off, ran to meet him with an overflowing love, even more tender than was felt toward the son who had never been in such sin and suffering. So the angels in heaven rejoice. So, in the parable of the Good Shepherd, he rejoices *more* over the lost one restored than over the ninety and nine that went not astray.

The grand aim of all this is to teach the most guilty and despairing that a pure and just God loves them even as sinners, will receive them tenderly, and pardon all their past sin when repented of and forsaken. The Gospel says, only return to your heavenly Father, and become obedient children, and all your past sinfulness shall be forgiven, and you shall be received *as if you had never sinned.* And this can be done, and yet God be just, owing to Christ's atoning sacrifice.

Moreover, the obedience demanded as the indispensable element of justifying faith is not *perfect* obedience, but only the *abiding*, *controlling* purpose to obey, which will frequently be attended by failures and shortcomings. For none but God can decide, in all cases, what is right as *best* for all concerned. Man will often fail to do right from mistakes, ignorance, and forgetfulness, even when his great desire and purpose is to obey in all things.

But the Gospel brings comfort for this also. It says: "Do not be discouraged by failures in duty; repent, and go forward again in your purpose and efforts to obey, and all the past is forgiven, and you are accounted as dear and obedient children, and all for Christ's sake." What he has done and suffered enables God to be *just*, and yet thus to justify, or love and accept as just persons, all who believe in and strive to obey his dear Son.

This, it will be noticed, is not the Catholic theory, that a man is made righteous by Christ's righteousness flowing into him; nor is it the theory of Luther, that man can have no righteousness at all, but only have Christ's righteousness "imputed" to him.

It is the common-sense doctrine that a weak, ignorant, and sinful child is loved in spite of his faults; and when he is trying earnestly to do right, his failures are forgiven, and he is accepted as a dear child; and all he does that really *is* right is so valued and received as a precious offering.

What really is good as to motive and act is accepted as *our* righteousness, and we are to be rewarded for it. What is deficient or wrong is forgiven for Christ's sake, as soon as it is confessed and repented of, with a sincere purpose to avoid the sin in future.

We will now examine the Epistle to the Romans with reference to the celebrated passage from which originated the theory of transmitted depravity for Adam's sin.

In the first chapters of this epistle we find it taught that both Jews and Gentiles know enough of God and his laws to deserve punishment for disobedience to known law; and that no one, not even Abraham, can be regarded and treated as righteous (justified) on the ground of sinless obedience to all the laws of God, natural and revealed.

Then follows the Gospel plan of salvation, both from sin and its punishment, through the atoning sacrifice of Jesus Christ and by faith in him. The first part of chapter v. exhibits some of the benefits to those justified by faith; then, at verse 12, comes the celebrated passage in which Adam and Christ are compared.

In much of what precedes this passage the apostle has reference to those who are justified in the widest sense, being believers. But this comparison has relation to the whole race.

Christ, in a certain respect, has caused the whole race to be regarded and treated *as if* they were not sinners, just as Adam, by introducing sin and consequent temporal death, caused all, even infants, who have not sinned against known law, to be treated *as if* sinners.

To a world of perfect beings just beginning existence, the direction would be, obey the laws of your Creator and be forever happy.

To all our race, after they are sinful, the same offer is made, and thus they are treated *as if* righteous. To them it is said, begin to obey the laws of your Creator, and you are as if you had never sinned. All that is required for your eternal happiness is that you have a controlling purpose to obey the laws of Christ your Lord and Creator, and then all your past and your future shortcomings are as if they had never been.

It is as if a family were relieved from a bill of attainder; their privileges are restored, and all they have to do is to *receive* the gift. Thus it is with mankind. They are relieved from the necessity of being punished for *past* sins whenever they choose to accept the gift by repentance.

In the most limited sense of justify, the whole race are justified by Christ's mediation. In a more extended sense, those who have true faith are justified; they not only have the bill of attainder removed, but they have accepted the terms, so as to *receive* the gift of their paternal home and privileges.

Moreover, it is taught that Christ's mediation not only saves from the penalties of past sins, but is the real influencing cause of that righteousness of character and conduct which eventually will secure eternal life to all who have true faith in Christ. His character, example, teachings, and the motives he has revealed, secure that love and gratitude which lead to final *perfect* obedience. In this sense Christ *makes* those who believe in him righteous in character.

In this, which may be termed the common sense interpretation, it will be seen that Christ does more good to all men than Adam did evil to all.

But in the interpretations given by both Catholic and Protestant theologians the passage is made self-contradictory.

According to both, an awful evil by Adam was done to *all* men; the good done by Christ was only to the very small part regenerated.

Thus, in exact contradiction to the text, Adam did far more evil to the race than Christ has done good.

The reader now is requested to take this passage (Romans, v., 12, to the end), and notice the *facts* stated, and also to observe that there are no theories to explain or account for these facts.

Thus verse 12 states the fact that sin entered by one man, and death by sin. But whether Adam caused sin and death simply as any father, in causing the existence of a family, causes all the events that are consequent, we are not told. The *how* is not explained. Theologians have invented the theory of a transmitted depraved nature, which has no warrant in this or any other part of the Bible.

Verse 13 states that sin entered before revealed law, but that it is not imputed to those who sin against unknown law.

Verse 14 states that the consequences of sin come on all, even infants who have not sinned as Adam did against known law.

Verse 15 states that the good done by Christ exceeds the evil done by Adam.

Verse 16 states that the evil was by one offense, but the good done is a remedy for many offenses.

Verse 17 states that by one man's offense death (temporal) reigned over *all* men, and that much more good comes by Christ, especially to those who *receive* the gift provided for all.

Verse 18 re-states the fact that by the offense of one condemnation to death [temporal] came on *all* men, and that justification unto life came upon *all* men.

Verse 19 states that many were *made* sinners by

one man's offense, and that many shall be *made* righteous by the obedience of one. But it does not state *how* they were made so.

Verse 20 states that grace has done *more* good than the offense did evil.

Verse 21 states that as sin reigns causing death, grace reigns causing righteousness and eternal life.

The reader will now judge whether the death spoken of in this passage is to be interpreted as what the common people mean by this word—that is, death of the body, or, as theologians teach, (i. e.) death of the soul by a change in Adam's constitution of mind transmitted to all infants, to be partially remedied only by re-creation at baptism or by elective grace.

In presenting this interpretation of this famous passage, the writer aims not to establish a new philosophy to account for man's sinful character, but to escape the pernicious one established by theologians of past ages. The Bible gives no philosophy at all on this point, but simply states the facts of man's universal sinfulness, and the full remedy offered for it by Christ's life, teaching, death, resurrection, and the gift of the Holy Spirit. This is all that the writer deems important. But if men, in order to the giving up an old theory, must have some other, here is one that does not violate Scripture, and that does not oppose the moral sense and common sense of all men as does the one now taught by theologians.

In the *Conflict of Ages*, p. 372, it is stated that for four centuries after Christ, the Greek Church interpreted the death introduced by Adam to be only the death of the body, and not a depraved nature. Also that, before Augustine and Tertullian, this was the view of the Latin Church. Irenæus, the great opposer of heretics, so interpreted this passage. In favor of this view the Greek fathers are uniform. Muenscher gives passages in proof of this from Justin Martyr, Athenagoras, Tatian, Theophilus Antiochus, Clemens Alexandrinus, Origen, Athanasius, Chrysostom, Cyril Hierosol., Titus of Bostra, Basil the Great, Gregory Nazianzen, Gregory Nyssenus, Nemesius, and Epiphanius.

This statement has never been disputed; and thus it appears that the earliest Greek fathers, who best understood their own language, in which this passage was first written, never have sanctioned the interpretation of theologians.

The following, from Neander's History, shows that this theological theory very probably started from a mistake in translating this passage in Romans v. into Latin. He says:

"In considering the scheme of doctrine which prevailed among the Latins, it is important to notice that in their ancient translation of the New Testament (the Vulgate), the words in Romans, v., 12, correctly translated in the English Bible 'for that all have sinned,' was incorrectly rendered in the Vulgate '*in quo peccaverunt*,' (i. e.) '*in whom* all have sinned.' This furnished some apparent ground for the representation that all mankind sinned *in* Adam, as taught by Augustine, and adopted by the Romish Church."

The question is not whether all men are depraved *in character and conduct.* This all agree in. The dispute is in regard solely to *the cause* of this depravity—whether it is caused by a depraved constitution of the mind or by something else. Theologians teach that it is caused by a disordered mental constitution. In denying this theory we do not deny depravity of man, and we are not required to point out the causes of it. But if this is insisted upon (as it usually is), then there is another mode of accounting for it which does not implicate God as a being who prefers sin and misery to virtue and happiness.

One of the most important principles of common sense is that nothing is to be practically assumed as true without evidence. Any man who sent his ships or wares where there was *no* evidence that he could find a market would be deemed insane.

But in supporting a theological theory resting mainly on a false interpretation of Rom. v., its defenders have been obliged to *assume* several very important facts without *any* evidence, and thus to contradict common sense.

One assumption is that God can and has created

the minds of angels and our first parents on a more perfect pattern than that of infants. No proof of this can be found in the Bible or out of it.

Another assumption without proof is that the infliction of pain and death on infants is evidence of their ill desert. This is not so, inasmuch as Christ suffered pain and death, though perfect in all respects.

Another assumption without proof is that God never did or can suffer. We have no knowledge of God's nature on this point but from analogy and from revelation. Analogy teaches that God's mind is like our own, with susceptibilities of suffering such as we have. The Bible uses every form of language to assure us that God suffers with and for his creatures. In the face of this evidence, and without *any* proof, theologians teach that God never has suffered.

If God is a sympathizing and "long-suffering" being, the susceptibilities of suffering are a part of his eternal nature which he did not cause. And all created in his image must have the same. Christ, the only perfect being who dwelt on earth, had these susceptibilities, and "was made perfect by suffering."

Liability to suffer, then, is a part of the eternal nature of God, and all free agents in this respect are made in his image.

In the preceding we have given an analysis of

Paul's teachings in an epistle of which the chief aim is to set forth the Gospel, or good news that he was called to preach to the Gentiles. The following is added for the purpose of settling the question as to what the words "righteousness" and "the righteous" mean, as used in the Bible.

The revelations of God are made in the language of common life, and words mean what *the people understand* them to signify when they use them. *Right*, in its widest sense in common use, means *according to some rule* for securing any design.

God's design in creating his vast family is to secure their highest happiness or *best* good. To accomplish this, all his children must obey the grand law that each shall choose what is *best* for all concerned, instead of what each one desires most for self. And, in forming this estimate, the interests of *eternity* are to be regarded of first account. None but the Infinite mind can judge on this infinite scale. And so man needs a revelation from God of the rules of right action. These rules are to be accepted with a practical faith (i. e.), a controlling purpose of obedience.

While the Bible contains the chief rules of right action, many specific rules can be gained only by experience, and by a correct application of the revealed laws of God to specific cases. For example: when God commands *honesty*, man has still to decide in multitudes of varying cases what action *is* honest; and the correctness of such decisions depends on the mental development, experience, and correct reasoning of our race as it advances in knowledge and civilization.

This being so, all men in all ages will continually misjudge as to what is right, even where there is a full purpose of obedience to all God's laws.

"The righteous," then, in the Bible use of the term, are not those who are *perfectly* obedient to all God's laws, for none are and none can be. But those are counted righteous who maintain a *controlling purpose* of obedience to the laws of the Creator. And, on account of what Christ has done and suffered, God can be *just* in justifying those who are sinners by transgression of law, but righteous as possessing this controlling purpose of obedience.

Besides the difficulty as to how God can be just, and save from punishment for past sin, Paul discusses another difficulty. We all perceive the *fact* that children are born with diverse mental constitutions, and some of them apparently much better than others, while these peculiarities are transmitted from parent to child. Thus some have a nature or constitution in which conscience seems to predominate, while a desire to please others, or to make others happy, is small. Others have the benevolent impulse very strong, but have little conscience in regulating it. Some have the sense of justice very strong, with little of the element of mercy;

while others are tender and merciful, and have little of the element of justice. Some also are very high in intellectual gifts, and some are very low.

Why some are formed so much superior to others St. Paul in part informs us when he teaches that we all are designed to be parts of "one glorious body," each one so perfectly benevolent as to rejoice in the gifts of another as much as if they were his own; that the *best* good of this great body demands that there should be diversities of grades, a foot as well as a head, and that all the humbler parts rejoice in the glory and honor given to the higher, and are equally benefited as parts of the great whole.

In this epistle the apostle recognizes the *fact* that some, also, are placed by God in more favorable *circumstances* than others, as was Jacob and his descendants in comparison with Esau and his descendants; and that this arrangement of advantages is made on principles which are not revealed to us, and so are "a mystery," to which we must all bow in humble trust in the Great Creator, who declares that he is not willing that *any* should perish, and that he is doing all things in perfect wisdom, and love, and mercy.

The mistake made in the theological system based on a depraved nature inherited from Adam is, that these manifest diversities in mental constitution transmitted from parent to child, which all may be *good* if properly developed and controlled as parts of a great system of social and intelligent beings, are confounded with a supposed *depraved nature*, in which all infants are alike, instead of being different from each other.

According to the theological dogma, all children are just alike in a depraved nature transmitted from Adam, preventing them from loving and serving God acceptably till it is re-created.

And theologians fail in not noting the difference between diversities of constitutional endowments, all of which are good when regulated aright, and a uniformity of nature in all so *bad* that it can not be regulated aright, but must be changed in order to right action.

One other point will give light on this subject. Theologians have decided that "concupiscence (i. e., desire) is of the nature of sin." This is a fundamental mistake; for the higher and nobler a mind is, the more strong desires and impulses it has to control; and the sinning of such a mind is not in having the strong desires, but in failing to control them aright. Stupid and phlegmatic persons have not half the temptations of desire that agitate those of noble intellect, quick perceptions, and vivid imagination; and, as a general rule, it may be stated that the nobler are the natural endowments of a person the more "concupiscence" exists to be controlled.

The Lord of Glory, when he put himself in the condition of a man, in that hour of agony when the powers of darkness were allowed to bewilder and affright, prayed earnestly, and, as it were, with great drops of blood,

"O my Father, *if it be possible*, let this cup pass from me; nevertheless, not my will, but thine be done."

Here was the *perfect man* and the Almighty Creator earnestly desiring to escape suffering, and yet choosing to undergo it, if necessary to that great good of his creatures which he came to accomplish. This is the sublime proof that a perfect mind may desire what it would not be right to choose, and that the height of virtue is to choose, not what we most desire for self, but what the Omniscient Mind sees to be *best for all concerned*, often involving the greatest self-sacrifice.

We now notice the texts in which the word *nature* is used in reference to sinful character. Before referring to them, we need to mark the meaning which mankind give this word in common use. The *nature* of a thing, as understood by the common people, as well as philosophers, signifies the *powers* created by God which are the *cause* or *reason* of its qualities or actions. Thus the power which the eye has to see is created by God, and this is the cause or reason why the eye sees. This power to see is the *nature* which God created.

But the eye has no power to see when it is in

darkness, though it has the power of seeing given by construction. The constitutional power of seeing is given by God in creating the eye, while the power of seeing by having light may be given or withheld by man as well as by God. Thus it is the nature of the eye to see when there is light, and not to see when there is no light. This illustrates the two modes in which the word *nature* may be used in reference to the infant mind.

The question is, are young children so made that the cause or reason of their sinning is that their minds are depraved in *constitution*, or do they sin for want of proper development, training, and advantages? Is the mind *made* wrong, as an eye would be when it could not see, light being present; or is it perfectly made, and does not act right for want of the light of knowledge and appropriate training?

Men also use the word *nature* sometimes to include all circumstances and events, as well as the constitution of things. Thus we say that any thing acts *according to its nature* when it acts *as it usually does* according to past observation and experience. If, according to universal experience, all children sin, we say it is the *nature* of children to sin, or they have a *sinful nature*—a nature that insures sin.

But such language does not decide the question whether this universal sinfulness in children is owing to a wrong constitution of their minds, or to their want of knowledge, development, and training.

We now are ready to examine the only two texts in which the word *nature* is used in reference to men as sinners. The first is this:

> "For when the Gentiles, which have not the law, do *by nature* the things contained in the law, these, having not the law, are a law unto themselves: which show the work of the law written in their hearts, their conscience also bearing witness, and their thoughts the mean while accusing or else excusing one another."—Romans, ii., 14, 15.

This, it is plain, refers to the *constitution* of the mind as made by God. And here it is said that "the Gentiles do *by nature*" the things required by law—"the work of the law is written in *their hearts*." Surely this is not a text that can be employed to prove that the minds of young children are made wrong as to *constitution*, but rather the contrary; for it says the Gentiles, as heathen, *by nature* obey God's law, and that it is written in their hearts.

The only remaining text in which the word *nature* is used in reference to the sinfulness of man is Ephesians, ii., 3: "And were *by nature* children of wrath, even as others."

Here the *second* use of the word nature is appropriate. The apostle says that those he addressed were all living in that course of sinning which is according to the common experience of man, as all men *naturally* do when they have not the light of the Gospel. This text shows that, according to the nature of things, as the world is and ever has been, men sin; but it does not teach that the *reason* or *cause* of this sin is that their minds are *made* wrong, but rather that it is for *want* of "the light of the *knowledge* of the glory of God as it is revealed in Jesus Christ."

One other text is usually quoted to prove a depraved nature transmitted from Adam, viz.:

"Lie not one to another, seeing that ye have put off the old man with his deeds, and have put on the new man, which is renewed in knowledge after the image of him that created him."—Colossians, iii., 9, 10.

Alford, a Greek scholar and commentator of the highest reputation, thus translates and explains this text: "Lie not toward one another, having put off the old man with his deeds, and having put on the new, who is continually being renewed toward perfect knowledge, according to the image of him that created him" (i. e.), being renewed, not by *full* knowledge, but *toward* it, so as eventually to attain a full acquaintance with the Divine will, the result being the image of God in man.

He adds this emphatic condemnation of the common theological use of this text:

"New creation of the spirit unto fullness of knowledge and truth, the highest form of which would be the perfect knowledge of God, is regarded by the apostle as *analogous* to man's first creation. As he was then made in the image of God *naturally*, so now spiritually. *Restoring the image of God as in the first creation* is an idea foreign to Scripture. It is not to restore the old, but to create the new, that redemption has been brought about. Whatever may have been God's image in which the first Adam was created, it is certain that the image of God in which Christ's Spirit re-creates us, will be as much more glorious than that, as the second man is more glorious than the first."

In this text, the *mode* in which men are new created is expressly stated: they are "continually being renewed *toward* perfect *knowledge*," the final result being the image of God; that is, we are to be spiritually re-created by *knowledge* of God and his will, not by a physical reconstruction of our minds, making us like Adam when he was first created.

Alford says that this last idea of restoring God's image as it was at first in Adam, which is now the common theological one attached to this text, "is an idea foreign to Scripture."

We are now led to inquire what Bible proof there is that Adam, or the angels, or any finite minds were created with any *better* minds or with any *different* minds from those of infants.

As it respects the angels, only two texts are employed to prove that they were created with diverse minds from infants. These are:

"And the angels which kept not their first estate, but left their own habitation, he hath reserved in everlasting chains under darkness unto the judgment of the great day."—Jude 6.

"For if God spared not the angels *that sinned*, but cast them down to hell, and delivered them into chains of darkness, to be reserved unto judgment."—2 Peter, ii., 4.

The application of these texts to this question all depends on the word "sinned."

In the Bible "sin" is used in three senses. In the first it signifies *transgression of law*, either known or unknown; in the second it signifies transgression of *known* law; and in the third it means a *habit* of sinning, or a sinful *character*. It is in the first use that it is said,

"If we say that we have no sin, we deceive ourselves." —1 John, i., 8.

It is in the third sense that it is said,

"Whosoever is born of God doth not commit sin; he can not sin, because he is born of God."—1 John, iii., 9.

Now the question is, did the "holy" angels never sin in the first sense? "Holy men of old" all sinned in that sense, and yet they are called holy as much as the holy angels. There is nothing that requires us to give the *first* sense to the word "sinned." There is nothing that forbids us to give the *third* sense.

The argument of analogy would lead us to suppose that God may have created all angels with just such minds as infants, and that, after ages of training, the result was the same as in the human race (i. e.), two classes, the holy angels and the sinful angels; just as the Bible speaks of holy men and sinners. Let the word "sinned" have the third sense, and all that these texts teach is simply the *facts* that there is a class of holy angels as there is of holy men, and another class of sinful angels who have not "kept their first habitation," but are "cast down to hell," just as the Bible says sinful men will be.

This being so, the assumption that the angels were created with any better *nature* than that of infants is without any evidence, while the evidence of analogy is against it.

The evidence offered that Adam's nature was created better or in any way diverse from that of his descendants is the following:

"And God said, Let us make man in our image, after our likeness; and let them have dominion over the fish of the sea, and over the fowl of the air, and over the cattle, and over all the earth, and over every creeping thing that creepeth upon the earth. So God created man in his own image, in the image of God created he him; male and female created he them."—Genesis, i., 26, 27.

"Lo, this only have I found, that God hath made man upright; but they have sought out many inventions."—Ecclesiastes, vii., 29.

That Adam was made in God's image signifies that his constitutional powers and faculties were like those of his Maker, so that all that was needful to perfect virtue and holiness was the *right use* of these faculties.

The short history of Adam and Eve in Genesis gives no evidence of any superiority to their posterity, in character or conduct, resulting from a supposed holy nature.

If any infant boy and girl, placed in a genial clime and safe garden, should grow to adults, and become parents, their history, probably, would be a reproduction of that of our first parents. The first intellectual effort stated is the ordinary one of young children in trying to give names to the animals around them. The first moral development recorded is their eating what they were commanded not to touch, as most young children do. Next came a false excuse; and then Adam cast the blame on Eve, and she turned it on to the serpent. Then God made clothing for them of skins, their infantile skill reaching only to aprons of fig-leaves.

And this is all there is recorded on which to found the splendid intellectual and moral endowments supposed by theologians to have been given our first parents at their creation.

As to the *consequences* of their disobedience, all that we find threatened in Genesis is expulsion from Paradise, the subordination of woman, pain in child-bearing, toil in supporting a family to man, and physical death to both.

When it is said, in the one other text quoted to

prove man's original righteousness, that God created *man* upright, it includes the *whole species*, and, if it proves any thing on the subject, it proves that infants were created as perfect as Adam was.

As to all the texts usually quoted to prove the extreme sinfulness of all men, they establish this *fact*, but do not set forth the philosophy of it. Not one of them teaches that the cause or reason of this sinfulness was a depraved nature inherited from Adam. This is a theory established in the age of Augustine, and not stated *any where* in the Bible.

In regard to the texts quoted to show that, owing to this depravity of nature, all that a child feels and does is sin, and only sin, till regeneration ensues, the Bible is written not for and about infants, but for and about those who have knowledge enough to sin against known law, either natural or revealed.

That men go astray from the womb, "speaking lies," all allow to be Oriental figurative exaggeration, meaning that men begin to lie about as soon as they can, as a general fact. "Shapen in iniquity and conceived in sin" is a similar Oriental expression not to be taken literally.

So when mankind before the flood are spoken of as having "every imagination evil and only evil," it can not be taken literally as referring to all men, for then it would include Noah.

When the carnal mind is described as one that is full of evil and *can not* please God, it signifies that while men are in the class of habitual sinners, living only to please themselves, they do not and *can not* please God in the same sense in which it is said that he "that is born of God can not sin." But these texts do not teach that every moral action of unregenerate men is sinful and displeasing to God.

In the Bible the *heart* often signifies the *chief aim* or ruling interest and purpose. When this is simply to gratify self, it is a carnal heart—a heart of flesh; when the chief aim or purpose is to please and obey God, it is a spiritual heart.

We are born again when we give up self-gratification as our main end, and *to do right* and thus to please and obey God become our chief concern.

The carnal mind, set to please self, is enmity with God—is not subject to law—can not be; for when it is thus subjected it ceases to be carnal.

In 1 Corinthians, iii., 14, it is written, "The *natural* man receiveth not the things of the spirit of God, for they are foolishness unto him; neither can he know them, because they are spiritually discerned."

This passage, which is usually employed to prove that men, before they are regenerated, can not understand the truths of Christ's religion, was addressed to those brought up amid the vices and ignorance of heathenism; and it simply teaches that all men, while in this state of darkness and sin, can not rightly appreciate the pure and self-denying religion of Christ. It says that man as he *naturally* is, and by the light of nature, without any Christian instruction and training, "receiveth not the things of the Spirit of God."

These are the passages of the Bible which are chiefly used to prove transmitted depravity of nature in young children, and a nature so entirely depraved that, previous to its re-creation, all that they do "is of the nature of sin."

The aid of some of the most learned commentators and professors in Biblical criticism has been sought by the writer, and, as yet, no case has been pointed out where the meaning here given to these proof-texts is not warranted by the correct rules of interpretation, and authorized by some of the most learned critics.

A great difficulty on this subject results from the fact that the theory of transmitted infant depravity has been so connected with theories invented to explain the philosophy of the Atonement, that it is imagined, by those trained in these theories, that to deny them involves the denial of Christ's atoning sacrifice.

The distinction between facts and philosophy removes this difficulty also.

The fact that God loves us; that he is not willing that any of his creatures should perish forever; that he has made a *sacrifice* to the extremest amount we can conceive to save us, is proved when God so loved the world that he gave his well-beloved and only-begotten Son to suffer and die for us.

We can not conceive of any thing more painful, any thing that requires more bitter sacrifices of feeling, than for a parent to give up an only and well-beloved child to undeserved shame, suffering, and death. And the history of the humiliation, sorrow, and painful death of God's only and well-beloved Son is set forth as the proof that God loves us even while we are sinners, and is *not willing* that we should perish.

There have been various theories invented to explain *why* it was necessary for Christ thus to suffer, and *how* his death avails to save us. Some of these theories are very childish and absurd, and all of them might be given up, without at all lessening the influence of the great central truth of the Gospel, that God tenderly loves us, even as sinners, and has *proved* it, in that he gave up his only-begotten and well-beloved Son to suffer such dishonor, sorrow, and death to save us. That he has done this is proof also that there was some *impossibility* in saving us any other way. The very prayer of the suffering Savior proves it: "O my Father, if *it be possible*, let this cup pass!" The cup did not pass, and so it was not possible to save us any other way.

There is no need of any explanation of the *causes* of this impossibility. It may be that with our present measure of development and knowledge we could not understand all the causes of this "great mystery" of God manifest in the flesh.

To illustrate the foregoing, suppose, in an awful tempest, a ship is driven among terrific breakers on to a rock-bound, inaccessible coast, where, surrounded by rocks and whirlpools, no passage for escape can be discovered.

Soon a man is discerned toiling down the jagged cliffs. Bleeding and exhausted, he reaches the deck, presents a chart to guide, and dies.

They examine the chart, and find their own position exactly drawn, and also "a strait and narrow way" set down as the sure and only chance of escape.

In such a case, common sense would discern these facts: that the messenger knew that there was such danger as warranted the risk of his life to save; that he was very benevolent in character, and that he loved them with that best love which *suffers* to save from harm. Moreover, his chart, as the *only* chance offered for their escape, should be followed.

The sufferings and death of this messenger, then, proves his benevolent character, his love to those he came to save, the reality of great danger, and the duty of following his instructions.

Suppose, also, that on his person are found evidences that he is the beloved and only son of a powerful king who knew all the risks of this mission of mercy. Then this transaction would prove that the father also was benevolent, loved the sufferers, and earnestly desired their escape.

Now suppose the officers of the ship, instead of following the chart, began to speculate as to whether this was really the son of the king, and how it came to pass that a king so benevolent allowed them to get into such a dangerous place on his shores, and what was "the origin" of this evil. Would not the sailors resent this folly? Would they not insist that all this philosophizing should be deferred until they had found "the strait and narrow way," and escaped from their dangers and sufferings?

And does not this illustration fairly exhibit the great mistakes of theologians in giving so much time, thought, and effort to propagate and defend their various theories as to the philosophy of man's sinfulness and danger?

Do not both Old and New Testament alike teach, "Let the wicked forsake his way, and the unrighteous man his thoughts, and turn to the Lord, who will have mercy upon him, and to our God, who will abundantly pardon?"

So again in the Gospel we are assured that "in every nation, he *that feareth God and worketh righteousness* is accepted of him;" while, for Christ's sake, all past sins can be forgiven as soon as true repentance is found.

CHAPTER SIXTEENTH.

THE TRUE CHURCH TRAINING.

THE *true Church*, in its widest sense, consists of all, in every age and in every world, who are, in aim and purpose, united with God in training his vast family to obey the laws of virtue and happiness.

The Bible contains the early history of the true Church in this world.

The antediluvian period was the infancy of this Church, when the race, with inexperienced educators, was struggling to gain the physical knowledge necessary for its earliest development. Long life was given that the experience of ages might be treasured in the teachers of mankind, and yet this resulted in such monstrous wickedness that the whole race was destroyed except the family of Noah.

While ages rolled on, his descendants became nations, of which Egypt and Assyria took the lead in the developments of civilization. In this long period we find first the family of Shem, and then of Abraham, alone constituting the true Church of God, while all the nations around were sunk in degrading idolatries.

Next to the patriarchal period came Israel as the

first organized nation that worshiped the true God, and became teachers of righteousness to other nations.

Preparatory to this, they were instructed in the arts and wisdom of Egypt, then the most civilized nation.

Next, they were removed, amid the pomp of astounding miracles, and placed in the centre of the civilized world, the great thoroughfare between the East and West.

Here they were organized as confederate republics, under a central government in many points resembling our own. Each male was a landholder in fee-simple, and unable to alienate his property from his family. Every sale of land was for a period ending with the Jubilee, when, amid blowing of trumpets and general rejoicing, every man regained his inheritance. A tribe was set apart as ministers of religion and teachers of the young, and supported by tithes from the other tribes.

This was the only nation on earth whose civil and religious laws required that all widows, orphans, and strangers should be supported by their neighbors; the only nation required by its laws to educate their servants as they did their children—to give them weekly periods of rest, and frequent festivals and holidays, and, if discontented, to protect them when escaping, give them support, and not to allow them to be forced back into unwilling servitude. The beasts of burden, and even the birds, were protected from cruelty by law.

There, in the centre of the known world, this nation held forth the oracles of God, and received to citizenship all who would become his true worshipers. So far as one nation could be made the educators of other nations, the Israelites held this office.

While other nations excelled in many of the arts of commerce and civilization, they were sunk in degrading vices and the most debasing religions. The nation of Israel stood in their midst a solitary witness of the true God, teachers of righteousness to the surrounding world.

This mission related solely to the duties of this life, without reference to the risks and dangers of the future state. Although, by tradition, the belief in a future life, in which the good would be happy and the wicked miserable, was preserved, yet all the sanctions of the Jewish laws were temporal, as more effective in that stage of development. Temporal prosperity was the reward of obedience to God's laws, and temporal miseries were the penalties for disobedience.

This period corresponded with that of school-training in childhood, before our duties resulting from the risks of the spiritual world are made practical in efforts to save others. Thus the Jewish dispensation is called "a schoolmaster to bring us to Christ."

But, "when the fullness of time had come," in preparing mankind for another advance, Jesus Christ came and "brought life and immortality to light."

Then, for the first time in this world, the true Church was instructed in its highest mission as the co-laborer with God to save our race from the dangers of the future life; and these so dreadful, that every earthly plan and hope, in comparison, are to be of no account.

This enlarged plane of duty was not revealed to those who were training men in the preparatory stages. They walked by faith in some future Messiah, whose aim and mission they dimly foresaw. It was this to which Christ referred when he said, "I call you not servants, for a servant knoweth not what his Lord doeth, but I have called you friends."

This is to say, now my Church are to understand the great end for which they are to labor—the great principle to govern all individuals, all nations, and all worlds — the great *law of sacrifice*, demanding that each shall make the *best* good of the whole, and, in reference to the *eternal* state, the first concern, and be ready to suffer even to the death to save, as far as possible, the whole family of God.

The Lord of Glory came to teach this great law, not only by word, but by his blessed example, while he endured poverty, shame, sorrow, and death to save the whole world from the awful dangers of the life to come. And when his mission was completed, his parting injunction to his Church was, "Go ye into *all* the world, and preach the Gospel to *every creature.*"

At this period the world was filled with "gods many and lords many," as contending deities, and the grand question was, Which is the supreme Lord whom all must obey?

A few poor, uneducated men, of a despised nation under the proud Roman empire, came forth and proclaimed a crucified Jew to be the supreme Lord of all the earth, of all gods and of all worlds, the Creator of heaven and earth, the only Lord of faith and practice.

The first effort of the Christian Church was to establish this chief doctrine of religion. To confess Christ as Lord involved the loss of character, livelihood, and comfort, and often brought the cruelest persecution and a violent death. And yet it was made imperative on all, not only to believe on Christ, but to profess his name by baptism and by joining a Christian community; and whenever the parents of a household joined the Church, their children became members, and were liable to the same disabilities and sufferings.

In this state of things, persecution secured the elevation and purification of these communities as nothing else could have done. Few would profess to believe Christ as only Lord except on strong conviction, while the weak and wavering would soon fall away. Thus the earnest and faithful, beset with danger, despised and afflicted, gave up this world as their chief good, and lived as seeing things invisible.

But when the Christian Church gained wealth, honor, and power, it decayed in spiritual life; even as in succeeding ages, while the periods of trial and persecution have been marked with strong Christian growth, ease and prosperity have brought spiritual debility and decay.

The persecutions under the Roman emperors, the suffering periods of the Reformation in Germany, in France, and in Scotland, and the Puritan struggles in Old and New England, evolved a vigorous piety and heroism never developed in prosperity.

At such times men are forced to give up their faith and hope of heaven, or resign earthly comforts and plans; and, having made the great sacrifice, the temptations of ease and worldly good are supplanted by the invigorating influence of the world unseen.

But the higher and more difficult development of Christian growth is to advance with increasing civilization and refinement, receiving the best gifts of this life, and yet carrying the self-denying and self-controlling principles of Christ's religion into the minutest details of every-day life. The Christian Church has yet to learn its highest lesson—to receive prosperity, riches, and honor with the same spirit and the same views as the primitive Church when accepting persecution, shame, sorrow, and death.

To live for the salvation of the world and not for self, to use every art and every means of refinement and culture, not for self-enjoyment as the chief end, but as the means of raising our fellow-men to the highest social, intellectual, and moral development, this is the noblest and most difficult achievement reserved for the Church of the future.

But, in order to this, there must be a basis of religious motive, which, as yet, never has had its true and appropriate presentation. This basis is *danger* in the future life—danger, not to self chiefly, but to the whole family of man. To this must be added clear views as to the mode of escape, and as to the agency of every one in aiding to save others.

In all practical matters it is danger which decides all questions of right and wrong, wisdom and folly.

Thus, if a company are on a journey of pleasure in a land of law and order, in a season of calm and sunshine, when all are in health and with abundant means, all questions of wisdom and rectitude would be settled without reference to any danger.

But suppose this party in a hostile country, beset with cruel and artful savages, surrounded with dangerous morasses, traveling unknown woods, and bearing with them young children, feeble women, and wounded and weary companions.

In such circumstances, what would be proper and right for the party of pleasure would be folly and wickedness for the endangered travelers. Each decision would cease to be, not as to how the most pleasure could be found, but how surrounding dangers can be best escaped. Wakeful nights, exhausting toil, ceaseless care, in one case, would be folly and sin; in the other, wisdom and virtue.

And the measure of motive and duty would be proportioned to the danger and to the ability of each to aid in saving others. If there were no danger at all, then one course would be wise and right. If there were a little danger, still another course would be right. If the danger were immediate and awful, still another standard of duty would occur; and the motives and obligations would be strong or weak, just in proportion to the degree of danger.

Again, if nothing could be done to escape, no motives or obligations for exertion would exist. If there were a little chance of escape, there would be some obligation and motive for exertion. If the way of escape were sure to all who would make the required efforts, both for self and for others, then the motives and obligations would be at the highest point.

Suppose, moreover, that a portion of the endangered party were instructed in a sure but difficult path of escape, and made the guardians of the rest; that they knew that some must be irretrievably lost, and suffer a dreadful death; and that the number who escaped would depend on the watchfulness, toil, and care of those who knew the true mode of escape; then it is clear that the measure of wisdom or folly, right and wrong, in the conduct of these guides would be not only diverse from those who were in no danger, but diverse from those of their companions who had no such knowledge and responsibilities.

Again, suppose a diversity in belief of these guides both as to the degree of danger and as to the paths of escape, this would materially increase the danger and the difficulties.

This example enables us to estimate the position of the Church of the past and the present in reference to the dangers of the eternal world.

Some have taught that there was no danger at all in the future life; some that there was some danger of temporary evils, they knew not exactly what. Some have taught a danger the most awful conceivable, even an eternal existence of torment.

Again, as to the way of escape, some have taught that baptism and Church rites were indispensable; others that they are of little or no avail. Some have taught that *faith* is the indispensable requisite, but have differed as to what it is. Some have taught that a new created nature is the indispensable way of escape, but that men can do little or nothing to secure it, all being decided by elective grace. Some have taught that the "means of grace" are available to secure regeneration; others that there is little efficacy in their use.

Meantime the great world, that is to be trained and saved by the instrumentality of the Church, has been growing more and more skeptical as to the dangers thus proclaimed, and more and more doubtful as to the assumed claims of the contending Church organizations.

The great principle of Protestantism, that every man is to be his own interpreter of the Bible, is becoming more and more a practical power, not with the learned and great chiefly, but rather with *the people.* Especially is this the case in this nation, where every minister of religion, every editor of a periodical, every professor in any college or school, is dependent on the people for support, and thus is to be judged by the people as to the theological opinions that shall be supported by their earnings.

As liberty and intelligence have increased, the people have more and more revolted against theological dogmas that contradict common sense and wound the tenderest sensibilities of the soul. In Europe, the whole French nation, at one time, rose against the Catholic Church, and banished it from the land. In Germany, *Rationalism* has extended widely over both the Catholic and Protestant churches.

In England we now find not only learned professors and doctors in the highest places of the national Church, but even ministers and missionary bishops, assailing either the Bible itself, or the doctrine of man's future dangers as revealed in it. And, after passing through the lower ecclesiastical courts, the question has been appealed from the Court of Arches to the Queen in Council, whether "justification by faith," in the churches of her vast realms, "on which the sun never sets," shall be accepted in the Catholic, or the Protestant, or the common-sense meaning. And this grand question of eternal life and death is not to be decided by the clergy, but by a woman and a mother, assisted, not by ecclesiastics, but by her legal and lay councilors.

In this country, the institution of the Puritan Church, which divides religious assemblies into professed saints and sinners, the one allowed to have children baptized, and the other shut out from what the majority of Christendom in all centuries has regarded as more or less essential to right training through life and to safety at death, has been a constant cause of disquiet and skeptical debate.

At the same time, the Unitarians, led by such men as Channing; the Transcendental school, led by such as Emerson; the semi-Infidel school, led by such as Theodore Parker; the Humanitarian school, led by such as Garrison; the Universalists, led by such as Chapin and Greeley, have all been attacking "the Church," and the theological system on which it rests. They are either openly assailing the Bible, as sustaining a system at war with common sense, or are so interpreting it as to lessen the sense of danger in a future life.

In consequence of all this, there is a subtle, undefined skepticism spreading through every grade of society, and especially in the class who really are the leaders of thought and opinion. The claims of the Church and the claims of the Bible are questioned now as they never were before, by some of the best as well as the most learned and wisest of mankind.

The most fearful aspect of all is the influence of the writings of the outspoken, and the whispered mistrust of the more cautious, on the young, who are now in a course of training. The extent of secret or open infidelity in our colleges and schools is probably beyond any thing ever conjectured by the religious world.

The result is an evident diminution, both in the churches and without their pale, of a sense of *danger* in a future life, on which is based the distinctive feature of the Church of Christ in distinction from the Jewish Church. The great masses of intelligent and benevolent men are saying aloud, or in their secret thoughts, "We can know little or nothing of the future state; let us learn to live aright for this world as the best way to prepare for another."

Thus the new standard of duty introduced by Christ when he "brought life and immortality to light," is set aside for that of Moses and the prophets, who were training the Church in its stage of childhood for its limited sphere. The great doctrine of Christ, that men are to live to save our race from the danger of the future world as *the business of life*, to which all else is to be subordinate—that they are to train their children to be self-denying *martyrs* in this great labor—is fast passing away, both in the churches and the ministry.

Suppose that the example and teachings of Christ were suddenly to be followed by the majority of those who *profess* to be his followers, and that obedience to his parting command to "Go into all the world, and preach the Gospel to *every creature*," became the chief object and interest of life—suppose, still more, that all their children were anxiously and diligently trained to this as their future *business in life*, to which all else must be subordinate, and that *sacrifice to the death for the world's salvation* was the great motto to regulate all the thoughts and plans of their educators, what inconceivably great and various changes in all the hopes, fears, plans, and daily pursuits of the Christian churches would appear, and how they would instantly be transformed into "a holy nation, a *peculiar* people." And the grand motive power that would effect this great change would be the *dangers* of the future life, and the ability of each one to save others from these dangers.

This view of the great principles that are to regulate the *true Church training* of the future will give but an imperfect view of their workings when carried into details. A brief indication of some of these particulars is all that can here be attempted.

It will be assumed that the chief end of the Creator is not to make happiness or enjoyment for his creatures without reference to quality or amount, but that it is to make the *most possible* happiness and of the *best* kinds.

Jesus Christ came to teach the right way to do this; the great comprehensive rule being that each one deny himself daily by living for the *best* good of the great whole; not in reference chiefly to the enjoyments of this life, but mainly in reference to the *dangers* of the future life.

In aiming at this, all will be regulated by this principle of common sense, that where there is any great impending danger, we are to choose the path which offers *the most* evidence of safety, whatever may be the attending doubts and difficulties.

Inasmuch, then, as Jesus Christ is the *only* human being of reliable character returned after death to this life to teach us what is to be encountered in the invisible world, and inasmuch as we can see that following his teaching tends to the *best* good of all even in this life, on the lowest ground ever taken by those who dispute his divine character and authority, guided by this principle of common sense, children will be trained to obey his teachings as the path which offers *the most* evidence of escape from the awful dangers he has disclosed.

Inasmuch, also, as happiness-making for the whole of our race, and of the best and highest kind, is to be the aim of all, every mode of enjoyment that adds to individual happiness will become *a duty*, unless it can be shown to interfere with the best good of the whole for time and eternity. As the converse of this, every mode of individual enjoyment that *tends* to diminish the best good of the whole will be banished as *a sin* against God and man.

Guided by these general principles, all the pursuits and even the amusements of life will be regarded as religious *duties*, as much so as acts of worship. Working and playing, eating and drinking, dress and all kinds of expenditures, theatres, operas, cards, dancing, wine, tobacco, every thing that gives health, comfort, or any kind of enjoyment, will be brought to the test of these principles. Does this pursuit, *as now practiced*, tend to the best good of *all concerned*, or does it involve temptations and injuries that do more harm than good to the whole? Does this pursuit, when regulated as it can be and will be, give pleasure to the individual without injury to the *best* good of the whole?

These questions will be applied in the family, in the school, and in the pulpit, till eventually children will be trained to regulate themselves by the great law of *self-sacrifice*, while yet they are permitted to enjoy in the highest measure the gratification of all the desires and propensities of their nature, in due measure and at proper seasons.

There will be no such division between *morality* and *religion* as has often been stringently enforced. The teachings of Christ as to this life will be regarded as a part of religion as much as those special duties owed to God and his worship. Training children to be truthful, honest, kind, obedient, and self-sacrificing, will be deemed a part of the religious education as much as those portions now regarded as distinctively so.

Every thing that tends to make men *happy* will be enjoined as a duty when it does not interfere with the best good of others.

Works of taste, music, painting, architecture, floriculture, poetry, the drama, the dance, the opera, all that tends to promote enjoyment, will become *duties*, and be regulated by rules that secure the enjoyment without injury to the good of the whole; and the churches will take the lead in the discussions and influences that eventually will write "holiness to the Lord" on all long-perverted sources of enjoyment.

And in this course it will be found that more

difficult self-denial and self-sacrifice will be demanded than ever was practiced even in seasons of persecution and martyrdom. At such periods, one act of renunciation of the world placed a man out of the range of its temptations. But to live in the world, to receive prosperity, wealth, and all their involved temptations, and yet maintain the highest standard of self-sacrifice for the spiritual and eternal welfare of the whole world, *this* will be found a far higher elevation of moral and religious excellence.

The experience of our nation the last three years is a most striking illustration of what the change will be when the Church understands and assumes its high mission, founded on the dangers of the future life.

Our country has been enjoying freedom, ease, and prosperity for fifty years, and the sense of *danger* has had no part in the motives that were influencing national character and pursuits.

Meantime the Church has joined with the world in the passionate rush after wealth, honor, and pleasure. The last twenty-five years has exhibited a career of prosperity and self-indulgence that has alarmed every reflecting mind; and the question has often been pressed in private and in public, Are we too, like Greece and Rome, to be debilitated and demoralized by civilization and prosperity, and be supplanted by races less civilized but more vigorous?

The Church of the present offers little in its history the last thirty years to warrant much hope from its agency. Its past action, through its organized bodies as well as individual agencies, on one matter alone—*slavery*, has been a sure index of its weakness in resisting the influence of wealth and selfish interests. Can any man say that the majority of the Christian Church organizations have, for the last thirty years, been teaching by *example* the doctrine of Christ, that every man is to practice self-denial and self-sacrifice, even to the death, in order to raise our whole race, including the African, to the highest degree of intelligence and virtue?

But suddenly a sense of *danger* has shaken the nation like an earthquake. Not only liberty, but the very life of our nation has been threatened. In this grand emergency, what deeds of self-sacrifice, what developments of heroic devotion have been evolved! Hundreds and thousands have given up ease, and home, and money-making, and been enrolled to offer life itself to save from these merely earthly dangers.

Enrolled in ranks, each with its subordinate and superior officers, who exact unquestioning, unfailing faith and obedience, till at last the whole vast body is moved by one controlling mind as its head—one who decides for all and each which shall have the post of comparative ease and honor, and on which, as unknown privates, shall fall the forlorn hope and certain death—all are animated by the same one idea to *save* our country at any and every hazard.

In the family circle, too, the needle and all the outdoor implements of labor are enlisted in the same effort to raise the funds and supply the needs of this vast array who are to accomplish this great salvation.

What an exact emblem of the true ideal of the Christian Church! Soldiers of the Cross—that is, soldiers to be marched to the bitterest self-sacrifice, and to certain death, if need be—soldiers who are to give up ease, and honor, and friends, and life itself—soldiers marshaled under various leaders, with the Lord of All as the Great Captain, all enrolled to save, not our country alone, but *the whole world*, not from temporal, but from eternal dangers.

CHAPTER SEVENTEENTH.

BIBLE BASIS OF TRUE CHURCH TRAINING.

It having been shown that *danger* in the future life is the basis of the true Church training, a brief view of this danger, and of the mode of escape, will be presented, as exhibited in the teachings of Jesus Christ and his apostles.

These instructions were given in the language of the common people, and the words mean what the people understood them to mean when Christ used them.

This language of the Jewish people has, in our New Testament, been correctly translated into the corresponding language of our own common people. In deciding on the true sense of every passage, we are to *use the same rules that the people employ in common life.*

Most words have more than one meaning; for example, the word *judgment* sometimes signifies a faculty of the mind, sometimes the decision of a judge, and sometimes a punishment inflicted for crime.

Words often are used *figuratively;* as when *anger* is called a fire, or an artful man a fox.

The rule of common life for deciding when a word is figurative or literal is this: *Every word is literal except when that meaning contradicts the known nature of things or the expressed opinions of the writer, in which cases it is figurative.*

Thus, when *anger* is called a fire that burns the soul, the literal meaning contradicts the known nature of the things spoken of, for the soul can not burn, and so the expression is figurative.

The words *eternal* and *everlasting*, in their literal sense, mean time without end, but in their figurative use they mean only time without *known* or *specified* end. When these words are applied to God and the soul, the literal sense is the true one, because it does not contradict the nature of the things spoken of; but when applied to the hills or to man's anger, the figurative sense is the true one, because the literal sense contradicts either the nature of the things spoken of, or other declarations of the Bible.

The same word is used sometimes in a wide and sometimes in a limited sense. Thus *punishment*, in the wide sense, signifies *all* the evils that follow wrong-doing, either natural or statute. In the limited sense it means only the voluntary statute penalties added to the natural ones.

In such cases, the rule of common life is this: *The widest sense is the true one, except when the limited sense is indicated.*

Thus *punishment*, in the New Testament, in reference to a future life, always is used in its widest sense, signifying *all* the evils, both natural and statute, that follow wrong-doing, because the limited sense is not specified.

These are the rules, made, not by learned men, but by the common people. These are the rules to guide in learning the dangers of the future state from Christ and his apostles.

But the spiritual state is one of which men have had no knowledge, and so have no words to express its diverse experiences. In such a case, all that can be done is to employ pictures and illustrations that will convey the truth *as nearly as possible.*

A parent, to keep young children from playing in a place infected with destructive miasma, might set up a horrid figure and call it *miasma*, and tell the children if they went into the forbidden place *Miasma* would kill them. This would convey the truth as nearly as it is possible to a young child.

Thus, in regard to the spiritual world, all revelations must be by figures and illustrations not to be taken as literal. Thus, "the worm that dieth not," and "the fire that is not quenched," convey the idea of great suffering that has no end. But the figures used are not to be taken in the literal sense, because it would contradict the nature of things, for a spirit can not be burned, or gnawed by a worm.

Before applying these rules to the New Testament, we need to notice a singular mistake made in the English translation.

In the Old Testament there is no reference made to a place of punishment in the future life. The Hebrew word *Sheol* signifies the *place of departed spirits*. The words *Heaven*, *Paradise*, and *Hell* never are used in reference to the dead in the Old Testament.

In the New Testament the Greek word *Hades* is used for the place of departed spirits, being synonymous with the Hebrew word *Sheol*.

The Greek word *Gehenna*, in the New Testament, means the place of future punishment of the wicked. It occurs seven times in Matthew, three times in Mark, once in Luke, and once in James.

The word *Hades* (meaning only the place of departed spirits) occurs twice in Matthew, twice in Luke, twice in Acts, once in Corinthians, and four times in Revelation; and in all cases it means the same as *Sheol* in the Old Testament. It *never* means the place of punishment of the wicked; and yet the English translators (perhaps from fear of the Romish doctrine of Purgatory) used the word *Hell* both for Hades and for Gehenna, thus making many texts appear to speak of Gehenna when they do not.

At the time of our Savior, the Jews held that in Hades the good dwelt in Paradise, and the wicked were separated from them and confined in a place called Tartarus. They held, also, that there is to be a final day of judgment, when the good will go from the paradise of Hades to heaven, and the wicked from the Tartarus of Hades to eternal punishment in Gehenna.

When Christ spoke the parable of the rich man and Lazarus, his object was not to teach the doctrine of future eternal punishment in Gehenna, for, if it had been, he would have used the word Gehenna. Instead of this, he taught that in Hades, the place of departed spirits, one so low and miserable as Lazarus was in this life, was happy, while the rich man was miserable. He implied, also, that at least some who do not repent in this life will be miserable in Hades, as was the rich man; but nothing is said in this parable as to what transpires between the hour of death and the day of judgment.

In 1 Peter, ii., 19, 20, it is said that Christ went and preached to the imprisoned spirits in Hades, and we may infer that he would not do this unless some were to be benefited by it. But what the effect of this preaching was we are not told.

When Christ said to the thief on the cross, "To-day shalt thou be with me in Paradise," he knew that the Jews understood the word Paradise to mean, not heaven, but that portion of Hades where the good are.

No Hebrew and Greek scholar will question these statements.

With these preliminaries, we are prepared to examine the teachings of Christ and his apostles as to the dangers of the world to come and the mode of escape.

When the forerunner of Christ appeared it was to "prepare the way of the Lord," whom he announced as one coming "thoroughly to purge his floor and gather his wheat into the garner," and "to burn up the chaff with unquenchable fire."

In Christ's opening Sermon on the Mount he declared that those possessing certain virtues will gain "the kingdom of heaven," "see God," and be "called the children of God."

On the contrary, he described others who "shall be in danger of hell fire" (Gehenna fire), and he exhorts to the most severe sacrifices lest we "be cast into hell" (Gehenna).

Then follows instructions as to what man must do to secure heaven. These requisitions are the most elevated and most difficult. For example:

"Love your enemies, bless them that curse you, do good to them that hate you, and pray for them which despitefully use you."

"Be ye therefore perfect, even as your Father which is in heaven is perfect."

"Therefore all things whatsoever ye would that men should do to you, do ye even so to them; for this is the law and the prophets."

"Enter ye in at the strait gate; for wide is the gate, and broad is the way, that leadeth to destruction, and many there be which go in thereat; because strait is the gate, and narrow is the way, which leadeth unto life, and few there be that find it."

"Not every one that saith unto me, Lord, Lord, shall enter into the kingdom of heaven; but he that doeth the will of my Father which is in heaven."

"Many will say to me in that day, Lord, Lord, have we not prophesied in thy name? and in thy name have cast out devils? and in thy name done many wonderful works?

"And then will I profess unto them, I never knew you: depart from me, ye that work iniquity."

Next follow exhortations not to lay up treasures on earth, but rather treasures in heaven, and to "seek first the kingdom of God and his righteousness." This sermon concludes with a picture of utter ruin to those who hear and do not according to these teachings.

Next after the Sermon on the Mount we find in chapter viii.:

"Many shall come from the east and west, and shall sit down with Abraham, and Isaac, and Jacob, in the kingdom of heaven.

"But the children of the kingdom shall be cast out into outer darkness: there shall be weeping and gnashing of teeth."

In chapter x. Christ again teaches of those who refuse the words of his disciples, "it shall be more tolerable for the land of Sodom and Gomorrah, in the day of judgment, than for that city."

Again, verse 28:

"Fear not them which kill the body, but are not able to kill the soul; but rather fear him which is able to destroy both soul and body in hell (Gehenna)."

In Matthew xiii. we have the parable of the sower thus interpreted, verses 37–43:

"He that soweth the good seed is the Son of man. The field is the world; the good seed are the children of the kingdom; but the tares are the children of the wicked one. The enemy that sowed them is the devil; the harvest is the end of the world; and the reapers are the angels. As therefore the tares are gathered and burned in the fire, so shall it be in the end of this world. The Son of man shall send forth his angels, and they shall gather out of his kingdom all things that offend, and them which do iniquity; and shall cast them into a furnace of fire: there shall be wailing and gnashing of teeth. Then shall the righteous shine forth as the sun in the kingdom of their Father."

Again, verses 49, 50:

"So shall it be at the end of the world. The angels shall come forth, and sever the wicked from among the just, and shall cast them into the furnace of fire: there shall be wailing and gnashing of teeth."

Again, in chapter xvi., we find, verse 27:

"For the Son of man shall come in the glory of his Father with his angels; and then he shall reward every man according to his works."

In chapter xxiii. we find heavy woes denounced on the Scribes and Pharisees, concluding thus, verse 33:

"Ye serpents, ye generation of vipers, how can ye escape the damnation of hell (Gehenna)?"

In chapter xxv. of Matthew are parables teaching the great fact that there are to be hereafter two classes, represented by wise virgins taken into the feast, and foolish ones shut out—the faithful servant who entered the joy of his Lord, and the unprofitable servant cast "into outer darkness: there shall be weeping and gnashing of teeth."

This chapter ends with a solemn description of the great consummation, verse 31:

"When the Son of man shall come in his glory, and all the holy angels with him—and before him shall be gathered all nations."

Then is described a separation into two classes according to their *deeds.* One class is adjudged, "Depart from me, ye cursed, into everlasting fire prepared for the devil and his angels," and the other is commanded, "Come, ye blessed of my Father, inherit the kingdom prepared for you from the foundation of the world."

And it is concluded with these awful words from the Savior himself:

"And these shall go away into *everlasting punishment,* but the righteous into life *eternal.*"

These teachings of Christ, as recorded by Matthew, are repeated by Mark and Luke with more or less distinctness.

In John, v., 28, 29, the Savior again instructs thus:

"Marvel not; for the hour is coming in which all that are in the graves shall hear his voice, and shall come forth; they that have done good unto the resurrection of life, and they that have done evil unto the resurrection of damnation."

These are the teachings of the Lord himself. His apostles repeat the same solemn doctrine. In Acts, xxiv., 15, we read,

"There shall be a resurrection of the dead, both of the just and unjust."

In Romans, ii., 16, Paul speaks of the day when God shall judge the secrets of men by Jesus Christ. And again, 2 Corinthians, v., 10:

"For we must all appear before the judgment-seat of Christ, that every one may receive the things done in the body according to that he hath done, whether it be good or bad."

Again, in 2 Thessalonians, i., 6–11:

"Seeing it is a righteous thing with God to recompense them that trouble you; and to you who are troubled rest with us, when the Lord Jesus shall be revealed from heaven with his mighty angels, in flaming fire taking vengeance on them that know not God, and that obey not the gospel of our Lord Jesus Christ: who shall be punished with everlasting destruction from the presence of the Lord when he shall come to be glorified in his saints, and to be admired in all them that believe."

Again, in 1 Thessalonians, iv., 16:

"For the Lord himself shall descend from heaven with a shout, with the voice of the archangel, and with the trump of God; and the dead in Christ shall rise first: then we which are alive and remain shall be caught up together with them in the clouds, to meet the Lord in the air; and so we shall ever be with the Lord."

The Apostle Peter teaches thus: 2 Peter, iii., 7, 10, 11, 12:

"But the heavens and the earth, which are now, by the same word are kept in store, reserved unto fire against the day of judgment and perdition of ungodly men. But the day of the Lord will come as a thief in the night; in the which the heavens shall pass away with a great noise, and the elements shall melt with fervent heat, the earth also and the works that are therein shall be burned up. Seeing then that all these things shall be dissolved, what manner of persons ought ye to be in all holy conversation and godliness, looking for and hasting unto the coming of the day of God, wherein the heavens being on fire shall be dissolved, and the elements shall melt with fervent heat?"

The Apostle John concludes with these pictures of the final consummation. Revelation, xx., 11–15:

"And I saw a great white throne, and him that sat on it, from whose face the earth and the heaven fled away. And I saw the dead, small and great, stand before God; and the books were opened; and another book was opened, which is the book of life; and the dead were judged out of those things which were written in the books, according to their works. And the sea gave up the dead which were in it; and death and Hades delivered up the dead which were in them; and they were judged every man according to their works. And whosoever was not found written in the book of life was cast into the lake of fire."

Revelation, xxi., 5, 7, 8:

"And he that sat upon the throne said, Behold, I make all things new. He that overcometh shall inherit all things; and I will be his God, and he shall be my son. But the fearful, and unbelieving, and the abominable, and murderers, and whoremongers, and sorcerers, and idolaters, and all liars, shall have their part in the lake which burneth with fire and brimstone, which is the second death."

Revelation, xxi., 23:

"And the city had no need of sun, neither of the moon to shine in it; for the glory of God did lighten it, and the Lamb is the light thereof. And the nations of them that are saved shall walk in the light of it. And there shall in no wise enter into it any thing that defileth, neither whatsoever worketh abomination or maketh a lie, but they which are written in the Lamb's book of life."

Revelation, xxii., 14:

"Blessed are they that do his commandments, that they may have a right to the tree of life, and enter in through the gates into the city. For without are dogs, and sorcerers, and whoremongers, and idolaters, and whosoever loveth and maketh a lie."

In view of this solemn array of declarations from the Lord himself and from his apostles, it is one of the many evidences of the influence of feeling and wishes in the interpretation of the Bible, that there is such a variety of opinions as to the revealed dangers of the future life.

As before stated, in the face of such declarations, some maintain that there is no danger at all; that all men, however wicked, at death go directly to eternal blessedness in heaven. Others, not quite so bold, teach that there is some danger of some sort of punishment to some of the worst kind of men, but that all the rest go to heaven. Others hold that it is a very uncertain matter; and that, as we can know little or nothing of what is to befall us in the eternal state, it is of small practical importance. Others hold that the whole race of Adam at death go directly to hell, and suffer eternal torments for sins committed in this life, with the exception of a comparatively few regenerated persons in Christian lands.

The diverse modes of interpretation by which these various opinions are maintained are all dependent on the sense given to the words *sin* and *punishment.*

In previous pages it is shown that the common people use the word *punishment* to mean not only the voluntary statute penalties of God and man, but the *natural consequences* of violating the laws of nature, which are fixed and eternal, either by the will of God or the eternal nature of things.

So the word *sin*, in common use, means transgression of any of the laws of God, either of nature or statute.

The whole system of the Catholic Church is based on the assumption that the government of God is like that of the civil state, which punishes all crimes with a given voluntary penalty, and not that of a parent, who punishes only as the *best good* of the child requires.

On this Catholic theory, it is taught that God's *justice* requires that a statute penalty be inflicted for every transgression of God's laws, either natural or statute, in addition to the natural penalties of sinning. This punishment is to be inflicted on some one, either innocent or guilty. If the innocent is willing to bear it, then the guilty may escape; but so much pain must be inflicted *somewhere* for every sin committed, in order to satisfy God's justice.

The final state of those guilty of mortal sins unrepented and unforgiven is settled at death, and they go to suffer everlasting torments for the sins committed in this short life.

Those who escape mortal sins, or have had them remitted, go to Purgatory, and are punished by statute penalties till God's justice is satisfied, either by their sufferings, or by the sufferings of Christ and the saints placed to their account.

The most common Protestant interpretation has been that for all those whose ruined nature has not been re-created by God, their final state is decided at death, and they go to eternal torments, as a punishment for the sins of this short life.

Revolting from both these theories, some of the Universalists have taught that there is to be no punishment at all for sins of this life, but all at death go to perfect blessedness. Others of this sect teach that there is to be a period of purgatorial punishment for the wicked, and then all our race are made holy and happy forever.

Another class hold that the good go to eternal blessedness, and the wicked are annihilated, and these are saved from all evil or punishment of every sort in a future life.

Still another view, founded on the common-sense interpretation of these and other passages, is, that God and all free agents made in his image are subject to pain and evil by the eternal nature of things which God did not create; that the only way to escape endless pain and sorrow is to obey the laws of virtue and benevolence as God himself obeys them; that Jesus Christ came to save from the natural penalties of law only by saving men from sinning; that the natural penalties of the eternal laws of mind reach to the innocent as well as the guilty, God himself sorrowing for the sins and sufferings of his children; that Christ, in this world, bore the punishment for the sins of men by suffering the natural consequences of their wickedness, reaching both to the innocent and guilty; that Christ came, not to interrupt the natural penalties of sinning to the innocent as well as guilty, but to submit to them as a sufferer from the sins of those he came to save; that he suffered in no other way, though perhaps in greater degree, than his followers often have done, when disgraced, tortured, and slain; that "the hour of darkness," when he prayed in fear and agony, was like what his followers often have endured when God's ways seemed dark, and they were overwhelmed with doubts and fears, as well as with physical suffering; and that Christ's followers are *punished* for the sins of those they strive to save, amid self-denials and rebuke, as Christ was—not by *voluntary* penalties inflicted by God, but by the *natural* penalties of the laws of the material and spiritual life, involving the good as well as the evil in consequent suffering.

No attempt will be made to controvert either of these views; but the reader is requested to ponder these questions:

Have we *any* reliable information as to the invisible world and the future destiny of man except the teachings of Christ?

Is there not *some* evidence that he died and returned from the place of the dead, and that his character as a reliable witness is equal to that of any human being of whom we have any knowledge?

Do not his teachings, interpreted by the rules used by the common people, declare the following facts:

That, at some future period (it may be thousands of ages hence), all mankind are to be *judged* by Jesus Christ, and be separated into two classes, according to their character and conduct—the one class to dwell with God and good angels, and the other to be confined in the world of sin and suffering with bad angels?

On the other hand, is there *any* evidence to be found, in these or other passages of the Bible, that the hour of death is the time when the final character and destiny of *all* men is decided, so that, *at that time*, all go either to heaven or to hell? Are there not some passages that forbid this idea?

Are there not some passages that indicate that *some* bad men, such as Judas, and *some* good men, such as Paul, decide their eternal destiny in this life?

Is it taught that, when Christ preached in Hades to those who lived before the flood, either that he had or had not any success?

Is it taught that, after death, men either will or will not have any farther chances to secure eternal life? Is not the matter left in entire darkness, with only the assurance that, to those who hear the Gospel, *now* is an accepted time and day of salvation, without any promise for the after life?

Is it not taught that there are diverse degrees of faith, and that there is danger even to those who have some measure of faith, of perishing for want of the requisite amount? Are we any where told how far we may fall short and yet escape? Are not those who are Christians exhorted to fear and to strive as if in great danger, and to make it their chief concern to save themselves and their fellow-men?

Is it taught in these passages or elsewhere that the punishments of the future life will be any other than the *natural* results of conduct and character in a world from which all the good are withdrawn and where all the wicked are confined?

Is there any rule of language that justifies the idea that *everlasting punishment* means the *end* of all trouble and pain, as would be the result of annihilation?

Is it possible to find any language that will more clearly express the idea that a portion of our race will *exist forever sinful* and consequently miserable, than is presented in these selected passages?

Is not the way of escape from this awful danger the *faith* which includes not only an intellectual belief in the true God, but also a *controlling purpose* of obedience to his laws, both natural and revealed?

Do not the "love" and "repentance" required as the terms of salvation also include *as their chief element* the controlling purpose to please God by forsaking sin?

In other words, is it not clearly and repeatedly taught that man can be saved from future eternal dangers only by an *inner* principle or purpose of obedience to God's laws, exhibited by "*deeds*" or "*good works*" as the chief element?

Is it not plainly taught in the Bible that the number of those who will escape the dangers of the future life depends on the exertions and faithfulness of the followers of Christ?

Should not these momentous questions be answered only after a diligent examination of the New Testament, with all solemnity and faithfulness, as deciding the issues of eternity for self and all that are dear?

CORRESPONDENCE.

THE author, having occasion to state the theological doctrines held by the chief religious denominations in this country, has been very desirous to secure perfect fairness and correctness in such statements.

For this end, proofs of the preceding portion of the work were sent to persons who, for influence and discrimination, rank among the leading minds in each of these denominations, most of them being personal friends. After receiving their criticisms, the fourteenth and fifteenth chapters were rewritten, and the two following were added.

A considerable portion of the resulting correspondence is inserted in the following pages as farther exhibitions of the topics discussed, and in a form more interesting than the didactic.

All indices that might identify the writers have been suppressed, so that it will be optional with all whose communications have been inserted how far such identification shall be permitted.

L

From Rt. Rev. Bishop ———, of the Episcopal Church.

"My dear Madam,—I return your article as you desire, and acknowledge gratefully the regard which, in revising it, you have shown to the suggestions of Bishop ——— and to my own.

"Practically, your position is of the greatest interest; and no one can have seen how deeply settled in the New England mind, in thousands of instances, is the doubt whether God really has any purpose of love, except toward a chosen company, without being prepared to sympathize with your past struggles and your present desires.

"Theoretically, I think that the more you allow your convictions to take their mould from the language of Holy Scripture, and of the experience of all Christians, the more will you be inclined, without diminishing the paramount importance of religious training, to ascribe its efficacy emphatically to the grace of the Holy Spirit; not arbitrarily bestowed, but in answer to prayer, and in fulfillment of a promise and covenant.

"I do not uphold all the doctrines of St. Augustine; but all that deplorable history of Dr. Payson's treatment of his daughter was based on a doctrine no older than the last century, and unknown to any extent out of New England.

"The corruption of man's nature lies not in the original construction of mind, nor yet in the absence of means and motives, but in the loss of moral power and the perversion of the affections, which all experience shows to result in the individual from indulgence in sin, and, even in individual peculiarities, to some extent hereditary.

"The Church teaches that we inherit this from Adam, and do not simply imitate him and follow his example. To suppose this is a merely negative thing, arising from the want of knowledge, training, and motives, is the Pelagian theory, and, as such, is distinctly condemned in our Articles.

"One higher than the highest says that we must be born again—born of the Spirit. The Puritan mistake is not in insisting on this, but in making it an empirical thing at a certain time in mature years, with distinct consciousness and with certain phenomenal circumstances or infallible results, to be judged by a purely experimental standard; and a thing, too, which is bestowed on some and withheld from others, without reference to the Sacrament of Baptism as a means and symbol to the Church as the family of God, nor to the universal redemption as securing a grant of grace to all.

"The basis of our hope from Christian nurture is in this grant of regenerating grace to all who will but receive it, of which the baptism of infants is to each the sign and pledge, and one of the great means; and not the idea of merely surrounding the soul with knowledge and motives, which can not of themselves call forth the moral power which it has lost.

"I wish the last two sentences on page 101 were qualified. These are not 'logical results' of that simple doctrine. Through the redemption of Christ, God can counteract and remove this inherited evil, whether through or without baptism. Let me commend to you those golden words of Thomas Fuller, 'If we can not perceive the manner of things, no wonder we can not conceive the methods of grace in infant souls.'

"Is it not quite as merciful, and much more philosophical, to suppose a *depraved nature* and a counteracting grace, both of which we all see in their fruits, as to suppose no depravity of nature, and yet no single case of innocence preserved?

"And now, my dear madam, will you permit me to ask your attention to one point, which must, I think, prove that there is in your system a most grave deficiency. From first to last, hardly any mention occurs of the Holy Spirit. Your own views, I believe, are stated uniformly without any allusion to that blessed name. Admit Him, and His power, office, and work into your system, and the change will be effected which I desire.

"You have thought too much as a mere educator, and in antagonism to a metaphysical distortion with which we are all but too familiar. There is something beyond education and closer to the heart than knowledge. *Veni Creator Spiritus.*

"You will not, I trust, think me too frank in this expression of my opinion. It is uttered with the most cordial respect and esteem, and with such sentiments I beg you to believe me,

"Yours very sincerely, ——— ———."

From the Author in reply to the foregoing.

RT. REV. AND DEAR SIR,—Your criticisms on the communication and proofs were most gratefully received, both in respect to the matter and the manner.

I have long regarded myself as an inquirer rather than a teacher on the great subjects which have been presented to your attention, and my chief hope of success has been based on the very doctrine you so earnestly recommend to my attention—the aid of the blessed Spirit, the help and comforter of all who are seeking for the truth. But I expect this aid only while using the means He has indicated, seeking with a humble and teachable spirit assistance not only from God, but from my fellowmen.

If you will recur to page 48, you will notice what, perhaps, you did not observe, that I distinctly recognize the aid a child will receive from the Holy Spirit in all efforts to become a true follower of Christ.

My idea on this subject is that the Spirit of Truth, in moral culture, is like the sun in the natural world, an ever-warming and vivifying agency, never withheld from faithful labor, while without it we should be as helpless and hopeless as would be the gardener without the sun. The grand difficulty I am striving to meet is the doctrine that the soul of a child, when given to its parents and teachers, is a ruined seed, from which no training or culture can educe any thing but poisonous fruit until its "nature" is changed through a physical rite or a new creating process of God's Spirit.

Instead of this, I believe that the heavenly Father, and the blessed Savior, and the gracious Comforter have done, and are doing, all that needs to be done on their part, so that nothing is now wanting but for parents, the Church, and the children to do theirs.

In the Bible the Church is represented as the bride of Christ, who is to train his children for heaven; and the closing words of our Savior in the Apocalypse expresses this consoling and blessed truth as his last and best blessing:

"I, Jesus, have sent mine angel to testify unto

you these things in the churches. The Spirit and the Bride say come; and let him that heareth say come; and let him that is athirst come; and *whosoever will*, let him take of the water of life freely."

You speak of admitting an opinion into my "system," as if I were a theologian constructing a theological system. Instead of this, I am more like the poor negro in the story of Uncle Tiff, when asked by his young mistress what part of the New Testament she should read to him.

"Well, now," said he, "I wants to find out de shortest way I ken how dese yer chil'ens to be got to heaven."

I have taken the Bible as an educator for a practical end. I have prayed for the aid of the blessed Comforter, and then sought its meaning by applying the same rules of language as are used by the common people in daily life; and, finally, I have asked those who are counted the wisest and best to point out wherein I have made mistakes, and after this course I have come to the results which you have seen.

I am constructing a theological system in no other fashion than the poorest and humblest is bound to do, who has access to the written Word of the Lord.

It is true that I have published two volumes that may, in one sense, be said to contain a system; but what I was aiming at was to show that doctrines have been fastened on the Bible contrary to common sense, and destructive to the eternal interests of little children.

In all this I was not attempting to make a system, or to account for the "origin of evil." All these efforts are to escape from the "presumptuous" attempt of theologians to do so, and from the "system" of theology which has resulted.

If we may but banish this "presumptuous" theory, and all the "systems" founded on it, I and all others of "the people" can return to the place where Christ and his apostles left the matter.

But this most cruel method is always taken by the defenders of the Augustinian theory. They assume that *God* has taught it instead of Augustine, and that all such reasoning is against God, presumptuous, and irreverent.

You say again, "One higher than the highest says that we must be born again — born of the Spirit."

I think, my dear sir, that I hold the sacred truth conveyed in these words as really as any Calvinist of the straitest sect. The infant is born into a strictly animal life. Its intellect, as well as its moral powers, are all dormant. It is as impossible for it to know and obey God as if it were destitute of an intellectual and moral nature. These powers are to be developed and trained under parental care; the knowledge of God, and of the numerous laws of the physical, intellectual, and moral world into which the infant is introduced, are to be communicated by a slow and gradual process.

The child is first to learn its earthly parents, and then be trained to obey them, as the indispensable preliminary to love and obedience to the heavenly Parent. This inability of the child is not owing to its "evil nature," but to its ignorance and imperfect development.

The child first must learn to take care of *self* before it can learn to take care of others, and its first period of existence includes this as the only possible exercise of its powers. Gradually it learns that other beings suffer and enjoy, and, by a slow process, it can be trained to know its neighbors, and then to know God, and to submit to those laws that involve painful self-denial for the good of others.

When a child has arrived at that point in its training in the family that its will is lovingly subject to its parents, it is "born again" spiritually, as much as is possible in that imperfect state of development. Its life is now as different from what it was when a mere sport of infant impulses and desires, and entirely uncontrolled by reason and conscience, as the infant period is diverse from that before birth.

Christ's declaration, "ye must be born again," was addressed to adults, and not to infants. To those Christ was addressing, a sudden change from a life of disregard to God and his laws to one of love and obedience was possible, and was correctly represented by the figurative language of a new birth. In regard to infants, the change from ignorance and disobedience must necessarily be a slow and gradual progressive one, and dependent not merely on divine influence, but greatly on educational training.

It is just at this point where I find the Calvinistic system, and the Puritan churches founded on that system, involve influences so unfavorable to the right training of young children, that I turn to the Episcopal Church, not because it is entirely free from the doctrine of the transmitted depravity of young children, but because, in both its theory and administration, this doctrine is divested of some of its dangerous tendencies. In this Church, *practically*, every infant is received as a lamb of Christ's fold to be *trained* to mature Christian life.

But in the Calvinistic sects, *practically*, every young child grows up with the feeling that he is out of the fold, and not to be taken in till God chooses to re-create his soul, and thus remedy the evil done by Adam.

In what you say of the "corruption of nature" in infants, there is the same difficulty as I pointed out in my *Appeal to the People*, Chapter XXXII., where I claim that all theologians holding this dogma contradict themselves, in one place affirming depravity of the constitution of infant minds, and in another place denying it.

Does not your letter present another instance of this kind? For you say, firstly, that "the corruption of man's nature lies not in the *original construction* of the mind." This is just what I say, and for which I am called Pelagian; that the original construction of an infant mind is, as God made it, *perfect*, and not corrupt or depraved.

Next you say what seems a contradiction, viz., that the depravity of infant nature "consists in the loss of moral power."

Now "moral power" is the power of being influenced by motives. The only conceivable way of losing this power is by losing all those outward objects that excite our susceptibilities, or else by losing some of these susceptibilities. For example: a man may lose moral power by the removal of all those outward influences that excite to virtuous fefort, or he may lose it by having the susceptibilities that are excited by such motives altered or destroyed. In scientific language, the "objective motives" may be removed, or the "subjective motives" may be altered or destroyed.

Now you say that this loss of moral power is "*not* the absence of means and motives." That is to say, it is not the want of the objective or outward influences to virtuous action. If this be so, is there any thing left but the susceptibilities which, as "moral power," can be lost?

That you really mean this appears when you say that the corruption of infant nature consists in "the perversion of *the affections.*" What can this mean except that the susceptibilities of the infant mind are perverted and depraved, and thus "moral power" is lost?

I think, if you will candidly examine this statement which you sent me as to what infant depravity *does* and does *not* consist in, you will perceive it to involve a direct contradiction.

This same kind of contradiction, I think, you will find in all theologians, Catholic and Protestant, who attempt to state first in what infant depravity does *not*, and then in what it *does* consist.

I have tried, again and again, the most acute Calvinistic and Arminian metaphysicians I could find, to obtain a statement of what the depravity of infant nature does and does not consist in, which does not involve an exact contradiction.

The only mode of avoiding the acknowledgment of this has been, either to refuse to prepare such a statement, or else a refusal to *define* the terms used. And so uniform has been this course of evasion, that I feel quite sure that there is no theologian of *any* school, Catholic or Protestant, who will publicly offer such a statement, and agree to *define* the terms used *as sanctioned by proper authorities.*

In saying this, I imply nothing which is disrespectful or disparaging. I believe that theologians

of all schools, who think the most clearly, are most embarrassed by the difficulties involved in this doctrine of transmitted depravity, and that they avoid any public acknowledgment because they are not yet suitably prepared to take the *practical* course that may be involved in such a public development as would thus be hastened.

I am at a loss to know your meaning in what you have written in regard to the baptism of infants. You seem to agree with the Thirty-nine Articles that God, having power to create a perfect nature for infants, chooses not to do so, and thus they come into life, not with the constitution of mind which God gave to Adam, but with one so depraved that a child has no power "to do good works" pleasant and acceptable to God till "grace" is imparted by the Holy Spirit.

You say "the basis of our hope in Christian nurture is in the grant of regenerating grace to all who will but receive it, of which the baptism of infants is to each the sign and pledge, and *one of the great means.*"

Now it is impossible for any infant to be "willing to receive" this gift, for it knows nothing of the matter. The only hope, then, is from baptism, which is secured only to a small portion of infants in most Protestant churches in this nation, where only the children of those professing to be regenerate are baptized. All infants out of Christian lands, and all in Christian lands not baptized, in your view, as I understand it, have not this gift of regenerating grace, and, as the consequence, most of them live a life of sin, and then go to eternal perdition.

Furthermore, you state that God can counteract and remove this inherited evil either through or without baptism, and you quote Fuller with approval as saying, "If we can not perceive the manner of sins, no wonder we can not conceive the methods of grace in infant souls."

You add, "Is it not as merciful, and much more philosophical, to suppose a depraved nature and counteracting grace, both of which we see in their fruits, as to suppose no depravity of nature, and yet no sign of innocence preserved?"

Here, at least by implication, you teach that sinful actions flow from a depraved nature, as a polluted stream from a polluted fountain, or a poisonous plant from a poisonous seed, while all virtuous actions spring from an implanted principle called regenerating grace; and that the mode of this loss or bestowal is what we can not perceive or understand. You allow that God *can* bestow this on all infants either "with or *without* baptism," and you concede that all sin flows from the want of this, which God can and yet does not bestow on all infants.

Here comes up the grand difficulty. Where is the goodness or justice of a Creator who for ages has been continuing this awful evil on infants for Adam's sin, when he has power to give them as perfect a nature as he gave to Adam, and withholds it when he knows that the consequence, in most cases, will be ruin to the child in this life and forever?

Is this as any human father would treat his new-born infants? And did not Christ come to reveal God to us as a *father*—one who loves us all, in spite of our sins, as a tender parent loves a child?

What father would withhold the rectifying grace from a helpless babe, knowing all the dreadful risks, and certain sin and misery consequent on this denial?

The Episcopal Church is the only large Protestant denomination in this nation that by its practice assumes that all the little children of the parish are lambs in Christ's fold, entitled to baptism as those who can be *trained* to virtue and piety. Still, the larger part of its clergy teach that baptism is an indispensable prerequisite to some spiritual gift that remedies some injury to the child's mind, and increases its chances of escaping eternal ruin.

Both Catholics and Episcopalians gain some proselytes by this theory. They say, "Come into our parish, and you need join no Church as regenerate persons in order to secure a remedy for this dreadful evil done to your infants." But many a mother and teacher must reply, "I can not. The father of these children believes no such doctrine—regards it as a superstition derogatory to God's character as a loving and tender heavenly Father—and he will not let his children be trained to believe it."

While this doctrine does draw some into the Catholic and Episcopal churches, do you not fear that it is exerting a silent, steady influence in drawing the highest as well as humbler classes away from all churches and to latent infidelity? Alas! I know many of the best and noblest who are thus repelled.

* * * *

From Rt. Rev. Bishop ——, of the Episcopal Church.

"DEAR MADAM,—I have read the two volumes you had the kindness to send to me—*Common Sense applied to Religion*, and *An Appeal to the People.*

"It was impossible to read them without admiration of the mental vigor and the honorable frankness by which they are distinguished, or without sympathy with the many struggles of the heart which they reveal.

"To give any extended opinion on the contents of two such books would require, not a letter, but days of oral, or volumes of written discussion. With your repugnance toward the hard-hearted system which has predominated in New England I quite coincide; but you will find it easier, as usual, to destroy than to build.

"Without entering into any discussion, and without presuming to hope that any suggestions of mine would modify your deliberate conclusions, I will but state a few of the points that have been uppermost in my thoughts while I read and after I had finished the volumes.

"Is it really any satisfaction to the mind to be told that Omnipotence *could* not prevent all the evil that is in the world? If Omnipotence could not prevent it, in whole or in part—if this is absolutely the best which could have been—what is this but a sort of predestination, only of blind necessity, not of a wise will?

"Is it not the fact of the existence of evil and the prospect of its eternal existence that forms the real difficulty, never yet solved but by the appeal to our own consciousness of ignorance and our reverential submission? Have not all discussions of this kind a somewhat presumptuous character?

"Has not the Augustinian system, in the respects in which it is painful to you, been almost always held, except here in New England, *as if it were not held at all?* Is not this a legitimate way of holding doctrines so mysterious and abstract, if they are to be held at all—that is, if believed to be true—just as the theory of predestination, apart from all scriptural authority, should not at all affect the conduct of any person of common sense?

"Have all your arguments any force whatever against a system which does not ascribe to man, in his natural state, any other inability than that of turning to God and rendering him acceptable service—religious, spiritual, pure service? Does not all experience establish the certainty that man is naturally under precisely this inability?

"Is it of any importance, as to this question, whether the impulse through which the inability is rectified come, as you suggest, from training human and divine, working as if from without, or, as the Christian Church with one voice declares, from within, from the Spirit of God? Is not the latter a much more inspiring, ennobling view, and does it not correspond with the literal statements of Scripture?

"If the Spirit be supposed to be freely, widely, generally bestowed on the youngest as well as afterward, and this to be expressed, and pledged, and made sure by baptism, do not your objections fall to the ground?

"If our Lord sent apostles, and thus instituted a ministry, can it be quite right to treat that ministry with so little regard, and to forget that 'they watch for souls' and 'have rule over their brethren?' And is it altogether best to appeal to 'the people and the secular press' as safely and more to be trusted?

"Is it not possible that a mind accustomed to distinct analysis, and to the development of great principles, and to the practical work of instruction, rather than to the laborious investigation of details or to learned study of language and of history, may, for that very reason, be sometimes and somewhat disqualified for looking on all sides of subjects like these?

"In a little while we shall know, and in the mean while can we too carefully or too prayerfully stem the danger of inciting in others, especially in the young, a habit of daring and self-sufficient speculation on themes so mysterious as the depths of the human nature and the divine?

"These, my dear madam, are the thoughts which occurred to me while I read and reviewed your arguments. I do not present them as arguments on the other side. 'Augustinianism' I do not undertake to defend. But I should be sorry that you should find no more honored or more scriptural alternative than 'Pelagianism.'

"'Not of ourselves, it is the gift of God; not of works, lest any man should boast.' In some form let us hold this fast. I am, with very great respect, yours sincerely, ——— ———."

Letter from the Author in Reply to the foregoing.

Rt. Rev. Sir,—I thank you for the attention you have bestowed on the volumes I sent, and still more for the kind and Christian manner in which, by your criticisms and queries, you have endeavored to aid me in the search after truth.

In reply to these queries, I would say that "the existence of evil, and the prospect of its eternal existence," *is* "the real difficulty," and the one we encounter as much without revelation as with it. It is one which, on any theory, should lead us to our Creator with a humble "consciousness of ignorance, and with reverential submission." And in all I have written, my aim has been not to construct a theory or "system" that removes this difficulty, but mainly to escape a presumptuous theory and system invented by man which increases it a thousand fold.

I find, out of the Bible as well as in it, that awful evil exists; that in this short and painful life I and all I love are involved in it, while there are dreadful forebodings of the future. What are we to do? is the agonizing cry of humanity in every age and nation as this awful fact is felt in every aching heart.

We look into the Bible and read, not a theory of the origin of evil, but a way of escape from sin and its penalties. Christ, the Creator, the Lord of Glory, comes to his suffering creatures, and tells us that by his life, teachings, death, and resurrection, he has secured a sure way of escape both from punishment for past sin and from its continued dominion. This way of escape is, so to believe on him as only Lord of faith and practice, as to *become obedient* to his teachings.

At the same time, with awful and decided language, he assures us that whoever has this faith will be happy forever, and whoever has not will be miserable forever. And his great command is, "Go into all the world, and preach the Gospel to every creature."

But Augustine and his followers arise and inquire, What is the origin or cause of all this sin and suffering? And so they frame this theory. God made angels and Adam with perfect minds. Adam sinned and ruined his nature, and then God made such "a constitution of things" that Adam transmitted to all infants his ruined instead of his original nature. Christ came to be punished for the sins of those who have this ruined nature new created, and also to purchase the influence of the Holy Spirit to do it. Those thus re-created are to be forever happy in heaven, and all the rest are to be consigned to endless suffering and despair in hell.

Now, reverend sir, my aim has been, not so much to construct another theory of the origin of evil as to escape this one, which was formed by fallible men in a dark and cruel age, and forced upon the Bible by Romish popes and councils.

I claim that the Bible does not teach that angels or Adam had any more perfect minds than infants, nor does it teach that Adam ruined his nature by sinning, nor that he transmitted a ruined nature to his posterity.

I show, in the volume *Common Sense applied to Religion*, that by reason alone we can prove the mind of man to be perfect in constitution, and that, if the Bible does teach the Augustinian theory, it nullifies its claims to respect as a revelation from God, and man ought to give it up and revert to the teachings of reason, as exhibiting a wiser and more reliable Creator, and a better system of religion.

You ask, "Have not all discussions of this kind a

presumptuous character?" I reply, The presumption is in those who have manufactured a system so contrary to our moral nature and common sense, and not in discussions to overthrow it.

You say it is easier to destroy than to build. This would be to me a sorrowful conviction were I expecting to build any thing. All I ask is the Bible, free from that false and mournful system that so long has obscured its tender and consoling truths.

You ask "if it is any satisfaction to be told that Omnipotence *could* not prevent all the evil that is in the world," and, if this system "is absolutely the *best* that could have been, what is this but a sort of predestination, only of blind necessity, and not of a wise will?"

In reply, I claim that all theologians, of every age and sect, are alike in this, they limit the power of God by *a necessity in the nature of things.* They differ from me only in the points where they are forced to concede such limitation.

For example, all are obliged to concede that God's power is limited thus much. He can not begin to be. He has no power to annihilate his nature or his past experience. All say God can not lie or love sin. Thus all limit God's power *somewhere.*

All theologians also limit God's power in this wise: They affirm that he is perfect in benevolence and wisdom. This is saying, in another form of words, that God has not the power to make a system wiser or better than the one he has created. It is also saying, in still another form (meaning the same), that a system in which sin and suffering are a part, and in which there is just such and so much as we find, is the best that God had power to make; so that, if it were altered any way by him, it would be to make it worse.

When we say, then, that God "had no power" to prevent the sin and suffering that exist and have existed, without making still greater evil in changing the best possible system to one that is worse, we say what all Catholics, as well as all Protestants, say themselves, in one place or another; and therefore they are barred from objecting.

Again: there are some things ascribed to God by theologians which are direct contradictions, impossible, and absurd—what no mind can conceive of as true, much less can believe.

Of this class is the affirmation that God does all things *for the best;* that is to say, for the best and highest good of all. This is one side of the contradiction. Then they say that God (by a constitutional arrangement) caused all infants to receive a nature that inevitably leads them to do wrong, and thus to destroy happiness, when he could have created them so that their nature would lead them to make happiness.

That is to say, God, having power to make *all* minds so that it would be easy and natural for them to choose right in all cases, and thus make the *greatest possible happiness* for all, has created all infants with a nature that inevitably leads them to choose the wrong, and thus to *destroy* happiness.

What is this but saying that creating infants so that they will destroy happiness is for *the best*, and will secure more happiness on the whole than creating them so that they will make happiness? Is it not saying, in other words, that destroying happiness makes more of it than increasing it, or that *less* is greater than *more?* And is not this a direct contradiction?

The proof that a being has not power to do a thing is, that he *wills* it to be done, and it is *not* done. If, then, God is not willing that any sinners shall perish, and still they do perish, it is proof that God has no power to prevent it. The best possible system, then, involves the utter ruin and loss of some who sin. The Bible teaches that God is not willing that *any* should perish, and yet that some will perish forever.

Again: the highest proof that a being is not willing that a thing should be, is that he *suffers* to prevent it. No sane person will suffer to prevent a thing that he can prevent by simply willing. To suffer to save is the highest proof of the fact that the sufferer could not save by willing.

To illustrate: A company of ignorant, disobedient rebels leave a good king, and go to an island where it is certain they will be shipwrecked. The king knows it, and sends his son to save them. The young prince goes, toils, suffers, weeps, and dies to save them. This proves that the king and his son love them, and were not willing that they should perish. It proves, too, that they could not save them by simply willing it.

This *sacrifice* might so affect the rebels as to win them back as loving and obedient subjects, as nothing else would have done. In that case, it would be properly said that nothing but the sufferings and death of the son could save them; that he was a "vicarious sacrifice," "suffered in their stead," made his father and the rebels one again (*i. e.*, made an "*atonement*" or "atoning sacrifice"), and that "by his stripes they were healed." Thus, too, the sacrifice of this son would "sustain law" by bringing rebels back to obedience.

Now suppose a document was found on the dead prince, with the royal sign and signature, stating that this whole thing was planned by the king to secure the shipwreck and also the death of the prince, in order to show forth his own justice, goodness, and mercy? Would not all who were thus rescued throw it aside as an absurd forgery? Would they not say that any person planning such a thing for such a purpose was fit for nothing but a mad-house?

A *rational* mind can not choose suffering (sacrifice) without compensating good. Such choosing is proof of insanity. God only knows the infinite, endless results of all acts of choice. He sees that pure, uncompensated evil would be the result of his choosing wrong, and so it is impossible for him to be tempted to any wrong (*i. e.*, excited by desire).

But finite minds can not measure future results —are "in darkness," believing evil to be good, and are thus excited to desire it; and they learn only by experience and by faith, that often what they desire as good, in the end is evil.

Christ had power to so connect himself with a human body (thus becoming a man) that his infinite faculties were, for the time being, limited, not in their nature, but their exercise. His hour of agony was the "hour of darkness," when, for the time being, he did not foresee all things, and thus was tempted in all points as we are.

The great thing taught in the incarnation and sufferings of Jesus Christ is, that sin and suffering are so inevitable in the eternal nature of things, that God has not the power to prevent them, and that *sacrifice* on the part of the pure, the good, and the innocent, to save the sinful, is inevitable; that God himself is subject to this law, and that to be a true follower of Christ involves suffering and sacrifice to save the ignorant and guilty.

You ask, "If this system is absolutely *the best* that

could have been, what is this but a sort of predestination, only of blind necessity, and not of a wise will?"

In reply I would say, that the chief point in which we are created "in the image of God" and above the beasts that perish is our *rational* free agency. The brutes have a power of choosing, but only those things which excites the strongest desire, thus making them subject to a blind necessity.

But man has the power of regulating his choices according to rule, the great rule demanding all to choose the *best* good of all concerned in view of an eternal existence. It is this power to choose contrary to the strongest desire or motive (*i. e.*, as it respects self-gratification), which is our *only* idea of rational free agency.

We thus, by our own nature, can understand that God also is a free agent, choosing according to rule, and not, as the brutes do, according to excited desires as stronger or weaker.

To conceive of God as having all the susceptibilities that man has, and that he regulates them, as man is required to do, by the great law of rectitude, so as always to choose what is for the best for all concerned, does no more destroy our idea of free agency in God than it does in man. Instead of this, it is a necessary part of our idea of a *rational* free agent.

You ask, in regard to the "inability" of the young

child of "turning to God and rendering him acceptable service," "if all experience does not establish its certainty," and "if it is of any importance whether the impulse through which the inability is rectified, come from training human and divine, working as if from without, or, as the Christian Church with one voice declares, from within, from the Spirit of God?"

I reply that, practically, there is a very great difference between a view that supposes the mind of a child able to turn to God whenever the appropriate knowledge, motive, and training are furnished, and one that supposes a preliminary new creating process indispensable, without which all motives and training are of little or no avail. What farmer would cultivate a plant that he was assured would yield only poisonous fruit unless its nature was changed by a new creation of God, till he had evidence of this change?

I regard the mind of the child as a perfect seed, needing only the good soil and careful training which man can provide, united with the warm sun of divine influence that is ever shed on all faithful labor. Thus there is both the outer and inner impulse, God and man working together to rear up plants of righteousness, both being indispensable to success.

You ask if my objections do not fail "if the Spirit be supposed to be freely, widely, *generally* bestowed on the youngest as well as afterward, and this to be expressed, and pledged, and *made sure* by baptism?" This will be some relief for those whose children are baptized; but more than half of the infants, even in Christian lands, are not baptized, so that remedy, whatever it may be, fails them.

If, as you intimate, the Spirit is "*generally* bestowed on the youngest," I should like to know whether you would teach, as the Methodist divines now are *seeming* to teach, that all the injury done to a child by Adam's sin is remedied by Christ? If so, then we are agreed that the infant mind is perfect as God first made it, and the name of Pelagian belongs to us both alike.

If you say you do not hold to a depravity of constitution, you agree with me. That is all that I deny.

If you say there is some cause for the universal sin of man, I grant it; but this does not oblige me to have a theory to show what the cause is. What I aim at is to get rid of a theory, not to prove mine the true one. I state mine, not so much to prove it as to show that we are not shut up to that of Augustine.

If it is urged that we see the fact, and must allow that at least some minds are badly constituted, and that this is transmitted from parent to child, I deny the fact, and say no one can *prove* it. Minds are parts of a vast system requiring diversity in orders and kinds. What is called a badly constituted mind can be regulated by the will, and *when* so regulated the person is higher in virtue than if not tempted by such propensities.

No man has a right to say that any child's mind is badly constituted as a part of God's infinite system of minds and worlds till he can so comprehend that system as to *prove* what he asserts. A man who builds a theological system on a theory for which he has *no* proof, acts as contrary to common sense as the man who sends merchandise to a port where he has *no* evidence that it is wanted.

In regard to the *entire* "inability" of man "to turn and prepare himself by his own natural strength and good works to faith and calling upon God," and that we have "*no* power to do good works pleasant and acceptable to God without his grace," no rational person ever denied it, in the only sense in which, as I suppose, the Bible teaches it.

An infant has *no* power to love and obey God, not because its mind is made wrong, but because the knowledge, training, and motives are wanting; just as the child has no power to see in a dark room, not because his eyes are made wrong, but because the light is not there.

Jesus Christ, the Creator of all things in heaven and on earth, formed us with capacities of knowing, loving, and obeying him, revealed his perfect laws, came to set us the example of perfect obedience, suffered to the death to save us, and ever lives to help and guide us by his Holy Spirit given freely *to all.*

This is "the grace" of Jesus Christ given for all; and those who have access to the light of this knowledge of the glory of God, know and can walk in the way of salvation.

How far those are benefited who do not learn this Gospel in this world, and what may be their chance in another state of being, is not revealed to man.

You ask if the Augustinian system has not been held almost always, except in New England, as if it were not held at all? I reply that all the Papal and Episcopal churches have held it a practical thing, inasmuch as they have intervened a theory of baptismal regeneration, or some other method supposed to restore to children and to the unregenerate some power to do works pleasing to God, and having *some* efficacy in securing regenerating grace.

But the Calvinistic sects have denied this power in their creeds and teachings, and left to most parents nothing but unconditional "election" as the basis of hope. The "covenant of grace," by which "the promise is to you and to your children," is usually taught to be a point of some hope for the infants of Church members, but for all other infants there is no way of escape from a life of sin, and eternal death as the consequence, but what rests on unconditional election.

You ask if it is not a legitimate way of holding doctrines so mysterious and abstract, as if not held at all, and so as not to affect the *conduct* of persons of common sense?

Is it not a strong evidence against such doctrines that persons of common sense are expected to *act* as if they were false?

On *any* theory, I can not perceive the wisdom or goodness of a Creator who, having the power to make all infant minds perfect, has constituted them so imperfect in nature that they must be re-created before they can turn to God and render acceptable service. It seems more inspiring, ennobling, and in agreement with Scripture that God creates all his children with perfect minds; not all equal and alike in endowments, but all perfectly fitted for a station of happiness in a perfect system, and needing only the knowledge, motives, training, and development which can not be created, but to secure which both God and man must act conjointly.

In the Bible God always speaks of man's agency in saving our race as what is as indispensable as his own. And he grieves and mourns over guilty creatures as ruined, not for want of what he had power to bestow, but for want of what man can provide and does not.

Your question as to my own personal disqualifications for looking on all sides of subjects like these introduces a point which is of great practical importance.

In our search after truth, as it seems to me, all that God requires is, first, a humble and teachable spirit—it is "the meek" whom he promises to "guide in judgment;" next, the use of the means in our reach; then prayer for guidance of the Holy Spirit; and, lastly, a decision according to the best judgment, not of other minds, but of our own.

When on all practical questions we have thus decided, we have done all that God requires. On many practical questions none but God can certainly decide what is right abstractly (*i. e.*, the *best* for all concerned in relation to time and eternity). He has given general rules to guide our decisions, and we are to apply these rules by the above method. When we have done this our responsibility ends. We have decided right so far as we are obligated so to do, and the results belong to God.

This subject in hand is a practical one to me, as it is to every teacher and parent. "Can these children, with the nature they possess at birth, be trained to true virtue and piety, or is nothing accomplished till God re-creates their depraved natures?" Are we to train infants as young Christians, to be developed into mature Christians, or are we to train them as depraved creatures, with the hope that some day God will regenerate them, previous to which there is no true virtue and piety to be expected?

I was not by natural taste a metaphysician or a theologian, but quite the reverse. All through my youth, however, I was accustomed to hear discussions, and my father's social nature sought my sympathy in all his theological debates. Then sorrow came and cut off the hopes of this life, and drove me to seek for religious consolation amid the stern teachings of New England theology, where it could not be found by me.

Then I became an educator, striving only to qualify myself for its sacred duties, and studying nothing but with this as the chief end. Thus I have been led to these investigations simply as a practical matter, bearing on my daily duties as an educator.

When I come to questions demanding learned research far beyond my reach, or when I find the knowledge needed hid in the Greek and Hebrew, am I then helpless, and obliged to take opinions on human authority? Not at all. On the contrary, I think I am better situated than any learned men, or metaphysicians, or theologians, who make these sciences their chief pursuit.

Do I want to know any thing in Greek, Hebrew, Chaldee, or Arabic? I have a brother-in-law under the same roof, who is learned in these, and is pleased to give his aid. In a very short time, I learn from him what are the diverse interpretations, and what are the arguments for each, and I then do not take his opinion, but judge for myself.

So, on questions of mental science, I have another brother who has made this his speciality, and who in a short time can point out the books, or give me an outline furnishing the arguments *pro* and *con* on any disputed question. In theology, also, I have for forty years been hearing and reading with my father and brothers, and all with a practical aim.

Now it is clear that, having the ordinary common sense of mankind, I have a better chance than any learned men, any metaphysicians, any theologians, to come to correct conclusions, and for these reasons:

I belong to no party; I have no restraints of synods, presbyteries; no parish, no theological school, no college, no newspaper, no magazine, that would be injured by my change of opinions. Where are the learned theologians and metaphysicians, the editors, or the clergymen who are as free from such biasing influences as I am? Would not almost every learned man in the nation lose his character, his professional position, and his daily bread, if he should fairly, as I have done, take the name of a Pelagian?

Not that I voluntarily assumed this name. Those who do not, or can not answer arguments, often call hard names, and it is to such that I was first indebted for it. Nor do I repel it. If Pelagius really did hold that infants are born with just such a nature as God created for them, and that this, like all his works, is perfect, and if agreeing with him in this is being a Pelagian, then I am content so to be called. The question of the propriety of the name belongs to those who have given it, not to me.

Your query as it respects the deference owed to the ministers of Jesus Christ, perhaps implies what is not correct as to the true impress of my words. I believe that the ministry have claims of deference and respect in all those matters in which Christ appointed them "to rule." In the interpretation of Christ's teachings they are *not* appointed to rule, but to *teach* all that knowledge which the people need to qualify them to judge for themselves. And when I appeal from the ministry to the people, it is only to urge this important distinction, that the ministry are to rule in conducting church affairs as presiding officers, but not in matters of opinion.

Every minister has a right to set forth his opinions and his interpretations of the Bible, and his reasons for them, and then the people are to be his judges as to whether he is right, so far as to be allowed to continue to teach thus. And if they judge him to be erroneous and dangerous, they, by their votes, can and ought to dismiss him from their pulpit.

There is not a pulpit, or a religious paper, or a magazine, or even a denomination that is not thus dependent on the people as their judges. Even in the Catholic Church in this nation, if all, or even a very large majority of the people, decide that their clergy are in the wrong, the clergy must yield, or lose character, and pulpit, and income.

And, although the ministry is and ought to be more learned and qualified to teach than the people in all that is needed for the true understanding of the Bible, I have already indicated the respects in which the laity have an advantage in the probabilities of forming correct judgments as to the true meaning of the Bible, *if* they will only make the proper exertion.

All I have written on the subject, in this view, I think, implies no want of respect to Christ's ministers. And my appeals to the people and secular press were aimed, not to lower this respect, but rather to lead those thus addressed wisely and humbly to use the power conferred on them by Him who has commanded *all* to "call no man master" but Christ, the Lord of all.

From Rev. Dr. ———, *of the Episcopal Church.*

"Dear Madam,—Your work strikes me as a careful and ingenious treatment of one of the most momentous of all subjects. For the most part I sympathize with its doctrines, and wholly with its spirit.

"There are some suggestions which, at your request, I will offer.

"1. It seems undesirable to make so formal a recognition of the vague and artificial distinction between High and Low Church. The *tendencies* which these names represent are real, but the existence of the parties is an evil which the best friends of the Church deplore, and are earnestly trying to remove. The actual lines of difference are so vague, and cross and recross in such confusion, that to attempt a two-fold classification under these names is both injurious and unjust. The work of our Church in this country is too important to be compromised by such pernicious partisanship.

"2. It will be painful to members of our Church, who have a knowledge of its history and relations, to hear it spoken of as a 'sect'—'an Arminian sect.' It is not a sect at all.

"3. I do not see that you make baptism an essential even to the *visible* Church; yet Christ makes it so, and St. Peter, to say the least. Suppose all baptized parents were suddenly cut off, and only their unbaptized children were left in the world, would there be a visible Church?

"You appear to think that the Episcopal Church, and Christians generally, would do well to root out the hope of some mysterious efficacy in baptism. But how is it possible to read and receive all the several passages of the New Testament which touch on this subject in their plain, 'common-sense' interpretation, without admitting that there is *some* 'mysterious efficacy' in it, and that Christ and his apostles teach that there is?

"'Except a man be born of *water* and the Holy Ghost.' 'He that believeth and is *baptized* shall be saved.'

"'The figure whereunto even baptism doth now save us.' 'The washing of regeneration.'

"Do not these expressions warrant our baptismal service in referring to the *water* as 'sanctified to a mystical washing away of sin?'

"I cordially agree with you that the Bible gives us *no theory* as to *the mode*, nor does it define the *degree* of the 'efficacy;' but its language is a strange delusion if it does not assert *the fact*. I adopt your own valuable distinction between *the fact* and the *mode* of the fact. The lowest Churchman, I believe, if he would not impugn the Gospel, admits *some* 'mysterious efficacy' in baptism.

"4. You seem to reject the idea that 'children are utterly unable to have any righteousness of their own.' I had supposed that all Bible Christians agree that no human being has any power, faculty, virtue, or grace, or even existence 'of his own,' or otherwise than by the gift of his Creator.

"On the whole question of the *fact* of depravity I am tempted to say more than you will care to read—more than you have asked for—more than I have time to write; but is it the part of 'common sense' to deny facts? And the fact is, that children are born uniformly selfish and prone to sin. Common sense and the Bible agree in that.

"You may refer the mischief to education, to which there are two answers. 1. Where did the bad educators and education come from? 2. If sin begins to come as soon as education begins, it must have been *in* before.* The world is full of hereditary transmitted evil. It is vain to say that this evil is not of a kind

* Here is a specimen of the Romish theory, that sin and righteousness are physical things to be put in and taken out, instead of the voluntary acts of rational minds.

to bring suffering—*real* suffering. It does bring it, moral as well as physical damage and loss. To make this inconsistent with God's goodness proves too much.

"5. More than once it has occurred to me whether there is not a grand fallacy underlying your whole argument as making 'common sense' a supreme arbiter and proper test of *spiritual* truth, thus ignoring the spiritual faculty—the *faith* organ—to which divine mysteries are addressed.

"What we call common sense is *one* noble power among other co-ordinate powers. All must work in harmony. But this one is not the highest, and revelation often makes its wisdom to be foolishness.

"6. In supporting your opinion that the Bible does not teach that men are depraved in their *nature* by or from Adam, you dispose of a whole set of texts by observing that they are an 'Oriental mode of expression, not to be taken literally.' This is an assertion only. And by the same rule of interpretation might not one expel almost any doctrine from the Bible?

"You will understand the freedom and conciseness of my comments. They are made only at your request, and rather with a desire to discharge my own conscience than with a hope to change your convictions. Pray take them in good part, and believe me cordially and faithfully your friend."

Reply to the foregoing by the Author.

REV. AND DEAR SIR,—Thanking you for the kind attention you have given to the pages I sent for your criticism, I proceed to notice the several points presented, which, to save repetition, I have numbered in your letter with corresponding numbers in my reply.

1. As to recognizing the distinctions of High-

Church and Low, while it is impossible, as you suggest, to draw any clear line of demarcation so as to make a two-fold classification of *persons*, you allow that the *tendencies* represented by these names are *real*, and you must perceive also that they all result from this theory of transmitted infant depravity.

The clergy and laity of the Episcopal Church are not trained to metaphysical speculations, or to framing philosophical theories. Their creed in the Liturgy is one of *facts*, not including a single item of philosophy to account for these facts. But in the Articles and in some of the ritual has been added some things as facts which are not so, and from this combination results the tendency to Rome on the one hand, and to Calvinism on the other.

The *assumed* facts, warranted neither by the Bible or common sense, are that God has created minds *in nature* diverse from those of infants, being so perfect that holy actions *naturally* result; that he created Adam with such a mind; that Adam ruined it by sinning, and, in consequence of this, God caused such a constitution of things that Adam transmitted, not the holy nature God made, but his own ruined nature depraved by sinning.

This falsely is called a *fact*, and accepted as a "mystery" revealed by God.

Every parent feels that if God has done a deed which in any human parent would be called monstrous and cruel in the highest degree, he must *somehow* have provided some compensating remedy. The Romish Church and the High-Church Episcopal divines say it *is* done, and the mysterious remedy is *baptism*, and other rites and forms for this end. The laity, not trained to reason, only *feel* that if their infants are so injured, they wish to go where there is the best chance of a remedy. This makes the constant pressure and "tendency" to High-Churchism and to Rome.

In resisting this tendency, the opposing party teach that baptism and other rites do not regenerate the soul of the child, but only admit to certain advantages in the Church, and that real spiritual regeneration comes only by the new creating influence of the Holy Spirit, in connection with means and influences possible only to a certain degree of intellectual development, and also dependent, more or less, on "*elective grace*." Thus comes the tendency to Calvinistic views and training.

This struggle, and the parties resulting from it, can never cease till that false doctrine, originated in the Romish Church, and contrary both to the Bible and common sense, is relinquished as *a fact*, and treated as a pernicious philosophical theory having no claims to respect.

2. You object to my speaking of the Episcopal Church as a "sect." This word is defined in the dictionaries as a "religious denomination." Our Liturgy defines the Church in its widest use as

"the blessed company of all faithful people." The *local* Church, in the Articles, is defined as "a congregation of faithful men in which the pure Word of God is preached, and the sacraments be duly ministered."

Besides these uses, the word *church* is employed to express an organization of several local churches into one body. Thus the English National Church is one body composed of local churches; the American Episcopal Church is another distinct body of local churches, united as one by their constitution and General Convention. So the American Presbyterian Church is another body of local churches organized as one body. Each of these is a *denominational Church*, in distinction from the Church universal and the local Church. And, in common parlance, the words "sect" and "denomination" are used as synonyms. I think, after this exposition, no candid person in our communion will be pained that I have used the word "sect" as applicable to the Episcopal denominational Church, or deny that it is as properly applied to that as to any other denomination of Christians.

3. On the subject of baptism, I find nothing said distinctly in the New Testament in reference to *infants*. We see in the history that, for adults, it was the appointed mode of *professing* to believe in Christ as Lord, and thus of becoming members of a Christian community. Christ's saying, "He that believ-

eth and is baptized shall be saved," is equivalent to saying that believing and *professing* this belief are what is demanded of all his followers. But, as often it might be the case that baptism was necessarily delayed or omitted, it is *not* said he that is not baptized shall be damned.

In the history of the first century, it appears that baptism soon was withheld till the young convert or young children had received proper instruction, and yet they were members of the local Church. It seems, in the age of Augustine, that he was not baptized in early life, though his mother was a very devout Christian woman. From all I can glean on this subject, I should infer that, in regard to infants, the early Christians had diverse views and practices, just as we have now.

If we recur to the Episcopal standards, we find that a church is defined, not as an assembly of *baptized* persons, but as a "congregation of faithful men," using the word *men* in its widest sense, including women and children. According to this definition, any congregation of faithful persons, in which "the pure Word of God is preached, and the sacraments be duly ministered according to Christ's ordinance," is a local Church.

This definition does not state how much faith each of the congregation must have to be counted a "faithful" person. But as in all cases baptized infant children are counted as in the Church, and it is supposed that all are baptized in infancy in the Episcopal denomination, the whole *parish* are supposed to be the *Church.* And the actual amount of faith practically demanded is only so much as secures attendance as a part of "a congregation."

According to this definition, all that is required to form a *local* Church of Christ is for a number of believers in his religion to unite as a congregation, in which the *pure* Word of God shall be preached and the sacraments be *duly* administered.

But who is to decide whether the Word preached is "pure," and whether the sacraments be "duly" administered? Certainly, on the Protestant principle that every man is to be his own interpreter of God's Word, it is *the congregation* who are to be the deciding power. The Word must be preached and the sacraments administered according to the convictions of the congregation, and not according to the dictum of pope or ecclesiastical councils. Thus a local Church of Christ on the Episcopal theory, as set forth in the Articles, consists of men, women, and children who have enough faith in Christ to join a Christian congregation, in which the Word of God is preached, and the sacraments be administered according to the convictions of the worshipers. It becomes a local *Episcopal* Church only by adopting the forms and usages of that denomination. But it is a *Christian Church* when the congregation believes in Christ, and has the *pure*

Word preached, and the sacrament *duly* administered according to the judgment and convictions of the worshipers.

I suppose that our Savior laid such apparent stress upon baptism, not as a mysterious remedy for injury done by Adam to infant minds, but because, in human language, the sign and the thing signified are often expressed by the same term.

Baptism was the appointed sign or form of *professing* Christ which was demanded of all. A man must be "born of the Spirit" by a true and living faith, and he thus enters the spiritual family of God. He must also be "born by water," and thus enter the company of professed followers of Christ, and share their labors and sufferings; and whoever was unwilling to take this cross of a public profession was declared to be no true disciple. Thus we understand the declaration, "Except a man be born of water and the Holy Ghost he can not enter the kingdom of heaven." This seems to me the true meaning of this and similar passages, and I think the Liturgy and Articles of our Church warrant it. Still, there are some passages left in the baptismal service by Archbishop Cranmer that retain some of the Romish idea of a "mystical spiritual regeneration by water."

4. I do not reject the idea that "children are utterly unable to have any righteousness of their own," in the sense you seem to receive it. God

gives us existence, all our faculties, and all those surroundings which enable us to use them. In this widest sense, God is the author of every thing—every act of sin and every act of holiness in all his creatures. It is in this widest sense he himself says, "I create evil."

But this is very different from the doctrine that God, having power to make all infant minds perfect, has caused them to be made depraved by a constitutional transmission which he instituted. It is this, and not your statement, that I deny.

You ask if it is the part of common sense "to deny facts," as if I denied the fact of the dreadful *depravity of man* as exhibited in this world's history. I maintain this as fully as any one. The only thing I dispute is the theory which attempts to show the "cause and origin of this evil."

When you say that the *cause* of this depravity is the depraved nature of infants transmitted from Adam, and I deny that this is taught in the Bible, and that it is contrary to common sense, you seem to think I deny the *fact* of man's depravity. You are not the first that has made this mistake. I rarely know any person speak or write on this subject without exactly this confusion of ideas.

The Bible was written for *men* who are sinners by their own voluntary transgressions, and has nothing to do with the nature of infants. The Gospel comes to help sinful men, not to teach the "origin of evil," much less to teach that infants have a depraved nature, from which comes all their after sin and suffering, and that, too, when God could have given another and better nature, such as it is claimed he gave Adam, and such as would have saved infants from all the sin and suffering resulting from a depraved nature. It is this theory I deny, not the *fact* of man's depravity.

5. Your remarks as to "the spiritual faculty" need some explanation. I conjecture that you mean by this term a power or faculty that takes cognizance of things not of this world—the spiritual things of the world unseen.

All our knowledge on these subjects we gain solely by *revelations*, made in human language for the common people, which are to be interpreted by the common-sense rules employed in every-day life. I never supposed any special faculty was given to enable us to understand the language of the Bible, or to have "faith" in its revelations, on one subject more than on another. Perhaps, on more reflection, you will come to the same conclusion.

6. In regard to your remarks on the texts which I have claimed to be "Oriental modes of expression, not to be taken literally," I refer you to what I have addressed to my brother on that subject in pages following.

* * * *

Extracts from a Letter of an Episcopal Clergyman to the Author.

"I venture to direct your attention to a few points which strike my mind unfavorably.

"One is your representing theologians as teaching that the natural depravity of infants is an 'infliction' visited on the innocent descendants of Adam as a 'punishment' or 'penalty' for Adam's sin. Your treatise implies that God directly creates every infant mind, or soul, with a depraved nature arbitrarily inflicted as the punishment for Adam's sin. In this I think you do injustice to all theologians with whose writings I have any acquaintance.

"I suppose that the sin of Adam *can not but* affect his posterity, unless God, by an omnipotent act, should change the whole law of propagation which he at first impressed on the nature of man. 'Who can bring a clean thing out of an unclean?'

"Another point is your representing the Lutheran theory of justification as teaching that man can have no righteousness at all, but only have Christ's righteousness imputed to him.

"If you mean by this that no righteousness which a sinner supposes himself to have before his conversion is *the ground* on which God justifies him when he repents and believes, you are right, as I understand the matter.

"But if you mean that the Lutheran theory teaches that a man can have no righteousness at all other than Christ's imputed righteousness, you misrepresent that theory, as I understand it.

"In your remarks on 'concupiscence,' you seem to mistake both the theological and lexicographical sense of the term. Where do theologians teach that our natural 'desires' are in themselves sinful?

"One other point is that you represent the Gospel way of salvation as no more than this: Repent of *past* sin, have a controlling purpose of obedience for the future, and, for Christ's sake, God will receive and treat you as if you had not sinned.

"Your phrase of 'a controlling purpose of obedience,' as a substitute for the scriptural phrase 'believe on the Lord Jesus Christ,' does not satisfy me, although, perhaps, you might so explain it as to bring it into harmony with what the Bible teaches."

Reply of the Author to the preceding Letter.

The points to which you direct my attention involve simply a question of *fact*, to settle which we must turn to historic and theological writings.

One fact to be decided is not what you, as an individual, hold and teach, nor how you may explain and interpret texts and creeds. The question is, Do Protestant theologians teach that the depravity of infants is an "infliction," "punishment," and "penalty" for Adam's sin, as the people use and understand these terms as shown by our dictionaries?

You say yourself, "I suppose the sin of Adam can not but affect his posterity, *unless* God, by an omnipotent act, should change the whole *law of propagation* which he at first impressed on the nature of man. 'Who can bring a clean thing out of an unclean?'"

Here you clearly imply that God had power to make and to change "the law of propagation" by which Adam's depraved nature passes to infants, and causes the sin and misery of this world. You imply, also, that he had power to make the law of propagation such that Adam would have transmitted his original nature, as God formed it, instead of the one ruined by himself.

Now you have only to go to standard Catholic and Protestant writers to find that they teach that, if Adam had not eaten the forbidden fruit, the law of propagation would have been the transmission of Adam's nature as God first created it; that Adam acted for the whole race, either *in* him, or as their representative; and that when he sinned, *then*, and *for this act*, God impressed "the law of propagation" by which Adam's nature which he had ruined, and not the perfect nature God first created, was impressed on all infants, from which results their sin and misery. Now this was, as the people use the term, "an infliction," "a punishment," and "a penalty" for Adam's sin. All men say that attainder reaching to children is a punishment or penalty on these children. All say that the children of a drunkard suffer with him the penalty or punishment of his sins. I therefore claim that I use these words in their true sense as the common people understand them, and am sustained by all lexicographers in this use.

Now suppose God had made a "covenant with Adam," as theologians express it, in this wise: "Eat not of that tree, and you and all your posterity shall have perfect eyes and limbs; but eat of it, and you and all infants shall have blind eyes and dislocated joints."

Suppose, in consequence of Adam's eating, God established this cruel law, and all little children were crawling about in darkness, screaming, tortured, and helpless with dislocated joints, while all parents and nurses were in the same darkness and helpless misery. How then could you prove a benevolent Creator, or prevent the conviction that he is malevolent—especially so when you knew that by a word he could restore to all these sufferers perfect eyes and limbs, and, in spite of tears and prayers, he refuses the boon?

But what a trifle this would be compared to the temporal and the eternal misery which you yourself allow has been caused by "a law of propagation," established by the Creator, impressing on infants a depraved nature, from which comes all their sin and misery in this life, and eternal ruin in hell to all except the few regenerate; and that, too, when he has power to create every infant mind perfect in nature.

Will you, reverend sir, furnish any *evidence*, from the Bible or from any other source, that Adam's mind became depraved *in nature* by eating the forbidden fruit, or that God established any "law of propagation" of such a depraved nature to infants? So far as I can discover, this is a mere theological theory, without any evidence of any kind.

The fact that children have diverse constitutional traits, some involving more temptation than others, none will deny. None will deny that these are transmitted from parent to child, and that the sins of a parent often increase the constitutional temptations and difficulties of a child. But if these increased temptations are regulated by reason and conscience, the child becomes nobler in character and virtuous self-control than if no such difficulties were to be overcome.

These varieties in mental constitution, and the changes made by sinful parents in them, are to be judged of as a part of a vast system of rational free agents, in which whatever is best for the whole is best for each part.

No finite mind is qualified to pronounce any infant mind badly constituted in reference to an infinite system and eternal results which the Infinite and Eternal Mind alone can behold.

The question of the Lutheran theory of justification is also one of fact. The Romish Church taught that by baptism and penance the soul is actually *made* righteous, Christ's righteousness thus being poured into it.

The Protestant said no, it is not made righteous; it is only regarded and treated as righteous by having Christ's righteousness imputed when faith is imparted at regeneration. If there is any thing taught in human language, the Protestant standards do teach that we can have no righteousness of our own.

Your statement that a sinner has no righteousness which "is *the ground* on which God justifies him when he repents and believes," you may give as your opinion; but I see not how you can maintain that Luther and his followers did not teach that a man can have no righteousness at all except Christ's imputed righteousness. It is a question of fact, to be settled by appeal to authorities.

In regard to the words "desires" and "concupiscence," we are also at issue on a matter of *fact*, to be decided by an appeal to dictionaries.

On examining a standard English dictionary [Richardson], I find the following:

"*Concupiscence;* to wish for, or to desire ardently.
"*Lust;* generally, to wish; to desire; to like; to love."

I think you will find in all English lexicographers that these words, in their original and widest use, include *all* desires and wishes for any and all kinds of enjoyment, and for escape from all kinds of discomfort and pain.

Besides this general comprehensive sense, these words have had a more limited use, confining them to a certain class of desires on which the family state is based. And here is the place where confusion of ideas has existed from want of a clear distinction between "*natural desires*" and the *uncontrolled and sinful indulgence* of such desires.

For example, a young man is betrothed to a maiden, and loves her with the pure affection appropriate to that relation. But suddenly he discovers that she is his own sister. In this change of circumstances, his past love for his betrothed was not sin. On the contrary, if he controls and regulates his natural desires by the rules of rectitude and religion, he rises higher in virtue and piety than if no such temptations had occurred to be overcome.

I now can reply to your question, "Where do theologians teach that our natural desires are in themselves sinful?" I reply, that not only the Thirty-nine Articles, but most of the standard theologians of the Protestant sects, teach that "concupiscence and lust hath of itself the nature of sin." It is also equally true that the same persons contradict themselves, and say, as you imply, that "our natural desires are *not* in themselves sinful."*

I suppose all these contradictions would be removed by a clear discrimination between "natural desires" and the "uncontrolled indulgence" of these desires, when such indulgence would violate the

* The Presbyterian Confession teaches that "works done by unregenerate men, although they may be things God commands, are sinful and can not please God, or make a man meet to receive grace; and yet the neglect of them is more sinful and displeasing to God." Thus it appears that we displease God by *not* doing works that are sinful. The eighth article of the Episcopal Church also teaches that "works before justification have the nature of sin."

laws of God. I hold that our nature is such that our natural desires are none of them sinful, and that sin is never any thing but the voluntary transgression of law by the uncontrolled indulgence of our desires, when the laws of God demand that they be denied and suppressed as they can be by the will.

Your remarks on "the Gospel way of salvation" again involve a question of fact. You no doubt concede that the meaning of the word "faith" is that which the common people understand when they use it. The first pages of Chapter X. set forth this matter at large. More briefly, "faith" sometimes means mere intellectual conviction, without including appropriate feelings and conduct; and this is called a "dead faith." In a wider use, it signifies intellectual conviction and the appropriate feelings and conduct; and this is called a "living faith."

Now the question between us is this: when a man repents of past sin, and forms a *controlling* purpose of obedience to Christ in all things (that is, a purpose which *actually controls* his feelings and conduct), is this the Gospel way of salvation? If you say it is, then wherein does it differ from the Bible meaning of true and saving faith in Jesus Christ?

When the doctrine of the transmitted depravity of infants was established as the foundation of both the Catholic and Protestant theology, every part of this system was made to conform. Thus *faith*, *repentance*, and *love*, each of which is presented as indispensable to the Gospel way of salvation, were all made by theologians to include as their chief element, the regeneration or new creation of a depraved nature. This is not any part of the meaning of these words as used and understood by the people in common life.

But infant depravity being relinquished, then these words will assume their ordinary and true meaning, as understood by the common people.

True *repentance* is not only sorrow for past sin, but a controlling purpose to forsake it.

Love is not only pleasurable emotions toward God, but a controlling purpose to please Him by obedience to His laws.

Faith is a belief in God or in Jesus Christ, involving a controlling purpose of obedience.

In all three it is the *controlling* purpose of obedience to God and Christ that is the *distinctive* feature of "the Gospel way of salvation." If a man has this purpose, and it actually *controls* his feeling and conduct, is he not a true Christian? Can he be one without such a controlling purpose?

If Christ and God are one, is not every man a true Christian who maintains a controlling purpose to obey the will or laws of God? And is not faith in God and faith in Christ the same thing? Are not the laws of God and the laws of rectitude one and the same? If so, is not every child or adult, who habitually is aiming to *do right and avoid wrong*, in both feeling and conduct, a righteous person and a true Christian?

Is not this way of interpreting the Bible in agreement with the common-sense rules that the common people employ, for whom especially the Bible was written?

From Rev. Dr. ———, of the Episcopal Church.

"My dear Madam,—I have been profoundly interested in the pages of your book sent in proofs, though I have not been able to give the attention which a production so striking and original demands.

"Those chapters in which you develop the moral training of the household as in the same line, though on a lower plane, as that of the Church, I read with an assenting mind.

"Your exhibition of mental torture in the history of Miss Payson, to which ingenuous souls are subjected, is mournful indeed. This agony produced in willing minds, plastic to the influence of the Spirit, by the denial that the all-loving Father and the all-sacrificing Son do not utter their assurances in good faith, is perfectly heart-rending. My inmost soul rejects this imputation against that infinite love which exhausts all language to prove sincerity.

"There is one point that has often impressed me as a father and a pastor in reference to those brought up to feel that they are children of God, with the privileges and responsibilities belonging to that character. I think it will be found that when such, at confirmation, are called to renew the vows made for them at baptism, that their exercises, when brought to this decisive act, are very similar to those of persons trained to regard themselves as out of Christ's family, and only children of wrath.

"In children preparing for confirmation, I have found as deep a sense of sinfulness, as solemn self-inspection, as true repentance, and as deep a sense of the solemnity of this publicly entering into covenant with God, as ever exists in those brought up under a different system. At such a crisis, the soul of the child brought up to regard itself as a young and imperfect Christian gathers itself up to examine whether it has the true penitence for the past, and living faith and purpose for the future, that such a public and solemn enrollment demands.

"I think this an important point to develop with a view to satisfy those who believe, and justly, that none should assume their baptismal vows with any thing less than as a very solemn, soul-consecrating act, and as a momentous era in the history of the soul.

"So much for the book up to Chapter XIV. While entirely revolting from Calvinism, I have always accepted our ninth Article on original sin. I take the liberty of saying that I do not feel the force of your observation that the doctrine of transmitted depravity is a *philosophy* constructed from the facts of the Bible. It does not seem to me even an inference or a philosophy of facts so much as a truth wrapped up in or underlying them.

"If I say that all lions have manes, and roar, and have an appetite for flesh, I construct no philosophy in saying that these peculiarities are transmitted from lion to lion, and that this is the *nature* of a lion transmitted from parent to offspring. It is a law running through all nature that like begets like. 'Whose seed is in itself after its kind.' If this is implied, why should we not express it? These are my first thoughts on that point."

* * * * *

REV. AND DEAR SIR,—Your very kind and sympathetic letter was gratefully received, and its valuable suggestions duly considered.

I will first notice your remarks on transmitted depravity.

Your illustration of the nature of lions does not meet the case, inasmuch as we are discussing the question of the character of *free agents*, who have the power (which lions have not) of choosing either according to reason and conscience, or according to the impulses of desire.

There is no such *uniformity* of choice as you seem to imply. Sometimes a young child chooses right and sometimes wrong. It does not uniformly choose wrong, as the lion uniformly roars and eats meat.

Great confusion of ideas exists in all directions from want of this distinction between the *rational* free agency of man and the instinctive choices of animals. The infant begins life with the mere animal development first, but in due time comes the great moral element that makes him a child of God, created in his image an *immortal free agent.*

Your remarks on the subject of *confirmation* are most excellent, very practical, and therefore calculated to be very useful. And yet it seems to me that the churches of Christ at the present day have but a faint idea of what was the real original meaning of the Eucharist, or of the preliminary rites of baptism and confirmation.

Both baptism and the Eucharist were instituted when the Christian churches were adults, gathered from ignorant heathens or from bigoted Jews. It was at a time of fierce and cruel persecution, when *professing* to be a Christian risked the loss of all things valued in this life.

At the Eucharist the disciples understood the command to "show forth the Lord's death till he come," and "this do in remembrance of me," to signify that what he their Lord had done to save them they were to be ready to do to save others, even to *suffer to the death.*

The true meaning of these rites can never return to the churches of Christ until they have a clearer realization of their true mission as *suffering* soldiers of the Cross. When their infants are baptized as those to be trained for the *service of martyrs*, then baptism, confirmation, and the Eucharist will come before them with a high and solemn import such as now is unknown.

How children are to be trained at once to receive and enjoy all the blessings of this life, as I have supposed they are to do in the future, and yet to enter the career of suffering martyrs—this is the practical question that must meet every minister and every educator.

In this aspect permit a few suggestive questions. Do you not suppose it would cost as much self-denial to some of our clergy to deny certain lusts of the flesh—such, for example, as the use of tobacco—as it often cost the earlier Christians to give up their daily comfort and enjoyments? Not the same in kind, but one as difficult to meet?

Do you not suppose that the use of this poisonous stimulant is leading thousands of our young boys and young men to intemperance, to debility, to shattered nerves, to irritable tempers, and to an early grave? Do you suppose it possible to stem this dangerous self-indulgence in the young, in cases where their spiritual guides can not bring themselves to deny this lust of the flesh, and so can not preach this self-denial to others?

If all children were trained to indulge their wishes and desires only when their own *best* good and the *best* good of society were secured, would there not be constant and stringent rules of self-sacrifice and self-denial now unknown or unrecognized?

If children were trained to use all *property* and all *talents* for the *best* good of the world around them, instead of for the gratification of self and friends, would there not be a system of constant self-denial introduced that would equal any practiced in any martyr age? Not in kind, but in the difficulties involved?

Suppose it were *proved* to the consciences of many Christian men of wealth that they could do *more* to promote the *best* good of the world to unite and plant complete Christian communities in Tartary or the interior of Africa than to live as they do now, would not these Christians soon be "scattered abroad preaching the Word," with a measure of self-denial equal to or exceeding that of the first Christians?

From a Roman Catholic Priest to the Author.

"DEAR MADAM,—Yours of the 1st instant, with the proofs, were duly received.

"With this I send '*Aspirations of Nature*,' by J. T. Hecker; also an Italian pamphlet published in Rome, first in the 'Civita Catholica,' by the advice of Cardinal Barnabo, with the approbation of the censor of the press; and it has been read by the Pope himself. [In this work was a notice of the author's work *Common Sense Applied to Religion*, and also of her brother's work *The Conflict of Ages.*]

"The chapter on 'Original Sin,' in the *Aspirations of Nature*, was read in proof to Archbishop Kendrick, of Baltimore, the most learned theologian in this country, and pronounced by him to be perfectly orthodox.

"I am not going to deny that there are different schools of theology in the Catholic Church. Still, to your question, 'Do you not suppose that I can find quires of quotations from the decrees of popes and councils that will contradict the statement that the Catholic Church *does not* teach the depravity of man's nature?'

"I answer, emphatically, no! You can not bring one such quotation. I dare say most candid men, *i.e.*, those not conversant with Catholic theology, and conversant with the theological language of Protestants, would misapprehend some phraseology employed in some Catholic documents.

"But the words have a fixed meaning in Catholic theology, which is *a science*. The boundaries of faith are clearly laid down. All that the Church has decided can be clearly ascertained; and outside of that we are at perfect liberty to reason as much as we like.

"I assure you there can be no question that all the explanations I give you are derived from the most approved Catholic theologians, and have passed the censorship of Rome.

"You ask, If there are not several views of original sin and baptism in the Catholic Church, as in the Episcopal?

"To this I answer, as to the *substance of the doctrine*, no. The views of different schools of Episcopalians are usually contradictory. In the Catholic Church it is of faith that by Adam's sin the whole human race lost grace and the right to heaven, and that we are naturally incapable of any act in order to our restoration. It is of faith that baptism effaces original sin, regenerates, sanctifies, makes one the child of God and an heir of heaven. In a word, baptism is *a complete remedy* for original sin and for actual sin in adults.

"But the idea of an essential corruption or change of *nature* is perfectly foreign to St. Augustine and to every other Catholic theologian.

"The Calvinistic doctrine of total depravity is condemned by the Council of Trent.

"The best Catholic theologians state the matter in this way. God destined man for *super-natural* grace and beatitude, which are far above his natural condition, and capacity. He made Adam the representative and federal head of his race, and made the continuance of these gifts (super-natural) to the race contingent on his obedience. He lost them; and hence it is said that the human race sinned and fell with him. Although an infant is personally innocent, he is born in sin in this sense that he is born out of the order, lacking in perfection, and unable to attain the end for which God originally designed him.

"But because God has only deprived him of special favors above his natural condition, and to which he had no right, and has left him all his natural rights, he has done him no injustice. If he die in original sin, Catholic theologians teach that he will never attain the beatific vision, but will nevertheless be happy by a natural union with God; some say by enjoying the creatures of God.

"This is what I mean by the 'stain' of Adam's sin, in Latin 'culpa,' which, like the stain of illegitimacy or attainder, involve no actual sin.

"Your whole difficulty lies in your not understanding the Catholic idea of the two orders, natural and super-natural. If you can grasp that, you can see into the whole matter. You have not had the slightest idea of what Catholic doctrine really is. The decrees of the Council of Trent and Moehler's Symbolism will be a good beginning.

"Meanwhile, with my best wishes and kindest regards, I am truly your obedient servant,

"______ ______."

Reply of the Author to the foregoing.

REV. AND DEAR SIR,—I feel very grateful for the aid you have afforded me in regard to the views of Catholic theologians, especially for the work pronounced "orthodox" by such competent authority. I have examined the chapter on "Original Sin," and find that, in the first place, it agrees with Protestant theology in teaching the perfect constitution of Adam's mind. Thus:

"His soul was endowed with reason and free will. At the same time was added the *gift of integrity.* This adorned the soul with all the *natural knowledge* of which man was capable; no dangerous ignorance or defect of judgment; the will, in possession of perfect liberty, was upright and tended to good, without any inclination to evil. Adam was master of the sensitive appetites; with an equable temperament, always tranquil, *with no tendency to excess.*"

"All these rich gifts were held by Adam *on condition of not losing sanctifying grace.* Sanctifying grace elevated man's nature to a new principle of life and action. It infused into his mind and heart a science and virtue which transcended the order of nature. Man became a participator of the divine nature, and fitted one day to enjoy the beatific vision, which consists in gazing upon God's own essence."

"The effect of Adam's transgression was the immediate loss of the holiness and righteousness wherein he was constituted, which consisted in the gifts of integrity and sanctifying grace."—See pages 195, 196, *Asp. of Nature.*

The Council of Trent declares thus: "If any one asserts that Adam's sin injured himself alone, and not his posterity, and that the holiness and righteousness acceptable to God which he lost, he lost for himself alone, and not also for us; or that he, being stained by the sin of disobedience, transmitted death and corporal penalties only upon all the human race, and not *sin which is the death of the soul*, let him be accursed."—*Council of Trent*, Sess. v.

How is it, then, that, with these passages before you from your own infallible Church authorities, so honest a man as you are, can affirm that Catholic theologians do not teach the depravity of infant minds?

You say the infant "is born *out of the order*, lacking in *perfection*, and unable to attain the end for which God originally designed him." What is this but saying that God, who gave to Adam the gifts of integrity and sanctifying grace, making Adam's mind perfect in constitution, withheld these rich gifts from all infants, thus insuring their future sin and misery in this and a future life, and all because Adam disobeyed.

The author of the *Aspirations of Nature* thus comments, and his comments are approved by your highest theologian:

"What the fall did was to despoil man (*i. e.*, infants) of the gifts and graces which *were not necessary to his nature, which he had no right to claim.*"

You say also:

"Because God has only deprived him (each infant) of special favors above his natural condition, and *to which he had no right*, he has done him no injustice."

Here is the place where Catholic theology is at war with the common sense and moral sense of humanity. If there is any thing which a new-created being, brought into such terrific dangers as meet every new-born child, has *a right to*, it is all the helps and chances which a perfect constitution of mind would give, and which the Creator has, by your own concession, power to bestow.

What human parent could have the heart to deprive each of his new-born infants of "the gifts of integrity and sanctifying grace," and for no better reason than because Adam disobeyed a command thousands of years ago? And is the all-bounteous Father less tender of little children than we?

I am not helped at all by your mere verbal disguise of the natural and the super-natural. The common-sense difficulty still remains unrelieved.

None but a malignant being could inflict a *nature* on infants, no matter by what name, insuring sin and misery in this life and through eternity to most of our race, when he has power to give a "supernatural" nature that would increase their chances of escape from sin and its everlasting consequences.

The chief difficulty is not in regard to infants that *die* unbaptized, and thus lose heaven and "the beatific vision." It is for infants that *live* with a despoiled and ruined nature, as they do by millions, without even the poor supposed help of baptism to aid in keeping them from a life of sinning and consequent eternal ruin.

From a Roman Catholic Priest to the Author.

"Dear Madam,—I have read your proofs with a view of complying with your request, if possible; and the result is, I do not see any way of doing it.

"Your real object seems to be to write against the Calvinistic doctrine of native and total depravity, and in doing this you have constructed a theory of the origin of this doctrine which lays it at the door of St. Augustine and the Catholic Church. A correct statement of Catholic doctrine would be incompatible with this theory, and require the reconstruction of the whole book.

"I do not see any other way except for you to follow your own judgment, and let your theory stand or fall by its own merits.

"I think your doctrine is Pelagian, so far as I understand Pelagius's system, and the same with that of Dr. Taylor and Dr. Fitch. You are, however, far more candid than they are in coming out openly against Calvinism.

"In spite of my criticism of your theories, I have a great respect and sympathy for your honest and independent spirit, and for your desire to represent Christianity in such a light that the goodness and love of God toward all men, and especially toward little children, may be made evident.

"The history of Miss Payson is very touching and very true. I have no doubt that child loved God with all her heart at the very time her amiable but mistaken father was tormenting her so cruelly.

"I can not wonder that you are attracted by the doctrine of the Episcopal Church in regard to the lambs of the flock, and that you have thought you could work more happily in your sphere as a teacher of youth under that system. I think you will find, however, a great deal of mere theory never carried out.

"I wish you could see how admirable is the system of the Catholic Church in this respect. All the children, rich and poor, are taught to consider themselves Christians from the cradle. Every child is confirmed, and goes to confession and communion.

"Last Sunday, in our church, sixty children, between eight and fourteen, made their first communion; and more than sixty others received the communion with them.

"Besides these things required by the Church, there are many religious exercises and ceremonies adapted to their taste which a pastor can make use of. These children will cry bitterly if they are put away from communion, and they love their religion, their church, and their pastors above every thing else.

"I wish you could know as well as I do the innocence, piety, and grace with which some of these little souls are adorned. My paper is out and I must close.

"With great esteem and regard, I am yours very truly, ——— ———."

Reply of the Author to the foregoing.

REV. AND DEAR SIR,—I can scarcely express the wonder and perplexity that followed the reading of your letter, and the articles you sent soon after.

And so you maintain that Augustine, claimed by all Calvinists and the Jansenists as the father of their systems, does *not* teach the doctrine of the depravity of man's nature?

I went to the Encyclopedias, to the Church histories, to my brother's book, and found all against you. My brother says Augustine teaches that "men enter this world with deranged constitutions and disorganized powers of soul and body, their intellect darkened by sin, and blind to the true beauty of God and spiritual things; their wills in a state of moral impotence as to that which is holy and good, their propensities and passions deeply corrupt."—*Conflict of Ages, p.* 297.

I deny that this is the condition of infant minds, and then learn from an article written at Rome, read by the Pope, and approved by the censor of the press, that my position on this subject is approved. And now I learn from you that Augustine also agrees with me that the minds of infants are not depraved in nature.

But I think I have found the key which unlocks the apparent difficulty without injury to the honesty of the parties concerned.

If you will read Neander's history of Augustine, you will find quotations in the original from his voluminous works, showing that at the first period of his theological career he held opinions which he disowned and retracted at the last period. For once you will find a distinguished theologian *owning* his mistakes, and writing "Retractions" of his opinions. Thus it is that Augustine is and is not a Calvinist—does and does not teach the depravity of man's nature.

In thus contradicting himself, he does what all theologians have done, from Augustine to Dr. Taylor, in attempting to make transmitted infant depravity consistent with common-sense views of God's justice and benevolence.

Augustine's method of reconciling God's dealings with depraved infants as *just* is, that all the race existed in Adam, and *sinned in him.* This imaginary pre-existence and action of millions of infants, thousands of years before they were born, is a theory originated by Augustine, and transmitted to the present age.

According to this theory, God's Spirit, and thus his sanctifying grace, departs from every infant soul because of this sinning in Adam. Christ died to purchase the return of sanctifying grace, which, in the Catholic theory, is gained at or by baptism, also by penance and the Eucharist.

In Protestant sects we still hear imploring prayers for this lost "grace," without which the soul is dead to all spiritual life. The Episcopalian prays in one form and theory for this gift, the Methodist in another form and theory. The Calvinist Presbyterian hopes for it as an act of sovereign electing grace.

Common sense, rejecting all the theories, takes the little ones to Christ as a loving parent, who has given, in creation, all needed powers, and will give all needed aid in every effort to use these powers aright. In training the infant child to learn the laws of God and to obey them, the parent is as sure of the "sanctifying grace" needed, as the gardener is of the natural sun, given for all, and not alone for a few that are baptized. "In every nation, he that feareth God and worketh righteousness is accepted of Him."

What you have written of the little children under your care and the little Catechism which came with your letter, I have read with the deepest interest. I am truly thankful that there is so much that is good in both; and when I see in them what seem mistakes and evil tendencies, I remember how much of the same is to be found in the common Protestant methods with young children. Both sides have something to learn.

Christ's "little ones" are not alone the little children in stature, but all that great class of ignorant, undeveloped mind, which in this nation comes so extensively to the care of the Catholic priesthood. In the kitchens of my numerous friends in different parts of the land, and often in my chamber, I meet these wanderers from country and home; and as I seek their confidence and try to aid them in spiritual life, I find, with real thankfulness, that often they have faithful priests to care for them. Their books of devotion, their catechisms, and their instructions at confessional as to daily practical duties, I wish could be as faithfully urged on the same class by the Protestant clergy.*

* The author asks the attention of all who have Catholic servants to a little volume entitled *Guide to Catholic Young Women,*

In my sojourns with the just and the good of all sects in this nation, I feel more and more the sad effects of these fences in the garden of our common Lord, where each stands to point out the weeds in his neighbor's inclosure, instead of searching to remove them from his own. If these barriers could be so lessened that each could enter the other's field to search for the good instead of the evil, how much might be found to reward the search, and improve the humble seekers!

All such would probably find that they had more weeds in their own premises than they well knew how to dispose of.

It seems to me this conviction is more and more gaining ground among the most intelligent Catholic clergy, especially those of them who, like the author of *Aspirations of Nature*, have passed from cultivated Protestantism to your Church. The effort of this author to hide or remove all that is contrary to reason and common sense in his own communion, even though attended with some injustice toward others and some blindness to his own difficulties, must in the end lead to improvement. I re-

especially for those who Earn their own Living. A Protestant might think it wise to cut out two or three pages, in reference to employers, that could not be conscientiously offered to servants; but, with this exception, the work might prove a blessing to all of every sect in this condition of life. Any bookseller can procure it for any one by sending to D. & J. Sadlier, 31 Barclay Street, New York, through the Post-office.

gard such men as are writing for Bronson's Review and laboring in the Pauline missionary establishment in New York, as fellow-laborers in efforts to bring the Christianity of *all* sects to a more rational and common-sense standard.

Letter from a Roman Catholic Priest to the Author.

"My dear Madam,—Yours of the 16th, with the inclosure, I received only yesterday. I am glad to learn that the work I sent has reached you, for you must know that two years ago I made efforts to obtain your address and send a copy, but was unsuccessful.

"I send by this mail the translation you request of the article published in Rome noticing your work and your brother's.

"Your *Common Sense applied to Religion* and your *Appeal to the People*, as well as your brother's *Conflict of Ages*, I have read with singular interest, because the solution of the problems before your minds was one of the principal causes which led me into the Catholic Church.

"What surprised me in reading your brother's *Conflict of Ages* was the misstatement of the Catholic doctrine on the point in question. It was with great regret I found also that in your two volumes you assumed the correctness of your brother's statements. Had he known the Catholic doctrine concerning the fall, there would have been no necessity to have had recourse to the old condemned hypothesis of *pre-existence* in order to reconcile Christianity with the implanted principles of common sense. Had you known them, you would not have made the Catholic Church responsible for an error which she repudiated as strongly as you yourself have done.

"Your views concerning reason and the constitution of man will be found in every current Catholic treatise on philosophy. They are in accordance with the common opinion of Catholic theologians, and agree with the doctrines which the Church has taught, not only in the first three centuries, but in every subsequent century to the present time.

"The contest of the Church with the errors of

Protestantism and Jansenism was based upon these principles, which you regard as entirely original with yourself, and as having never before been enunciated in any age or language.

"That your own reflections should have led you so near to the Catholic doctrines, is only another proof of the harmony of those doctrines with the human mind.

"You will find it a difficult task, if not an impossible one, to show, as you speak of aiming to do, the identity of natural religion with revealed religion. It will be hard to prove that such a thing as a purely natural religion ever existed. Revealed religion not only reasserts those truths which are commonly classed as the doctrines of natural religion, but also makes known others which are entirely beyond the discovery of human reason.

"Be assured, dear madam, that I have a warm sympathy with your aims, and take a lively interest in your endeavors to reconcile the doctrines of Christianity with the dictates of common sense.

"Yours faithfully in Christ, ——— ———."

Reply of the Author to the foregoing.

Rev. and dear Sir,—Your letter and the accompanying document reached me safely. In reply, I would waive the question as to how far my brother and myself have been mistaken in stating the Catholic doctrine concerning the fall. That the Catholic Church has repudiated this doctrine, in the sense usually conveyed by Protestant formularies, I do not deny. That the decrees of the Council of Trent, deemed infallible by you, give us any better theory, can be decided by those who may take the pains to read the extracts I have made from them at the close of this volume.

I am more interested in the remarks you make on the subject of "reason," and the supposed accordance of my views, in my published volumes, with "every current Catholic treatise," and with "the common opinion of Catholic theologians."

I wish, in the first place, to rectify the impression that I suppose that I have made a *new discovery* in enunciating the principles of common sense, and the *test* by which they are to be identified. This is not what I claim. I only say that *a belief* in certain truths exists in all sane minds, and that these truths are to be identified by observing the words and actions of all sane men in the *practical* affairs of life.

Taking this test, I have drawn up, in short and popular language, certain of these truths as thus identified, and by their aid in the two volumes, *Common Sense applied to Religion* and *An Appeal to the People*, I have proved, as it appears to me, that all infants come into life with perfect constitutional powers of mind, as God made them, and not depraved. I can not learn that such an argument exists any where else.

Again: in the second volume, a *system* of natural religion is drawn out by aid of the principles of common sense, which is based entirely on the perfect constitution of the infant mind. I can not discover that such a course of argument has ever before been attempted, though I have sought for it of those who have access to the wisdom of Rome, as well as of Germany and Britain.

I did not aim to attempt, as you seem to suppose, to show that "such a purely natural religion ever existed," or ever would have been thus reasoned out without a revelation. I only attempt to show that, now that revelation has helped us, we can reason out such a system, and that it is coincident with that of the Bible, just as by the system of Newton, now that he has set forth the principles of gravitation, and shown us how to employ them, any bright young boy can demonstrate problems that he never could have proved without such aid.

In claiming to have done, in metaphysics and theology, something similar to this work of Newton in physics, I only am meeting the supercilious criticisms of certain editors, who have asserted that these arguments of mine are left unanswered only because they have long ago been demolished. No person, as yet, has ever pointed out any work in any language in which this course of argument has been either attempted or controverted. Paley's *Natural Theology* and Butler's *Analogy* are specimens of the same kind of argument; but neither of these writers have attempted to prove the perfect constitution of the infant mind, or based a system of natural religion on that as a fundamental position.

In saying this, I do not ignore the fact that almost all standard works on mental science recognize the fact of the existence of these principles of reason and common sense as a part of the constitution of the human mind. Nor do I forget that various writers have given various *tests* for identifying these principles, many of them very abstruse and impracticable, as you will see in the work of Sir William Hamilton on this subject.

I was led to this attempt thus: In all theological discussions there is a constant appeal to *reason* as the umpire. The Unitarian denies the Trinity, because he says it is contrary to reason.* The Protestant denies transubstantiation because contrary to reason. Miracles and angelic agencies are denied as contrary to reason, and so of many other dogmas of contending sects. This led me to inquire what is this "*reason*" to which all are appealing. Reid and Stewart shed the first clear light on the question, and proceeding forward thus guided, I have come out where I am.

And now will you allow me to tell you, without danger of your displeasure, that I can not find, in any of the volumes you have sent me, any thing that verifies your assumption in your letters to me that Protestantism denies the authority of reason

* On p. 100 of the *Appeal to the People*, it is shown that this doctrine, instead of being contrary to reason, is a fair deduction from one of its first principles.

any more than the Catholic Church? I concede that in the quotations in the *Aspirations of Nature* from Luther, Wesley, and Calvin, are stout denials of the authority of reason, and much that is a real denial of free-will. But, on the other hand, in all these same writers you will find contradictory statements affirming the supreme authority of reason and maintaining the doctrine of free-will. In the Old School Confession of Faith, which is the strongest of all Calvinism, in maintaining man's inability to do works of righteousness before regeneration, you find this:

> "God hath endued the will of man with that natural liberty that it is not forced, nor by any necessity of nature determined to good or evil."

Also this, which seems contradictory:

> "Man, by his fall into a state of sin, has lost *all ability of will* to any spiritual good accompanying salvation; so, as a natural man, being altogether averse from good and dead in sin, he is not able, by his own strength, to convert himself, or to prepare himself thereunto."

The Council of Trent says:

> "Man, by the sin of Adam, though he has power 'to *reject* the illumination of the Holy Spirit,' yet he *is unable, by his own free will*, to move himself unto righteousness."

Now wherein is the Roman Catholic decree on free-will very diverse from the Protestant forms?

It seems to me both Protestant and Catholic theologians are alike in contradicting themselves in their standard formularies, affirming free-will and the authority of reason in one place, and denying it in another.

In the extract you send me from Balmes's *Fundamental Philosophy* I find this recognition of one of the principles of common sense:

"Suppose some one to say that all we see is *nothing*—that there is *no natural world.* Whoever hears such madness knows not what to answer, but he repels it by a natural impulse; the mind feels that it is nonsense, without stopping to examine."

This is a recognition of a principle of reason and common sense similar to that which in my first volume, *Common Sense applied to Religion*, is expressed thus, page 23: "The *evidence of our senses is reliable;*" that is, we and all sane persons must act on the assumption that *what we see and feel is what it appears to be.* The moment a man loses reliance on his senses he is insane, and is so esteemed.

Now the Council of Trent, that you claim is infallible, has decreed thus:

"Canon 1, Sess. 13.—If any shall deny that in the sacrament of the most holy Eucharist there is contained truly, really, and substantially the body and blood, together with the soul and divinity of our Lord Jesus Christ, and so *whole* Christ, let him be accursed. If any shall deny that the *whole* Christ is contained in the venerable sacrament of the Eucharist, under each appearance and when they are divided, under *every particle* of each appearance, let him be accursed."

Now, as a true Catholic, how do you meet this? How can you hold that bread and wine are flesh and blood, without denying the principle of reason and common sense that our senses are to be trusted? Do you say that Christ commands us to believe thus? And is not this saying that Christ commands us to violate those principles of reason he implanted to guide us to truth and duty? And if we violate and deny them in this case, how are we to prove the authority of revelation, or that Christ has taught thus? Do not all miraculous revelations rest on the evidence of the senses, and how are you to prove Christ's authority by his miracles without this faith in our senses?

I have stated this argument, not with any expectation that it will cause any change of opinion in you or any other Catholic. There is a most singular hallucination as to the doctrine of *self-infallibility* that obscures the vision of most intellectual combatants on the field of theology.

I give your case as the illustration. You, at one time, constituted yourself a judge of the doctrines of the sect in which you were educated. You decide against it, as not in agreement with reason and revelation, as *you* interpret their teachings. You examine the claims of other churches, and finally select the Church of Rome as the only true Church. In this process you make yourself the judge of faith and practice, and the interpreter of the Bible and creeds, and you finally come to this decision—*the true Church is the one that agrees with you.* Then, by a singular self-deception, you imagine that you submit your judgment in faith and practice to the decisions of the Church that you have yourself selected because it agrees with you.

And Protestant theologians sometimes do the same thing. I once inquired the *reasons* of a certain opinion held by a learned theologian in a leading Presbyterian theological school, and in the reply I received, this friend remarked that "he was a man *under authority*, and that he should not dare to set up his individual opinion against the judgment of *the Church of God* in all ages." I showed this to a shrewd lawyer, and he quietly remarked that "the Church of God in all ages" to which he submitted was doubtless the Church *that agreed with him.*

Thus it is that, in spite of all their creeds and theories, even theologians of all sects, are obliged to resort to the great principles of reason and common sense in their own minds, and thus to carry out in practice the great Protestant principle that every man is to be his own interpreter of the Bible.

We are placed as free agents in a vast system where truth and duty are to be discovered by our own diligence, faithfulness, and honesty. All are liable to great mistakes; but he has the best chance who is the most *humble* and most *honest* seeker.

True humility does not imply a distrust of our natural capacity of judging, but rather a distrust of the biases of education, and self-interest, and intellectual pride.

If a man is more afraid of being convinced he is wrong than of being wrong, or is ashamed to own his mistakes when he finds them, he is under a bias that is fatal to the discovery of truth. If to this is added strong personal interests and prejudices entwined with long-established habits of thought and feeling, we can see how it is that theologians are rarely found to own themselves in the wrong, or to make any great or sudden changes in their systems; not that they are less honest than other men, but on that principle of civil law which forbids the most honest of men to testify, even under oath, where their own personal character and interests are involved.

It is on this ground that I have made an *Appeal to the People;* not as wiser or better than theologians, but as freer from embarrassing biases.

To the Author of the Conflict of Ages.

MY DEAR BROTHER,—On the subject of infant character there are but two positions possible; *i. e.*, the infant mind *is* perfect in constitutional faculties, or it is *not*, but is depraved in constitution. There is no third supposition possible. I regard you as the most able defender of the latter position, and as honest and fair as you are able. I therefore submit the following to you, and to all who hold the same view:

The doctrine of infant depravity necessarily involves a system of mental philosophy. Augustine, its church father, teaches that the faculties of all rational minds are organs to receive and appropriate what is gained by a mystical union and communion with God. What is thus received is called "grace," and without it the mind, even in its normal state, is incomplete and dead. Without this "grace" no holy desires and emotions will arise, and the "free will" is active only to sin.

Adam's mind was created perfect, and was filled with this "grace." He, by his "free will," sinned, and lost it. All infants were *in* him and sinned in him, and lost grace. Thus it is that all infants are born with minds dead as it respects all holy emotions, while their "free will" is alive only to sin. On this theory, *regeneration* is the return of that "grace" into the souls of infants which they lost in

Adam. The whole Catholic system rests on this theory, which has also been transmitted to most of the large Protestant sects.

For example, we find Dr. Hodge, the leading theologian of the O. S. Presbyterian denomination, states it thus:

"God regards and treats all men, *from the first moment of existence*, as out of fellowship with himself; as having forfeited his favor. Instead of entering into communion with them the moment they begin to exist (as he did with Adam), and forming them by his Spirit in his own moral image, he regards them as out of his favor, and *withholds* the influences of his Spirit. Why is this? Paul tells us why it is. It is because we fell *in* Adam. In other words, Adam having been placed on trial, not for himself alone, but also for his race, his act was, in virtue of this relation, REGARDED AS OUR ACT. God withdrew from us as he did from him; in consequence of this withdrawal, we begin to exist in moral darkness, *destitute* of *a disposition* to delight in God."

In the *Conflict of Ages*, page 90 and onward, it seems to me you have exhibited the same view. You say,

"There is a life of the mind. It involves an original and designed correlation to God, and such a state of the affections, passions, emotions, intellect, and will, that communion with God shall be natural, habitual, and *the life of the soul.* He who has been so far healed *by divine grace* as to reach this state, has a true ideal of the *normal* and healthy state of the soul."

Then, of the state of the mind of the whole human race, you say,

"The *whole mind* appears to be a wonderful system *in ruins.*"

The main difference between you and other theologians is not as to *the fact* of the depraved condition of the infant mind as diverse from what God first made it, but as to the *when* and the *how*. Augustine says *in* Adam, Dr. Hodge says *by* Adam, and you say *before* Adam. All seem to agree in the *pre-existence* and sinful action of infants before birth, resulting in the *loss of a union or communion with God*, and thus in the ruin of each infant soul.*

Regeneration, on this view, is the partial reunion of the soul with God, which, as you express it, is thus "healed by divine grace;" and after this healing you say a man can have "a true ideal of the normal and healthy state of the soul."

That God has not power thus to "heal" *all* infant souls none can suppose, for he who can create a perfect mind can *recreate* it. And yet you teach that all infants come into this life *unhealed*, while sin and suffering here, and eternal misery in the future life, are the inevitable result to millions of infants, consequent on this neglect to heal.

In regard to this system of mental philosophy and theology, the whole, as it seems to me, rests on *assumptions without proof*.

* Dr. Park and others teach that God established a system of constitutional transmission, so that parents transmit the depraved mental constitution which Adam caused in himself by sinning, instead of transmitting the perfect one God created. On this theory, infants never sinned before birth, and yet are punished with depraved minds, when God has power to create them perfect.

In the first place, it is asserted that the minds of all rational free agents are made on such a pattern that a mystical union with God is indispensable to their normal state and perfect action—an assertion without *any* proof, so that it would contradict common sense to adopt it.

All revelations from God are necessarily in the words of men, in the sense men use them. We have no other idea of a union of one mind with another except a unity of *desire*, *emotions*, *will*, and *action*. Of course, we can have no words to express any other kind of unity, and no revelation of any other kind.

On page 82 of the *Appeal to the People*, it is shown *how* the thoughts, desires, and emotions are controlled by *the will;* so that the only way to bring all the desires, emotions, and actions of minds into harmony or unity with God is, that each shall *choose* to be perfectly subject to his will and laws. Now God creates our faculties of mind by his omnipotent *natural* power, but he can create choices only by *motives* presented to the understanding and susceptibilities—that is, by his *moral* power.

But this theological system teaches such a unity with God at the beginning of existence, that holy emotions, desires, and affections flow out as the result of the created constitution, not as the result of a *voluntary self-control* in conforming to God's will and laws. It seems to me there is *no* evidence to sustain this theory, and no attempt to produce any.

Having assumed, without proof, that God created all minds on a pattern diverse from any known to us, theologians next assume that the minds of all infants have a depraved constitution, from which inevitably results sinful desires, emotions, and affections; and that no holy acts will occur till this depravity is remedied.

There is no evidence of this assertion; for, in order to decide whether a mind is perfect or depraved, it must first set forth what is a perfect mind as to constitutional powers, and then show that the mind of man is lacking in some point of this perfection. This has never been done.

In my two volumes is an argument, as yet unanswered, proving that the mind of man is perfect in constitution; so that, independent of revelation, we have evidence of the perfect constitution of the infant mind.

Those who resort to the Bible for proof of infant depravity employ the texts that speak of *man* (not infants) as "carnal," "fleshly," the "natural man," etc. But they only *assume* what ought to be proved, *i. e.*, that these texts refer to the created susceptibilities of infants injured in or by Adam, and not, as I claim, to the voluntary character formed by man in this life. All such texts prove depravity in man, both in character and conduct, and no one ever disputed this fact. The question is, not the fact, but its philosophy, or the *causes* of this depravity.

On the common theory, the *cause* is the state of the constitutional powers injured by sinning *in* or *by* Adam, or, as you say, *before* Adam. I claim that, so long as I accept the fact of man's sinfulness of character and the remedy provided by Jesus Christ, I am not bound to assign any cause. But if it is insisted that causes for this sinfulness be assigned, I think there are far more rational ones than this to be found in Chapter XXV. in *Common Sense applied to Religion.*

All the texts ever presented to prove that the cause of human sinfulness is a depraved mental constitution, are fitted to sustain my theory of causes as much as the common one, and, as it seems to me, far more so.

On the common theory, God, in regeneration, recreates or renews the constitutional faculties injured *in* or *by* Adam, and no true and holy love to God or man will exist till this is done. In my view, God regenerates or "sanctifies by the truth" communicated by parents, educators, and church ministries, aided by his Holy Spirit, who acts through these means. In the case of adults, this new creation often seems instantaneous. In the case of infants, young children, and most ignorant adults, it is a slow and gradual process.

Now all the texts usually quoted on this point are as applicable to my view as to the other. "We must be born again—born of the Spirit," expresses the regeneration of a human soul in *a voluntary self-consecration* to the service of God by obedience to his laws, as truly as it does a change of depraved constitutional powers.

An infant is born without any "heart" or "purpose" to love and obey its parents; but it has a good *nature*, which insures a heart of love and obedience, first to its earthly and then to its heavenly Father, as soon as the earthly educator performs his part of the new creation, for God is sure to do his part.

If a child is educated wrong, it grows up with a "carnal" heart. If it is educated aright, it grows up with a spiritual heart. The "natural heart," and the "fleshly or carnal heart," in my view, signify not depraved constitutional faculties of mind, but the state of every intelligent free agent destitute of knowledge, and love, and obedience to God, which *God*, *educators*, and *self* must equally unite to secure.

On the common theory, until a child's mind is new created, or "healed," in its constitutional powers, no true love and obedience to God will occur. But I claim that every thing in the child's mind is right, and ready for that training which, by a gradual process, will secure a knowledge of God and his laws, and a loving obedience to them.

On one view, every thing a child does till new created "is of the nature of sin." On the other, every act of intelligent obedience to God's laws is right in relation to the rule; and if the motive or intention is to do right, the act is good and virtuous in every relation.

On my view, an infant child begins to be a Christian as soon as it begins to act intelligently in conforming to the laws of God, with the intention to act right; and it grows in Christian life just as fast as its impulses and desires are controlled by a voluntary submission to the laws of true rectitude, which are none other than the laws of God. And an infant begins its Christian life long before it has any knowledge of God, while it is forming habits of loving obedience to its earthly parents, who are the agents, and should be the representatives, to the child, of its heavenly Father.

The important distinction between the inability from a lacking of constitutional powers and the inability for want of appropriate circumstances, needs to be constantly recognized. A child with perfect eyes is entirely without power to see so long as light is withheld, and yet he is perfectly able to see as it respects constitutional powers. So a child, at birth, has perfect ability to obey all God's laws in reference to its constitutional powers, while, as it respects knowledge, motives, and training, it is entirely without power to do so.

On the common view, the child's inability is owing, at least in a great degree, to the ruined state of its constitutional powers. In my view, it is owing to the want of "the light of the knowledge of God," of his lovely character and perfect laws, of their glorious rewards and fearful penalties, and, owing to this want as the chief cause, the child is estranged from God, and lives a life of ruinous self-indulgence and selfishness.

On one view, God creates man anew by an operation on his mental faculties, thus remedying the injury done by previous sinning *in* or *by* Adam. On the other, God creates man anew by knowledge, training, and motives, presented by educators, aided by his Holy Spirit; the grand motive of all being the knowledge of his character as a loving and long-suffering parent, exhibited by Christ as God manifest in the flesh.

On one view, holy love is an *emotion* flowing from the normal constitution of mind. On the other, it is a *voluntary* state of the mind, its chief element being the purpose *to do right*, which is the same thing as choosing to please and obey God.

This purpose may exist in a mind so bewildered by false teachings as to God's real character, that emotions of complacency and affection toward him are impossible. This was my own experience through all those sorrowful years when I was struggling with the theological system of New England. Escape from this system relieved all the difficulty, and I found it as easy to *feel* the delightful emotions that attend perfected love as to perform the actions that flow from the purpose to obey. Thousands of suffering minds, truly devoted to the will and service of God, have toiled, wounded and bruised, to call forth emotions that the very nature of the mind renders impossible, so long as the intellect is clouded by false views of God and his ways.

My chief difficulty in regard to *your* system is this—your only possible mode of proving that any minds were created more perfect than infants, or that infants are depraved, or their pre-existence, is by the aid of *revelations* from God; for by the light of nature alone you can prove neither of these points.

But I claim that, the depravity of all infant minds being assumed, and also God's power to make them perfect in nature, you are deprived of all evidence by which you can prove a benevolent creator, or a *reliable* revelation from him, and so are cut off from your only mode of proving infant depravity and pre-existence. For we can not prove a *reliable* revelation from God till we have first proved a benevolent Creator, inasmuch as a malevolent being would make revelations only for mischief and deception.

The works of God are the only proofs we have of his existence and character without a revelation. If, in attempting to prove his character and designs by his works, we should find all contrivances and designs fitted to give pain instead of pleasure; if light distressed the eye, and food and perfumes disgusted the taste and smell; if all children loved to inflict pain, and never enjoyed giving pleasure to others; if every arrangement of both matter and mind was calculated to inflict suffering, we should inevitably infer that it was the *design* of the Creator to cause pain to his creatures, and that his character was malevolent.

Now, on your theory, we come into existence surrounded by minds that are to live and act forever, and every one of them is so constituted that *by a depraved nature* they do evil rather than good. This being so, and these being the chief works of the Creator's hands—the *only* existences that can enjoy and suffer *forever*—how is it possible to avoid the conviction that the Creator, having power to make all perfect, is malevolent? and how could a *reliable* revelation to teach the way to truth and happiness be obtained from such a Creator?

In your *Concord of Ages*, I find a definition of *logic* as "the science of the laws of the faculty of systematic comprehension." You mean by this, I suppose, that mind has the faculty of so comprehending the various parts that can form a system as to arrange them into that system; that this faculty acts by certain laws, and that the knowledge to be gained of these laws is the science of logic.

I deny that this is the meaning of the word logic, as ordinarily used by mankind. All definitions of this word, in all dictionaries of all languages, teach that logic is *the art or science of reasoning*. This meaning is given in a variety of forms, but they all have the same signification. Sometimes the idea is expressed in this form: Logic, or reasoning, is the process by which one proposition is proved to be true by means of another already granted.

The reasoning in the *Conflict and Concord of Ages* is as truly a process of this kind as any other specimens. Let this be an illustration:

Suppose a traveler in a newly-discovered, uninhabited island, discovers a well stoned up, a well-sweep and pole, and a bucket complete all but the bottom. By an act of reasoning, he infers that the *intention* or *design* of the author of these contrivances was to draw water.

But suppose every thing is complete which will secure the drawing of water except the bottom of the bucket. By still another act of reasoning, it would be inferred that the author of the contrivance either had put in a bottom or intended to do so.

This will serve to illustrate your argument in the *Conflict and Concord of Ages.* You have shown that all previous systems of theology have failed in combining the works and word of God into *a system*, so as to avoid the necessary inference that the Creator is unjust and malevolent from *the nature* of his works.

You attempt a new theory of arrangement, combining the facts in the nature and action of matter and mind with the facts of the Bible into a system that *does* relieve God from this awful implication. The point, which is as indispensable to your system as the bottom of the bucket in the previous illustration, is the perfect nature of infant minds in a pre-existent state, that they ruined their own nature, and that this life is a new and merciful probation. You claim that this is the only possible theory embracing infant depravity which is consistent with a God of benevolence and justice.

But the assumption that God can create perfect minds and that all infants are depraved, renders a *reliable* revelation impossible, and thus breaks up your whole system by removing all that the Bible furnishes. For all minds known to us as the chief works of God, being ruined or depraved, he having power to make them perfect, prove him malignant, and thus one who will *deceive* by his revelations.

If this be so, your system all fails, both for want of evidence and as opposed by contradictory evidence.

As I regard the matter, all new created beings, angels or infants, begin existence ignorant of God and his multitudinous laws, all of which are first to be learned in order to be obeyed. Meantime, by the family, the church, and the Spirit of Truth, God is training all, and this world is the infant-school of our race. That the period of training to each human mind ends at the hour of death, is a doctrine made up by theologians, and not in the Bible. What transpires between death and the day of judgment, when the good and the bad are to be finally separated, is left in perfect darkness. The horrible doctrine concocted in the darkest ages, that every child and adult whose mind (depraved by or in Adam) is not new created, goes to eternal misery at death, is not in the Bible, and is soon to pass away by the use of that *common sense* in interpreting the Bible which God gave us for this very purpose.

I now come to the great practical difficulty involved in your system as much as in the common one, and which meets me especially as an educator, and that is the doctrine of the regenerating power of the Holy Spirit.

To me this doctrine is the most dreadful part of the system based on infant depravity, and one that brought the most conflict and dismay in my own past experience. To think that my Creator had brought me into such awful perils, with a mind that never would act aright till re-created; that eternal separation from my parents and dearest friends, and eternal sinning and misery in hell, was the alternative; and yet, with all my prayers and tears for a "new heart," he, *having the power*, *would not* bestow it—this bore upon my soul like a fatal incubus, impeding the outflow of any loving or grateful emotions. And when I had some hope that he had done the favor to me, the same dreadful implication followed for the sufferings and dangers of my friends. How can God be benevolent and refuse such a boon, *which he has full power to bestow?* It was the belief in his *power* that was the chief cause of distrust and dismay.

If a person should see a strong man watching little children who were sick and lame, and whenever one of them fell down from weakness he should plunge a pitchfork into it and throw it into a burning caldron, no possible representations as to his wisdom, power, and goodness could prevent the observer from regarding such a man with horror and disgust. And yet this is a trifle in comparison with that awful system which represents the Father of All sending into this world millions of infants who he foresees will grow up to suffer "the miseries of this life and the pains of hell forever," for want of a new-created nature which he can bestow and yet withholds.

My brother, we are before the public under solemn and painful responsibilities. Our father's biography is now before the world, in which he appears as a prominent defender of the New England system of theology and of the Puritan Church based on that system. And he earnestly trained all his children in that system.

And now you, his first educated son, even before

his death, have issued two volumes to prove that this system is contrary to "the principles of honor and right," unless the theory of infant pre-existence is added to it—a theory which he and all other theologians, after reading your arguments, have rejected.

Next, his oldest child has published two volumes to prove that *all* systems of theology based on the theory of infant depravity are contrary both to common sense and to the Bible.

Then our younger brother, both as minister and editor, has rejected the theory of infant depravity, and the whole system based on it.

Still another brother has issued a volume repudiating the New England theory of the atonement held by our father, and also maintaining infant pre-existence as indispensable to sustain the theology of most of the Protestant world.

And now, in the biography of our father, is exhibited not only his arguments in defense of the New England system, but its results in his own personal history and in his family religious training. In it we find that he was not baptized in childhood because his excellent and conscientious foster-parents did not secure that experience required to join the church, while through childhood he lived a prayerless life, without God and without hope. In manhood came agonizing religious struggles that destroyed health, and nearly exiled him from the ministry he sought.

Then we read the distress of our gentle mother, not trained in that hard system, when it was pressed on her conscience so as nearly to unsettle her reason.

Finally, we have the record of our father's experience in training a family. And was there ever a parent who, in the first period of family training, more perfectly exhibited the happy combination of strong and steady government with the tenderest love and sympathy, or whose children were better prepared to transfer the love and obedience of an earthly father to a Heavenly One?

And yet what a record of vain attempts for *twenty years*, not in a single case rewarded with success! What anxiety, perplexity, disappointment, and agonizing fear are there recorded on the part of the father, and what sufferings and vain efforts on the part of the children! And has not this experience been thus preserved to aid in the rescue of other such sufferers?

I can now show why I thus publicly address you. It is not to secure a public theological debate, for which I have neither taste nor ambition. It is in behalf of suffering parents and suffering little children that I make this plea. Thousands and thousands of Christian mothers, year after year, wake from the first happiness of maternal love to the awful fear that they are bringing into existence those dearer than life, who are "under the wrath and curse of God, and so made liable to the miseries of this life and the pains of hell forever." And this short, uncertain life given as *their only chance!* a fall, a mistake in food, a thousand daily accidents may end this precious life at any moment, and then *all is over!* The child, *no one knows at what age*, if not new-created in nature, goes to hell to spend *eternity* in hopeless misery!

No wonder that mothers often have declared to me that they would have gladly rescued every child they bore from such perils in the promised safety of an infant grave. Most dreadful of all is the common doctrine that there is no sure and certain mode of securing safety for a child. Even ceaseless prayers and faithful labors avail not, as is seen in many who, trained by most conscientious and prayerful parents, end life in infidelity or vice.

This it is that shakes the soul and drains the life-blood of mother hearts all over the land; this it is that terrifies and tortures young children in the family, in the church, in the Sunday-school, and in the reading of children's books. The mournful example introduced into these pages, except the early age, is but one of a thousand such.

This it is that is leading not only the young and ignorant, but multitudes of the mature, the wise, and the good to reject the Bible as supposed to teach a system so cruel and unreasonable; this it is which converts to infidelity in Christian lands far more than all our missionaries turn from heathenism.

My aim in all this is not to establish a system or a theory. What I seek is that the common people like me shall not be driven by theological and metaphysical reasoning and by church organizations to adopt such baneful theories in the religious training of the young. And when I present what seem better theories, it is not because they are deemed indispensable, but rather to cover escape from what has caused so much needless bewilderment and misery.

I address you, also, because I regard you as the most able defender of the doctrine of infant depravity, and at the same time so honest a man and good a Christian, that if you find that the *assumed* facts on which this theory is based can not be sustained by proper evidence, you will publicly relinquish the doctrine, and thus lend your aid to remedy the evils it has engendered.

The assumed facts to be proved are, 1. That the first created minds were diverse from those of infants in constitutional powers and condition, and on the normal and perfect pattern. 2. That infant minds are diverse from this pattern, and diverse from what God first created them.

If there is evidence of these two propositions, you, of all the men I know, are best able to find and present it.

If there is no proper evidence, you, of all the men I know, are most favorably situated, and most likely honestly to say so.

In conclusion, I deem it but justice to my father's memory to state that, although he never changed his *system*, his mode of administering it, as shown in his Autobiography, was greatly modified in later life; and he often told me that his earlier method with his own family was not the best.

In my own case, he sought an *emotional* experience that never came till his theological system ceased to be believed; and at last he relinquished the effort, and taught me and others that an earnest and long-continued purpose and effort to obey God's requirements warranted the suffering inquirer to assume the public profession of a Christian as one way to secure the emotional part of Christian experience. It was by such counsel that I became a member of his church, with no more evidence of Christian character than had existed in that long year of struggle and sorrow exhibited in his correspondence.

This is offered as an important appendage to that history, lest those younger ministers who may look to our father for an example as a parent and spiritual guide should take this part of his history as their model.

NOTE.—That there may be no injustice done to the system of mental philosophy held by the author of the *Conflict of Ages*, Note B, at the end of the volume, is appended.

To the Wife of a Professor in a Methodist Theological Seminary.

My dear Friend,—I have made my application to your husband and his associates through you, because I believe a special mission is resting on our sex in this emergency, and that you are "a representative woman" of that class by whom this mission is to be accomplished.

When our blessed Lord took the little children in his arms, it was the mothers who urged their rights, even against the rebukes of disciples and apostles. It is the mothers, especially such intelligent and influential mothers as you, who, I believe, are, in this day, to reproduce a similar beautiful and peaceful conquest.

When I had written the preface to my volume, *Common Sense*, etc., I consulted a very fastidious friend as to inserting that part including a sorrowful portion of my personal experience. His reply was, "Put it in; it will do more toward accomplishing your object than all your arguments." And so I have found it. And, in this volume, the history of one poor child will probably accomplish more than all my reasonings. Theologians, happily, are most of them parents, and have as tender hearts as any class of men; and we must use the policy of peaceful as well as cruel war, and assail them at the weakest point.

In my last communication from your husband, in his criticism on the proofs of Chapter XIV. of this work, he proposed an alteration that would imply that, in the Methodist denomination, infant children *are* members of the local church, though "not in *full* membership." The same thing is often claimed by many of the Congregational clergy at the present day, and was so assumed by the Puritan fathers, who first instituted the local church consisting of regenerated persons united by covenant and profession of faith. It was the logical inconsistency of this claim in regard to infants that originated the Baptist churches, and by which, also, President Edwards ended the practice of the baptismal "half-way covenant," and thus exiled most young children in this land from Christ's family.

Your husband states that the Methodist denomination, like the Episcopal, "administers baptism freely to all children offered at its altars irrespective of the church membership of parents." This is consistent with the doctrine now urged by your leading theologians, that *all* infants are members of Christ's church, as seen in the extracts pp. 163, 164 of this work. In this respect your denomination are and ever have been diverse from the Congregational churches.

But here is the inconsistency of the matter. If *all* infants are at birth members of Christ's church through his atonement, which has remedied the evil done by Adam to the *nature* of the child, then baptism is simply the outward form of acknowledging the fact, that every human being, even among heathen, is born into the church of Christ, and begins life a true Christian and fitted for heaven.

This is carrying the church membership of infants too far. No infant can be called a *Christian* child, as member of a Christian *local* church, except by the membership of its parents. The only sense in which an infant can properly be called a Christian, when its parents are in no way connected with a Christian worshiping assembly, is that of its birth in a Christian family and nation, in contrast with those born in pagan or Mohammedan lands.

I regard the Methodist Church, in its origin and system, pre-eminently the offspring of *common sense.* Wesley, its noble founder, was distinguished for that quality in all his career. When the National church was ruled by venal politicians and a worldly ministry, and he saw no other remedy, he broke away and formed a "society" of those who lived not for this world as the chief good. When he could get no ordination from the national bishops for his ministry, he took the common-sense ground that the members of a profession are the best qualified to decide who shall enter it, and to give license, and so he appointed ministers, and ordained them himself. When educated ministers were too few, he took the best he could get. When a settled ministry would not reach the poor and the dispersed, he established an itinerating ministry. Then he instituted the admirable class system, by which the humbler members are taught and watched over by the more advanced.

But Wesley was not infallible any more than the pope, and failed to foresee the operation of his system on the religious position and training of the young. And now, after experience has exhibited the defect, can not the good men who stand as leaders in his place, acknowledge, as he did, the mistakes of the church in which they were born, and as openly and decidedly break up all that is false or injurious?

If all infants are members of Christ's real invisible church at birth, should not all, when grown to a congregation who have enough faith in Christ to assemble to be taught his Word, be counted as members of his visible church so long as they have this faith? And are not all their infant children members with their parents? Why should that inner organization exist, called "the church," in distinction from "the congregation," from which all the lambs of Christ are shut out till certain officers pronounce them regenerated?

If a man finds his house untenable, there are two ways of remedying it: one is to insist publicly that it is perfect, and then stealthily each night change a beam or a room, till, all unobserved and unconfessed, he has a new and different house; the other way is honestly to say it is wrong, take it down, and rebuild it aright. Which would all just men say was the most honorable and Christian method? I leave you to make the application.

It seems to me that the Methodist and Episcopal churches will ere long be alike in assuming that all children are born into the church where their parents worship; that baptism is giving them the name of Christ, and thus acknowledging their rights to all the privileges of his church; that the communicants are the more advanced class, or elder children, who, in the nursery, or younger class, have learned to behave well enough to be allowed to sit at table with their parents. When this is done, then every part of parental, school, and church training, from infancy to maturity, will be one and the same course—all regarded as the *religious* training of a child of God—each part as important in its place as every other.

I now wish to indicate more distinctively one portion which I think Providence has assigned to our sex, and especially to such women as you, in this reformatory mission.

The employments of man are those that provide chiefly for the physical wants of the family, and the public wants of civil society and country. The profession of woman rightfully centres in the family state. She is the chief educator of mind, the nurse of the body in infancy and in sickness, and the administrator of the comforts and domestic economy of home.

Men have elevated their professions to *sciences*, demanding endowed institutions, abundant apparatus, and liberal salaries to secure the highest talents for training in these several duties. Woman, as yet, has not been thus favored.

And yet how much science is demanded for the right training of mind, the most difficult of all earthly duties! And what skill, and sagacity, and knowledge is needed in the charge of the delicate body of an infant, and the ever-varying responsibilities of a nurse of the sick.

If all infants were in the charge of highly-educated, conscientious nurses, instead of ignorant, unprincipled servants, how different the fate of thousands that meet an early death or a life of suffering. If all the sick were committed to nurses properly trained for their profession, how many would be restored to life and usefulness that now perish or live as burdens to themselves and their friends.

And so in domestic economy, what waste of food by ignorance and neglect, and what ruin of health by wrong selection and bad cooking! It is said, by those who know, that $10,000,000 annually is wasted in New York by want of economical care and cooking. Paris is fed better than New York on three fourths of the raw food, owing wholly to modes of economy and the style of cookery. And the reason is, that in Paris this art is made a liberal profession, securing the best scientific skill by honorable position and high salaries. But with us, cooking, like the care of infants, is committed to the poorly paid, ignorant, and vulgar, thus disgracing woman's profession.

And now thousands and thousands of well-educated, refined, and virtuous women are living as paupers on earnings that scarcely support life, while philanthropists are seeking still farther to widen the mischief by thrusting women into the professions of men.

But the only and true remedy for the "wrongs of woman" is to *raise her profession to a science, to train her properly for it, and to make it honorable and remunerative like those of men.*

The chief department of woman's profession is the *religious training* of the young. The past theories of theology, that make this prime duty of woman so nearly a hopeless undertaking, and which place the chief ministries for regenerating the human soul in the pulpit, have, more than any other influence, lowered the dignity and estimation of her profession.

So long as the infant soul is regarded as ruined and helpless by a transmitted depravity of nature that no training can remedy; so long as the system of mental philosophy resulting from this doctrine prevails, which makes *emotive* experiences, flowing from "a return of God's Spirit," or from a "new created nature," the distinctive feature of the "new birth," and the chief evidence of Christian character, the noblest part of woman's profession must be undervalued. It is from this comes the disparagement of that part of religious training which consists in securing prompt and cheerful obedience to the laws of God in the early periods of childhood, and that separation of morality and religion so frequent in the pulpit. From this comes the great contrast in the neglect of all the liberal institutions and endowments for woman's distinctive professions, which are bestowed with such excess of profusion on man.

When the ministers of religion shall teach that obedience to the laws of health in eating, drinking, and sleeping is a part of religion as much as going to church and private prayer; when they teach that amusement, *properly regulated*, is a *religious duty* for both old and young, instead of a sinful waste of time; when they teach that a woman who is training a child or servant to be an intelligent and healthful cook, is giving her a part of her religious education; when they teach parents that by a strong and steady government, combined with tender love and sympathy, they are workers together with the Holy Spirit in *regenerating* a child, when multitudes of other duties, now scarcely alluded to in many pulpits, are placed on an equality with prayer-meetings and missionary operations, then we shall find woman's professions made as scientific, honorable, and lucrative as law, medicine, and divinity; and when this ensues, woman will no longer need to seek the professions of men, because she will be in such great demand, and receive such liberal honor and emolument in her own.

To aid in hastening such a happy change, the *American Woman's Educational Association* some ten years ago was formed, of which I think you have been a manager, and to which I have devoted my life and time. Its aim is to secure institutions for women, in which *endowed* departments shall be established for woman's distinctive professional training, to correspond with the three professional schools of men—law, medicine, and divinity—and thus elevate woman's employment as a *science*, and also secure to her honorable and lucrative employment, such as men secure in their professions.

One institution on this plan was commenced at Milwaukee and *endowed;* but, before the experiment was completed, in a business crisis the endowment failed. This occurred about the time that this discussion was commenced by the publication of *Common Sense*, etc., and in consequence, during the past six years, so far as my agency is concerned, the enterprise has been intermitted. But the completion of this volume, and the restoration of such health as has not been known for many years, enables me once more to seek the co-operation of women of talent and influence in this enterprise for the relief of our suffering sex, by the elevation of our profession to a *science* and practice both honorable and lucrative.

One of the most effective modes of promoting this object is to aid in ending the false system of religious training based on the depravity and inability of the infant mind as consequent on the sin of the first human pair.

But you may ask, What can we of the Methodist Church do, when our teachers of theology, our ministers, our Sunday-school teachers, and our religious books, both for adults and children, all are based on this doctrine of a native helplessness consequent on the departure of God's Spirit for Adam's sin?

I think the difficulty is not to be remedied by attacking these things as all wrong and to be given up, but rather by a method of accommodation based on the distinction made in these pages between an inability from constitutional malformation, and an inability for want of knowledge, motives, and training.

While we can maintain that the *nature* of a child is perfect as to all those powers and faculties formed by its Creator, yet, so long as it is ignorant, ungoverned, and untrained, it is weak and helpless, and, so soon as intelligent free agency commences, is necessarily depraved and sinful both in character and action.

There *is* a helplessness in all minds that makes us dependent on God for aid, first in an ignorant and untrained *nature*, then in the mistakes and bad examples of educators, and then in the wrong-doings of the child, thus forming bad habits to be overcome. This helplessness, it can be carefully taught, is pitied and provided for by God, not only in all the "means of grace" supplied, but in the *ever-present* influence of the blessed Spirit, never withdrawn till all efforts and influences are seen to be useless, and then with real grief. And all the expressions from the pulpit, in the Bible, and in religious books on this point, can be explained to conform to this view as easily as to the old Augustinian theory, and with much more truth.

I urge this course on all mothers and teachers with such deep anxiety and earnest desire as mournful memories of the past sometimes make almost overwhelming. The records in my father's Autobiography have recalled so vividly the sufferings of his children under the soul-withering system he was so conscientiously administering, that I seem to feel that his disenthralled spirit must be urging my hand as I write.

I remember, in the period of great revivals under his ministry, through which all his older children had passed to maturity unchanged in spiritual life, his sixth child, now in heaven, came home from Yale College during a revival there, to see if his father's labors and prayers could not secure what he sought in vain elsewhere. He was an earnest, enthusiastic, conscientious youth, and his whole soul was absorbed in the desire to be "regenerated." For three days and nights, from his room in the centre of the house, we heard such wails and impassioned pleadings as made our home as solemn as the grave, while not one of us knew what to say or do for his relief; nor could we understand why a merciful God should thus withhold such a reasonable boon.

It must be that you have often witnessed similar mental agony, for I myself have seen the system under which you have been trained administered by similar methods. Only a short time ago I was in a large health establishment, where the excellent physician of your church labored as earnestly for the souls as for the bodies of his patients. I often observed there a pale and serious youth, conscientious, exemplary, and the son of a missionary. At one time I was told there was more than ordinary religious interest, and that this young man was among "the seekers." One day the physician was detained from an appointment with me nearly two hours, and when he came he told me he had spent most of this time in prayer and converse with this poor youth, who, he said, "was trying to get religion." Such occurrences as these, and such prayers as I heard in Methodist prayer-meetings there, used to wring my heart with vain regrets and longings.*

In both these cases, all this bitter sorrow would have turned to peace and joy had it been said by a spiritual guide in whom they confided, "Do not afflict your soul by such false views of your heavenly Father; for, so long as you really seek and desire to obey his will, you *are* a Christian, and his Holy Spirit has done and is doing all that you need. Go in peace; strive to sin no more, for all the past is forgiven, and you are an accepted and beloved child."

Will not you, and such as you, in your large and useful denomination, practically act on the admission of your theologians, that the young are lambs of Christ, already in his fold to be trained, not as "born under the wrath and curse" of their Savior, but as his dear children?

* Where do we find in the Bible any warrant for such impassioned prayers for God's Spirit to *convert sinners* as are often heard in periods of religious excitement? David prayed for *himself, when a saint*, "Create *in me* a clean heart, and take not away thy Holy Spirit;" and adds, "then will *I* teach transgressors, and sinners shall be converted."

Our Lord says, "After this manner pray ye;" and in this model prayer is a petition for daily bread, and none for the Holy Spirit to convert unregenerate men. Nor can we find any precept or example for such a prayer. The Bible represents the Holy Spirit as the Comforter, Guide, and Helper of *all* who seek his aid, and God as *more* ready to bestow the gift on *all* his creatures than parents to give bread to their children.

Extract of a Letter to the Author from a Female Friend.

"As to addressing my uncle on the subject of religion, I thank you, dear friend, for your kind interest, but I feel that one must be very adroit not to offend. He knows so *many* men in the church who are such arrant rascals in business transactions, that I think he feels that going into the church does not make men any better, and that he can be a good Christian quite as well out of it as in it. I know this is his opinion, though he rarely speaks it.

"Moreover, I feel myself so far behind him in all the graces which ought to adorn the Christian character, that I have not the face to say, 'Come where *you* can be made better.' He has received the same religious instruction that I have, and but for the observance of some of the mere externals of religion, I see no difference between him and those of us who are enrolled as church members. How much he loves his Savior is known only to Him who seeth in secret, but I really think he loves his neighbor better than himself."

Reply of the Author to the foregoing.

MY DEAR FRIEND,—I certainly did not propose to address your uncle on the subject of religion in reference to his own personal duties and relations. My wish was to ascertain how the views I hold would strike a man of so much intellect, common sense, and high moral feeling, educated in a Calvinistic denomination, and yet avoiding all the outward forms of religious faith. You can not understand, till you know more of my inner life and past history, how strong an interest I feel in that class of men represented by your uncle, some of them called infidels, some Unitarians, and some simply "unconverted moral men."

My wish in regard to your uncle was, without any personal appeal, to give him the views I have since presented to you in my proof-sheets, and then to have *you* make the private personal application to induce him to take a different practical course as to his influence and example in the *externals* of religion, where, in your view, is his only failure, so far as is seen by men.

I would address such a man as your uncle as a *Christian;* because, in the first place, he has the intellectual belief that Christ is Lord of faith and practice, which is the first part of true faith. Still more would I so address him thus on the ground that while "he that hath *not* the spirit of Christ is none of his," he that *hath* the spirit of Christ *is* his. And who in this world, by the only true test given by Christ himself, the *fruits*, or *deeds*, has the spirit of Christ, if not one whose life leads those that know him most intimately to say, as you do, "I believe he loves his neighbor better than himself?"

I should not ask such a man to "join the church, in the sense you understand it in the Congregational denomination, but I should try to secure his joining the *Episcopal* Church by simply becoming a stated worshiper. And I should urge this, not alone with the plea you suggest, "Come where you can be made better," but by another, which would be far more influential with one who so lives as to seem to love his neighbor better than himself. A man of such intellect, cultivation, and practical good sense, who in no form recognizes the Christian religion, throws the whole weight of his influence against it, and thus tempts the weak and erring, who need what perhaps he can do without, to courses that may end in ruin in this world as well as to increased risks for eternity. This is a motive that would have great and increasing weight the more it is considered by a man so sensible and benevolent.

But you will say he does not attend church, does not join in any outward forms of worship; nor can you say, from any certain evidence, that he prays, or has any form of acknowledging God; how, then, can he be a Christian? There may be reasons which, though they do not fully justify his course, may be not at all indices of a want of true Christian feeling and character.

I too have had a dear friend who had the high moral principles and exemplary life of a Christian, with these same deficiencies which you find in yours. The minister of the church he attended was a Calvinist, and preached total depravity and its connected doctrines according to the Westminster Confession. When he ceased going to church, he told me the reason was that the *preaching* there always tended to make him *a bad man;* that, after hearing it, he always felt unamiable, indignant, and especially repelled from his Creator as an unreasonable, hateful, and foolish Being, and *he could not help it.* So the least evil of the two was to stay away.

He was a man of clear intellect, with a tender, sympathetic nature, a keen sense of justice, and a natural abhorrence of all subterfuge and meanness. To him the doctrine of the ruin of all infants in Adam was shocking, and the various theories by which, as he said, God contrived to cast all the blame on Adam, seemed to him as mean subterfuges. The theory of the atonement, by which a human soul was joined to God the Son, and then made to suffer the punishment for sins committed by others, to his mind seemed, as he said, "clumsy, irrational, and childish."

And yet his was not the kind of mind that could go into theological and metaphysical dialectics. The clergy and theologians around him interpreted the Bible as teaching these views, to his mind so derogatory to his Creator, and so, *taking their interpretations*, he lost faith in the Bible as of any divine authority, though he admired and reverenced the character of Jesus Christ, and accepted his teachings as wise and good. His good common sense taught him that some kind of religion was needed by all, and that, of all others, that taught by Christ, whatever its imperfections, is *the best there is.* Therefore he gave his support to it, and wished his family to attend its ministries if they could gain any moral benefit from them. And thus he lived, and finally passed away, uncheered by any brighter hope than that which the wise and good of all ages may cherish from the light of nature.

These, our beloved friends, I regard as "representative men" of that great and increasing class who openly or secretly have become followers of Theodore Parker, or, as silent sufferers, have withdrawn from all outward forms of faith, and, like your uncle, conceal their secret thoughts to save their Christian friends from pain. This is the class of noble men who I believe such women as you are may, by the right kind of influences, lead into the Episcopal Church, and thus, in the end, to an open and happy Christian experience and profession. And for this end I wish to remove some of the many misconceptions in regard to this church.

It has been a matter of surprise to me to find not only how ignorant I have been of the true character of this church, but the extent of the misconceptions, not alone of others out of its communion, but of Episcopalians themselves.

I will mention, then, that, in the first place, it is a church which any quiet, modest, and virtuous man can join, and secure all its privileges, without being questioned or interfered with in any way by any person whatsoever.

For "joining the church," in the Episcopal sense, is simply becoming a stated worshiper in a congregation of that denomination. Whoever does this is entitled to all the privileges of that church, unquestioned and perfectly free as to both opinions and practice, so long as he is not guilty of "evil living"—that is, of acknowledged immoralities.

As this statement will be questioned both by those without and those within this church, I appeal to the Liturgy, Constitution, and Canons as what will sustain the affirmation.

The starting-point of these rules is, that *all* infants are entitled to church membership, and that all that is requisite to secure it for them is Christian sponsors to promise that they shall be educated to be Christians. If there are no parents or guardians, any Christian person can be sponsor. Baptism, to the infant, is the outward rite or form of publicly acknowledging its rights as those of *all* infants. It gives the *name* of a Christian, and the seal or credential of its claim, existing from the moment of birth, to be numbered as a child of God and an heir of heaven. According to this, every infant in the world has a right to be baptized as a child of God, and fails only for want of Christian sponsors.

According to the regulations of the Episcopal Liturgy,

"So soon as children are come to a competent age,

and can say the Creed, the Lord's Prayer, and the Ten Commandments, and can answer to the other questions of the Short Catechism, they shall be brought to the bishop."

Also:

"The minister of every parish shall either bring, or send in writing, the names of all such persons within his parish as *he shall think fit* to be presented to the bishop to be confirmed."

These rules leave a large liberty to the minister. But, to protect from any abuse of this liberty, the *congregation*, and not the communicants, are those who choose, not only the minister, but also all the lay delegates who make the canons, and regulate all the administration of the whole denomination in General Convention. Nor is it allowed to limit delegates to the communicants.

A portion of the clerical body have used this liberty so as to constitute themselves judges of the opinions and religious experience of their parishioners, and in those cases confirmation and access to the Lord's Table has often been regulated by the conscience of the priest instead of the parishioner. But this is contrary to the spirit of the whole ritual and constitution of the church, and in violation of the rule that no person shall be excluded from the Lord's Table except for "evil living."

But it will be urged that adopting the forms prescribed in the rites of baptism and confirmation, which must precede access to the table of the Lord, does in fact amount to the same thing as joining the Puritan Church, by professing to be regenerate and to believe a certain creed. Here the mistake is owing to not noticing the difference between joining a church and using the forms of one of its ordinances. Every regular worshiper in a local Episcopal Church is already a member of the church.

The forms and rules of baptism and confirmation, which are to precede access to the Eucharist, amount to no more than this, that the minister must find out and notify the bishop that those desiring confirmation are proper persons according to the rules of the church; and those rules exclude none but those guilty of "evil living," provided they can say the Creed, the Commandments, the Lord's Prayer, and the Short Catechism.

It is the duty of every minister to give instructions preliminary to confirmation, and here he can urge his own peculiar views and use his personal influence. But no one is bound to accept his interpretation of the Bible or of the forms of the church. Each person is free to put his own meaning to these forms, and no bishop, priest, or deacon has a right to interfere in any other way than by instruction and advice; and, if it is attempted, on complaint, the bishop is bound to interfere.

And here I would urge your attention, and, through you, that of your uncle, to what I regard as the distinctive excellence of the Episcopal forms.

They are all based on the assumption that the local church is *the school* of Christ, the great Master; that the ministry are subordinate teachers, and that the whole congregation are learners in different stages of advancement.

The forms of worship for the whole congregation express the highest style of Christian experience; not on the assumption that all who use them have reached this height, but rather that this is the model at which they are aiming. It is assumed that each worshiper, in using these forms, is trying to rise to a communion with the all-loving Father, and to a conformity to all his laws.

It is not professing to have attained any particular elevation of Christian character, but rather the use of the heaven-appointed mode of seeking the very highest attainments.

This is as true of the rites of baptism, confirmation, and the Eucharist as it is of the ordinary Sabbath forms. All these forms express the actual existence of the deepest Christian experience and highest Christian virtues; and yet it is probable that not a single one who uses them would dare to say that the experience thus expressed was fully attained, but only that it is desired and aimed after by the use of these forms, and by help from the blessed Comforter, who aids our weaknesses by these ministries.

Every man who attends the Episcopal Church

by that act acknowledges himself a believer in Christ as the teacher of the true religion, and thus is one of "a congregation of faithful persons," just as the worshipers in a mosque or heathen temple acknowledge their faith by this act of attendance on its public rites.

But whether a man interprets the Bible, or the Articles, or the Liturgy as any other man or body of men do, is a matter between himself and his Maker, and one in which no other person has a right to examine or interfere in any way. If he wishes to have access to the Lord's Table, and is ready to use the prescribed forms, the minister can present his own views and instructions; but, whether they are accepted or not, he can not exclude from any Church rites and ordinances except for "evil living."

This being so, it is the office of the minister to *teach*, but not to *judge;* to hold up the obligations of Christ's religion, but to leave the question of attainment to the inspection of God and the conscience of each worshiper. This it is that makes the Episcopal local Church a teaching or *educating* church, in contrast to the local churches of those sects which organize an inner association of persons supposed to be regenerated by a new creation of a depraved nature, and whose spiritual state is to be inspected and then decided by lay vote or by clerical judgment.

This Puritan method operates as it would in a school where a model class was organized called good scholars, while all the rest were classed as bad scholars, and no graded classes between. Every teacher can see how pernicious would be this method, especially so if the model class included some who were very poor and unruly pupils, and the bad class contained some of the most exemplary.

Thus it is in those churches that profess to exclude all but the regenerate, so far as church officers can judge or decide. The regenerate church often includes some of the most unworthy members of society, while some men, like your uncle, who show most of the spirit of Christ in their deeds, are ranked with those who are the unregenerate, and not Christians.

The attempt to introduce the same method into the Episcopal Church in this country, by calling the communicants "the church," in distinction from the rest of the parish, is as contrary to the spirit and rules of that church as it is to the example and teachings of the New Testament.

Nothing of this kind has ever been attempted in the English Church. In that communion all infants are baptized, and confirmation usually is administered in childhood. Thus the division between the truly pious and those who are not is decided, not by outward professions, but by *deeds.* Those who live a worldly, irreligious life are taught that they are children in God's family living in ungrateful rebellion, and all the congregation alike are exhorted to live up to the model exhibited in all the sacred forms of their church.

The history of Dr. Arnold and his Rugby school, and his sermons to young boys, are a most interesting illustration of the system of the English Church educational training.

Those sects which organize within the worshiping congregation an inner church, to which none are admitted till, after due inspection, some church officer decides that there is proper evidence of regeneration, present a painful alternative to that class of men represented by your uncle. Either they must submit to this personal inspection, and be publicly pronounced as regenerated saints, or they must be classed among the unregenerated sinners, who are spoken of as not *Christians.* All this may be escaped in the Episcopal Church.

I am aware of the repellances that such a man will encounter in a communion whose forms are not familiar. Moreover, if he goes to hear one class of ministers of the Episcopal Church, the Calvinistic system will repel; and if he goes to another class, the rites and forms of the church will be so dwelt upon and magnified in importance as to annoy.

But, ere long, with a very little aid and influence from a loving friend, the forms will become familiar, and soon their noble, simple, and elevated spirit will gradually and quietly secure a heart and intellect so fitted to appreciate and enjoy the beautiful, good, and true. And as to the preaching, a sensible and benevolent man, who enters the church with the right spirit, soon learns to take what is good and pass over easily what, to a captious spirit, would be offensive. There are many ministers in the Episcopal Church who go to neither of the above extremes; and in every denomination there are some ministers who tax the patience of their hearers by violations of good taste, or by doctrines which offend common sense.

In regard to the claims of some on the debated matter of apostolic succession and diocesan authority, it is a topic of little practical moment to *the laity*. The common-sense practice, adopted in all professions, of excluding unworthy pretenders by some kind of examination and license, all sects adopt and approve as it respects their clergy. The chief difference is as to modes of doing this thing, and the importance of these diverse modes.

In the English Episcopal churches there is a diversity of opinions on this matter, some holding that the diocesan form results from apostolic authority, and is obligatory; others holding that it is only, in their opinion, the *best* way as the general rule, but not obligatory. This latter view was the opinion of most of the first founders of the English Church, and is that also of a large portion of its highest dignitaries at the present time. In this country, also, there is a similar diversity of opinion, and an increasing tendency to drop the discussion of the subject. As to the laity, they are not required to adopt the Thirty-nine Articles, or any particular views on any disputed points.

As to "the Creed," which all are expected to believe, it is a simple statement of the great "facts" of the Christian religion, which all sects hold in common, without any of the theories which have caused their divisions.

There is not a sentence in it which a Catholic, a Unitarian, a Swedenborgian, a Quaker, and all our larger sects could not adopt in perfect good faith. The aim of this creed is to bring together all who believe in the Christian religion into worshiping assemblies *as learners* to be taught, not as accomplished Christians.

That the views of the author in this letter might be duly authenticated, proofs of it were sent to several of the bishops and other influential clergy of the Episcopal Church. To one of them the following letter was sent with the proofs, and his reply is appended.

Letter from the Author to Dr. ———.

REV. AND DEAR SIR,—Suppose the two gentlemen referred to in this letter had come to you with this statement:

We believe in Jesus Christ as the Lord of faith and practice, and feel obligated to obey his teachings. One of his commands is that we acknowledge our belief and obligations by the rites of baptism and the Eucharist.

But in most churches we can not thus obey Christ, except by professing to believe certain doctrines that we do not believe, and also by professing to be regenerate in a sense we can not accept as true of ourselves.

On examining the forms to be used for Baptism, Confirmation, and the Eucharist in the Episcopal Church, we find we can with good conscience adopt them, and we wish to obey Christ in these ordinances.

Upon this you inquire if they put the same interpretation on these forms that you do, and they reply, "We find no authority in the Liturgy, or constitution, or canons of the Episcopal Church for any church officer thus to interfere in this matter, and we deem it a question between God and our own consciences alone. We are ready to hear your opinions on the matter, and to receive your instruction in public and private; but on several points of faith we are not ready to set forth our creed to any person."

Would you feel justified in excluding from church ordinances such men, with such characters and such views?

Suppose, again, that one of them should say, as some dear friends of mine of the highest moral worth might do, "The Bible, *as interpreted by you and most Christian ministers,* I can not accept as the *authoritative* guide in faith and practice. I do not believe in the Trinity, or the Atonement, or infant depravity, as you and the clergy interpret the Bible.

"But I can accept the Creed used in the Episcopal Church, for I find no such doctrines there. I wish to obey Christ by professing faith in him as my Lord and Master, by the appointed rites of baptism and the Eucharist, and can use the required forms in good faith. I am ready to hear all your instructions, and do not expect to controvert your opinions, or lessen your influence by disseminating mine."

Would you be justified in excluding from baptism and the Eucharist for such statements?

Extract from the Reply to the foregoing.

"As to the first supposed case, I should *not* feel justified in excluding such men from the ordinances of our church, though I should feel bound to set before them very distinctly *my* view of the position they would assume before the world, as being supposed to accept the well-known Trinitarian faith of the church which they propose to enter.

"As to the second case, also, I should *not* feel justified in excluding even such a man, proposing, as he is supposed to do, not to enter our church for the purpose of holding, defending, and disseminating anti-Trinitarian views, but for that of conforming to the usages of our church, with a willingness to hear and consider her teachings. As in the other case, I should feel bound to impress on him *my* views of the position he would assume before the world.

"If, with a full understanding of my views, such a man were still willing to enter our church, holding these and connected points as matters of conscience between himself and God, I should not feel bound, nor even justified, in excluding him from church ordinances. Moreover, if I saw, from conversation and acquaintance with him, that he was really and truly seeking after fuller light, and desirous of finding rest in the real verities of Christianity, instead of being a prejudiced and captious fault-finder with old forms of faith, I certainly should receive and treat him with great tenderness and affection, and be particularly careful not to put any needless obstacles or stumbling-blocks in his way."

The following is from an Episcopal bishop, who criticised the proofs of the above letter:

"I like *the drift* of this letter so much that I wish you could make it more unexceptionable in its phraseology. You say 'every regular worshiper in a local Episcopal Church is already a member of that church.' This statement will be strongly objected to by almost every Episcopalian, inasmuch as the prevalent, or, I may say, the universal opinion is that we become members of the outward church in baptism, as we do of the spiritual church, by becoming partakers of Christ's spirit.

"It is, indeed, a singular anomaly that one may be an *officer* in this church, in one sense of the word—that is, a warden or vestry-man, and also a *representative* in Convention, in many dioceses, without being baptized or ever receiving the communion. How to reconcile all this I do not pretend to know.

"I feel that you are doing a grand work, and one that *touches the centre of things*."

I would ask this respected friend and my fellow-Christians of the Episcopal Church to consider these *definitions*, sanctioned by universal use, as shown in our dictionaries:

"*A Christian*—1. One who *believes* in Christ's religion; 2. One who *professes* to believe it; 3. One who by family and country is *supposed* to believe it; 4. One who so believes it as to *obey* its precepts."

Thus there is an *intellectual* faith, a *professed* faith, a *supposed* faith, and a *living* or *true* faith.

Now what I claim is that the Puritan Church is an attempt to organize the *invisible church* as those having *true* faith, so as to make men *judges* of Christian character, and that no such attempted organization exists in the Episcopal denomination. This all must acknowledge.

The question then is, Does the *local* Episcopal Church consist *only* of those who have professed faith by *baptism*, or does it also include all who profess faith by a *stated attendance* in a worshiping congregation?

I do not regard the question as one of much *practical* consequence, inasmuch as all the parish are supposed to be baptized in infancy. It is conceded that it is not required of a man to be baptized, confirmed, or to receive the Eucharist in order to be either a voter or an officer in a local Episcopal Church. Nor is there any such body in that denomination as corresponds with "the church" in distinction from "the parish" in the Congregational, Baptist, and Methodist denominations.

The same may be said of the local Presbyterian churches, *if they obeyed their rules and standards*, which always assume that the whole "congregation" is the *church*, and recognize no other church.

The attempt to organize the *invisible* church, now so common, never was made till the time of the Puritans.

In regard to what is said on the subject of the Creed and Trinitarian views, the following is offered for consideration:

Dr. Beecher taught that there are three Divine Persons, each having all the attributes of the Supreme Divinity—all three as distinct from each other as Peter, James, and John, yet mysteriously united as one God.

Dr. Bushnell teaches that there is one Divine Mind, and that the Trinity consists in the diverse relations and manifestations of this one mind.

Dr. Channing teaches that the Father alone has

all the attributes of Supreme Divinity; that Christ is God in another sense; and that the Holy Spirit is not a distinct divine person.

The Swedenborgian teaches that Christ is the Supreme Divinity, and that the Father and Holy Spirit are names of the same person in diverse relations and manifestations.

But the Creed required in the Episcopal Church at baptism and confirmation expresses belief only in these *facts*—in the Creator as "*the Father;*" in Christ as "our Lord;" in the New Testament history of his birth, death, resurrection, and his future judgment of the living and the dead; in the Holy Ghost; in the universal church; in the communion of saints, the forgiveness of sins, the resurrection of the body, and the life everlasting.

Here, it will be seen, there is no attempt to settle the Trinitarian question, but each one is left free to accept either of the above theories; nor is there a single article of this Creed which is not held in common by all Christian sects.

Supposing, then, a minister *should* set forth his particular view of the Trinity, and state that this is the view usually taught in the Episcopal Church, and that it will be *inferred* that all who are communicants will be *supposed* to hold this view, this surely imposes no special obligation, except, it may be, to state a contrary view, or to say that no definite opinion has been formed on the subject. A great excellence of the Episcopal Church is the *perfect liberty of conscience* afforded to all the laity, and the *greater* liberty afforded to its clergy than is permitted in any other Christian denomination whose local churches are organized as one body.

Any one unacquainted with the Constitution and Canons of this church will be surprised to find how strict are the constitutional rules that restrain bishops from abuse of power, and how much less power a bishop has than the unregulated *majorities* in many other denominations.

From the Author to a Mother.

MY DEAR FRIEND,—You ask why I have joined the Episcopal Church, and also why, in doing so, I was *confirmed.* The first question you will find answered in the proof-sheets I send with this. As to the rite of confirmation, I regard it, in reference to one of my character and circumstances, simply as a courteous compliance with the religious rules of the Christian family I enter, which there is no proper cause for refusing. On the same principle, were I a minister of another denomination, on entering, I should comply with the rules of this church as to ordination; not because I do, but because I do not deem any particular form very important, and so could conscientiously yield to the customs of the Christian community I should enter.

In reflecting on my own course in this matter, and also on the religious condition of your dear children, I am led to present, for your and their consideration, some reasons for their following my example.

Your children now are in a false position; one which does them injustice, and makes a false impression on them and on others, which is injurious to their feelings and to their character.

In your religious community they have been trained to feel that those who *profess* religion by "joining a church" are Christians, and those who do not are not Christians. In the Congregational churches the assumption is that young children are not lambs in Christ's fold, but those out of it, whose *natures* must be new created before they can be taken in.

It is true, your family training has not been after this pattern; but the pulpit ministries, the Sunday-school, the religious books for children, the religious conversation of most with whom they associate, all assume this view. Moreover, no one can be acknowledged as a Christian by access to the Lord's Table till church officers have examined as to evidence of regeneration and of belief in the creed of the church. Now your children do not believe in some important parts of the creed of your church, nor do they regard themselves as "regenerated" in the sense demanded by your church rules and customs.

Meantime, they see among their associates who are members of the church persons with all sorts of faults, from many of which they themselves are free. These are regarded as "regenerated," fitted for heaven, "lights of the world," the "salt of the earth," looking on others out of the church as sinners, destitute of religious principle, and on the way to hell.

The influence of all this is to throw them into an unconscious and almost resentful antagonism with their Christian friends, which has a repelling influence on both sides. No friend who is "a professor" can address them on the subject without an implied assumption of superiority, or as a reprover or adviser.

Now, in the Episcopal Church, all children are assumed to be young Christians—lambs of the fold to be trained to a *higher* Christian life. All regular worshipers and their children are *in* the church, and entitled to all its privileges on using the appointed forms.

What, then, is confirmation in this church? It is the child assuming the obligations taken by sponsors in its behalf at baptism.

And what is promised at baptism? Not that the sponsors will positively make the child a true spiritual Christian, but that they will see that it is trained to believe the Christian religion, and use other appointed means for the purpose of securing this end by the help of God. At confirmation, the children assume the same obligations; that is, that they will use the appointed means for becoming true spiritual Christians, with the hope and purpose of securing this end by God's help.

Thus "joining the church" in the Congregational denomination is being examined and voted into a close corporation as already true Christians and fitted for heaven. In the Episcopal form all children are *in* the church, and confirmation is a public acknowledgment of their obligations, and their desire and purpose to fulfill them in future by God's help.

True faith in Christ, or to be " a true Christian," involves, in the first place, the educational belief in Jesus Christ as Lord of our faith and practice, which sponsors can properly promise to secure.

Whoever has this faith has begun to be a true Christian, or taken the first step. Next comes the receiving and understanding of Christ's teachings. This also may be secured by educational training. Lastly, and chiefly, is *obedience* to Christ's teachings in *purpose*, *feelings*, and *conduct*. The union of all these makes a true spiritual Christian.

But to "feel and act right" and to "obey Christ" are the same thing, so that whoever is habitually trying to feel and act right is really trying to obey Christ, though the purpose may not be conceived of in that form of expression.

Your children are in the position that thousands of the best Christians are now in, who read the Bible, and hear religious teachings concealed in theological theories that veil the character of God and Christ in darkness, or present it in hideous distortions. Owing to this, all that *emotive* part of religious experience, which is usually sought as the chief evidence of piety, is chilled or destroyed. This was my experience for years, and would have continued so through life, had not these false and cruel theories been thrust aside.

Your children are habitually trying to feel and act right, as much so as most of those who are counted good Christians in every sense. Had they been brought up in the English Church, under such training as you have given, they would have grown up consistent and happy Christians from infancy. I know large families in the Episcopal Church where the parents will tell you that they never knew a time from the cradle when each child, according to its measure of mental development, was not a loving and obedient follower of Christ.

What I now would urge is that you influence your children to join the Episcopal Church, not as converted, regenerated saints, as understood in the Congregational sense, but as persons desiring *to be good*, and seeking the ministries of Christ's religion for this end.

Let them commence the outward acknowledgment of their religious obligations, and their wish and purpose to fulfill them, by the rite of confirmation, and they will feel relieved from all those fretting repellancies that now surround them, and, under more favorable influences, will come out into "the glorious light and liberty of the children of God."

One other point I offer for consideration. To complete a happy Christian character, *veneration*, *devotion*, and *personal love* to the Savior need to be developed, and these also are the result, more or less, of *training*. In the Episcopal Church these elements are *systematically cultivated.* When our Savior gave the Lord's Prayer—for all ages and conditions—he knew that the ignorant and the young could neither understand nor feel half of the sublime and comprehensive truths included in it. We are obliged to begin with *forms* adapted to a higher life than we possess, and by their aid we gradually rise to the spirit which should fill them. The Episcopal Liturgy is based on this principle. It is adapted to the highest stages of Christian life. The young and ignorant are trained to use it when they can neither understand nor feel much that their lips utter. But as years pass, the spiritual element is developed by this and other culture, till, in due time, the heart feels what the lips utter.

When we take those ancient forms, hallowed by so many beautiful and venerable associations—when *we ourselves* speak in our own ears such glorious words of love, devotion, penitence, and thanksgiving, we are taking the surest mode of calling forth and cultivating these beautiful and happifying elements of Christian character.

Through my past life, among my maternal relatives, I have been a frequent attendant on the Episcopal form of worship, but never joined in it except as Congregationalists ordinarily do. The effect of the change, when I began to take part in the responsive service, was very delightful and elevating, and I became a worshiper at church as I never was before. How singular that those sects which demand an emotive experience as the chief evidence of regeneration should have relinquished all the ritual forms most calculated to develop such an experience!

But you may say, "My husband's feelings and his connection with the Congregational denomination are such that I see not how I can go myself, or send my children to the Episcopal Church."

If this is an insurmountable difficulty, I would urge another course. Your minister is a truly good man, and the chief desire of his heart is for the salvation of his flock. Go to him with your difficulties, and ask him if he can not contrive some way to take your lambs into the fold. I have known several mothers in the Congregational denomination who have made this plea to their pastor: "Several of my children are as dutiful and conscientious as most adult 'professors.' They wish to be true Christians, and to obey all Christ's teachings, and yet they dare not come out before the 'examining committee' of the church, nor stand up in public profession, to be gazed at as among the converted saints. Can you not so arrange it that they may come into your church privately as those who *wish* to become true spiritual Christians, and are willing to use all the appropriate means of religious training? And if any of them feel that Christ's command, 'This do in remembrance of me,' is obligatory, can not this ordinance be allowed to my children without forsaking your ministry?"

The preceding letter, in modified forms, has been sent to several friends. The following is a specimen of some of the happy results of the course suggested:

"What a comfort it is to have *all* my children united in religious sympathy! I have never ceased to bless the day when they were confirmed in the Episcopal Church. It has been to them that *gradual education and progression* which they and I hoped for; and I see, every year, how the services and prayers *gain* on them more and more. One of them said to me the other day, that whatever care or trouble she might have when she entered the church, all fell away from her there, and she always came away happy. The *comfort* of it is every thing to her, and I see a steady progress in them all. I know not how to be thankful enough. All cares are light now these heavier cares are lifted."

The author disclaims any invidious comparison as to the *general* results of religious training in the Episcopal Church. The theory of infant depravity has developed its evil tendencies in this as well as in other denominations, especially in undue reliance on church ordinances, perhaps as injurious as undue reliance in other churches on sudden conversions and "revivals."

The distinctive advantage of the Episcopal Church

is that young children are regarded as *young Christians* already in the church, and in a course of gradual training to a higher spiritual life. Whenever, therefore, a parent pursues the methods of early training indicated in this work, all the influences of *the church* are adapted to encourage and aid.

But churches that exclude children as aliens, or enemies of God, till re-created, exert an influence disastrous and discouraging to both parents and children.

From the Author to some young Friends after their Confirmation.

MY DEAR CHILDREN,—I fear I shall not be able to join you on Easter Sunday, not from want of interest, but from fear of an excess of it beyond my physical strength. Let me comfort myself for the disappointment by sending you some words of encouragement and sympathy that I hope will aid you in "the ways of pleasantness" which you have entered.

Our blessed Lord describes his service as "a yoke" and "a burden," and yet declares it to be "easy" and "light," and what will give "rest to the soul." There is nothing more important to your success than a clear understanding of this, not only in its general form, but in specific applications.

In its most general sense, the yoke and burden of Christ is a daily effort to cease to live for self-gratification, and to take *happiness-making** for others as the chief aim, guided not by our own estimates, but by the teachings of Jesus Christ. He, our Great Exemplar, lived "not to please himself," but to instruct, comfort, and save others. This is the easy yoke and the light burden that brings rest to the soul.

* "Blessed are the peace-makers" would be more accurately translated "Blessed are the *happiness-makers*, for they are the children of God."

We are to do this, not by any great act of self-sacrifice, not by any sudden transformation of our "nature" by some mysterious new creating process, but by a daily, patient, persevering "bearing of the cross"—the crossing of our own desires for mere selfish good, and the sacrificing of them for the higher good of others. This is the general statement. Now for some of the specifics.

We are to follow Christ, not by stepping into some new sphere, but by first learning to bear our cross in the position we are in at the present time. We are to deny self, and make happiness for others in the every-day life around us. We are not to try to please every body in any way and every way we can devise, but we are to do it in the *best* and right way, and for this we need a higher wisdom than our own, even that which cometh from above.

What, then, are some of the daily crosses and self-denials we are to bear? Of course not what we like to do, but those things which are contrary to our tastes. When a person pleases us by agreeable qualities, or by kindness or favors of any kind, we have no chance to follow our Lord. "If ye do good to them that do good to you, what thank have ye, for sinners also do even the same. Do good and lend, hoping for nothing again, and ye shall be the children of the Highest." We follow Christ in bearing the cross, then, when we do not the things which we like, as pleasing to self alone, but things we do not like that do good to others.

God has placed us in the family state for this very end, that we may begin on a small scale, and learn by degrees this difficult lesson. We are to live for the best good of a small family, as Christ lived for the large family of this whole world.

Let us, then, take each member of the family where you are, and inquire wherein you can deny self and take up the cross; and in so doing we shall find that the Bible supplies us with rules for every case.

To begin with the eldest, we have one command that meets this case exactly: "Bear ye one another's burdens, and so fulfill the law of Christ." The burdens of the aged are many, and God preserves them alive when often they wish to die, for the very purpose of cultivating the Christian graces of those around them. They are weak in body, and we must lend our strength to do for them what they cease to be able to do for themselves. Their eyes fail, and we must read for them. Their hearing fails, and cuts them off from social enjoyments, unless we talk with them, not for our own gratification, but for theirs. Their body fails from disease or decay; their mind becomes weak, and perhaps gloomy and suspicious; their resources for enjoyment fail, and this tends to make them peevish and discontented.

All this is seen by the Good Shepherd, who cares most for the feeble of his flock. And so the Bible abounds with directions for securing honor, tenderness, and care for the hoary head. It would be a good exercise, if your patience should fail in such duties, to collect all the texts in the Bible on this subject.

I can not, in so small a space, enter on the specific duties of each family relation, but I must not omit, what is so often forgotten, our obligations to those often the humblest and weakest members of the household, the denizens of the kitchen. How often, especially in our great cities, do we find those who, as to mental development, are Christ's "little ones," in dark and comfortless rooms by day and night, while the chief aim of employers seems to be to get as much work out of them with as little pay as possible.*

If you had a dear little sister stolen from you in early childhood, and heard that, neglected and ignorant, she was toiling in such a family, what would

* The Catholic clergy are commanded to instruct their people not to join in Protestant worship in families, or to receive the Protestant Bible or books; but, as a compensation, they provide the Catholic Bible, and have prepared some most excellent reading for family servants. I wish all Protestant ministers and heads of families would examine the little work "*Guide to Catholic Young Women*," published by D. & J. Sadlier, New York, and give it to their Catholic servants, and then try to find one as good for Protestants.

be your feelings and conduct should she be returned to her home? But are not all in your household Christ's children, and does he not feel most tenderly and most anxiously for those who have been most neglected? Remember this when you go to your kitchen; seek the confidence and good-will of those who have no home, and no parental tenderness and care. Give them kind sympathy; try what you can do by furnishing suitable reading—by kind instruction, by patient forbearance; and daily seek to raise these children of God to a higher life. And remember those encouraging words of our Lord: "Inasmuch as ye did it unto the least of one of these, ye have done it unto me."

To you, my dear ———, I must be very brief.

The question you propose seems to amount to this: Shall you go to Europe, and seek enjoyment for self, or shall you go to ———, and find happiness in imparting good to others. I will not now advise as to this specific case, but rather give you some general views as principles to guide.

We are to live through eternal ages in a system in which the *only* true way for each one to find happiness is to make happiness for *others* as the chief end.

God is *training* us in this life for this career. Our first lesson is to learn by experience what makes self happiest, in order to learn what will make others so; then, in the family, we learn to make happiness for those we love, and in many ways to sacrifice self for the best good of the family. Some go through this family training petted and indulged, growing more and more devoted to self-happiness, and yet getting less and less. Others, by this training, are so prepared that they can advance another step, so as to be made happy in seeking the best good of those they do not love—the ignorant—the disagreeable—the neglected out of the family.

It is here that we begin to rise more entirely from the earthly to the heavenly; to become fellow-laborers with our Lord, who came "not to please himself," but to do good to "the evil and unthankful."

To make sacrifices for one's children, for family friends, for those we love, for those who please us by agreeable qualities—this is what even the heathen will do. It is only the followers of Christ who have learned "to do good hoping for nothing again," except that highest "joy" for which our Lord "endured the cross"—the joy of blessing and saving the poor, and miserable, and lost.

The highest sphere of all is for those who have not only a given development of natural and cultivated benevolence, but who also have a compass of intellect and an executive power that enables them to work on general principles, and on a larger scale than the family or neighborhood.

It is such who are to stand highest in the scale of being and of happiness, often even in this life—still more in the world to come. Such are to be "kings and priests."

Knowing your private history, your high position, and your grade of talent, I have often thought that Providence may be training you for such a sphere—a training that almost always includes *previous suffering.*

Still, as I see no immediate call to any other position than the one you now occupy, it is very probable that a visit to Europe, *if it does not injure you,* will prepare you for higher ministries. A year spent in a round of mere self-qualification is a dangerous preliminary to a career of self-sacrificing benevolence; but some can meet it safely, and, if so, it is a preparation for a higher sphere.

Do not think I would in all this assume that you will not marry, or advise you not to do so; that is the lot in which most women will be both the happiest and most useful. It is the lot most women would desire and prefer; for the happiness of the higher sphere none can understand or appreciate till they have been developed for it. But it is as much higher and nobler as wedded bliss excels the tiny joys of childhood; for the nearer we approach to God in character and action, the happier we are.

To a Congregational Clergyman.

MY DEAR SIR,—You say that you agree with the published views of my brother, as set forth in his sermons in the *Independent.*

This being true, you do not hold to a depraved nature of infants transmitted from Adam,* nor to the theories of atonement, divine influence, and regeneration that are based upon this doctrine.

But "the Puritan Church," which is founded on these theories, and must stand or fall with them, you *appear* before men to uphold, when in conviction you have relinquished it. You invite to the Lord's Table as fellow-Christians all who love our Lord Jesus Christ, and purpose to obey his teachings. This takes in not only Unitarians, Swedenborgians, Catholics, and Quakers, but many who are connected with no religious sect.

Yet still you shut out the lambs of your flock from the Church of Christ, and, so far as example

* "Each faculty, in its proper place, exercising its proper function, is right and good. God neither created *nor preserved* in man a single original faculty whose natural function is wrong. Man's conduct *is* wrong enough; but man's faculties, in *their nature*, all of them are right. Man is sinful enough; but it is *the use* he makes of his faculties, and not the faculties themselves, that make him so. A thief's nature is as good as an honest man's nature," etc.—*Sermon in Independent, Jan.* 7, 1864. *See also the Sermon on the Atonement and Justification, of July* 4, 1861.

goes, you influence others to do the same. It is for these I enter my plea.

My first reason for taking children into the Church is, that the exclusion which turns them away every communion season, and also many of their parents, as not members of Christ's family, revives and perpetuates pernicious impressions and associations which contradict your pulpit teaching. I will give as illustration a case of one I knew in early childhood and in after life.

As a child, this friend was generous, tender, and sympathizing, and possessed keen moral sensibilities. When only four or five years old, I narrated to her the tale of the Babes in the Wood, which threw her into an agony of indignation at the cruel uncle, and of sorrow for the suffering babes. Afterward, if I proposed to tell this, or any similar tale of wrong and suffering, she would always make her escape, and never listen.

When about eight years old, she resided some months with a cousin of the same age, where, in the street, were seen neglected and ignorant young children. She influenced her cousin to join her in teaching them in a daily school of an hour or two, and in after years she told me that every day she prayed to Jesus Christ to aid her, with the fullest confidence that her prayers were heard and answered.

Soon after this, a Methodist servant told the child

that her parents were Calvinists, who believed that all children were born "under God's wrath and curse," and, unless they were elected and converted, would go to hell, and be burning in a fire forever. To verify this, the Westminster Catechism was shown which was taught in her father's church.

She shrank from this horrible tale as she did from the story of the Babes in the Wood, and, for fear it was true, never told her parents what she suffered. From that time her religious faith and trust failed. The only thing that ever helped her, through after years of spiritual distress, was the feeling that *if* one so kind and good as Jesus Christ *was* God, he would somehow make all these dreadful things come right.

This is only one of many cases that have come to my knowledge of the mournful ponderings of young children over such terrible theories, while often they dare not reveal their distress, nor show the causes of changes in feeling and character that reach through life. Are not such sufferers those of whom their kind Savior said,

"Take heed that ye despise not these little ones; whoso shall offend one of these little ones which believe in me, it were better for him that a millstone were hanged about his neck, and he were drowned in the depths of the sea?"

Now what I urge is that the division of your parish into church and congregation, which on every communion season openly exiles children from the family of Christ, is based on this very theory, that children are born "under God's wrath and curse"—depraved creatures, that must be new-created before they can be lambs in Christ's fold. You may yourself oppose and controvert this opinion, but, so long as you continue the very organization made to sustain this doctrine, your acts nullify your words.

It is true, you openly and often declare, when you urge men to join your church, that it is not to profess to be better than other men, but rather that it is a profession of weakness and sinfulness that seeks the sustaining influences of church associations, and brotherly watch and care. But, if this be the ground of admission to your church, why exclude children, the weakest of all, and those most needing this watch and care? And why claim to be a church in the present Congregational sense when the distinctive thing on which that whole system rests is forsaken? And how are you to meet the charge of evasion and pretense in keeping a name and form, when you have forsaken the thing for which they stand?

When our Savior so strongly remonstrates against all that tends to weaken or injure his "little ones," it is not alone for children in stature that he cared. Many children in families and schools of high culture are more developed in mental powers than most adults in the ignorant and neglected classes.

These neglected ones are those for whose interests the Savior watches with more tenderness than for those more favored. The poor servant-girl in the cold garret and dark kitchen; the toiling unrequited seamstress; the young apprentice; the day-laborer—such are those whom Christ bore on his heart when in his parting message, as the chief evidence of love to him, he enjoined, "Feed my lambs."

It is in this relation that I ask you to look at another cause of "offense" to Christ's little ones. It is impossible for you to eradicate the long-established impression that your "church," in distinction from your "congregation," are persons whom God has regenerated by a new creation of their nature. The special duty of Congregational Church officers is to examine and decide who give proper evidence of regeneration and of belief in a given mode of interpreting the Bible, called a creed. All the texts of the Bible addressed to Christians are considered as belonging to church members, and not to those out of the church. The minister also addresses his church as a holy nation, a peculiar people on the road to heaven, while those out of it are regarded as impenitent, and not fitted for heaven. Thus it is that "the church" stand before these weaker children of Christ as true Christians.

In my office as an educator I often had under my training many commencing a new religious life, while my aim was to give them the highest standard, even that of Christ and his apostles. I endeavored to train them to a life of self-sacrificing devotion to the salvation of their fellow-men as the *chief concern* and the *future business* of life. But they "joined the Church," some in one place and some in another, and soon they found church and church officers living by a very different standard. And yet minister and all assumed themselves to be the peculiar people of God, and on the way to heaven. How, then, could these "little ones" lift up a standard higher than minister and church? It was vain to hope it, and so my labor was mostly in vain. Had there been no organized church of persons examined and pronounced regenerate, then *the Bible* would have been the only standard, and this would have drawn them upward instead of downward.

But there is still another heavier cause of offense against Christ's little ones. It is the rule and duty of the Congregational Church to cut off from its body those who cease to give evidence of regeneration, and of belief in the given creed. In your own church, if a man is openly a drunkard, your church officers, I suppose, would have him excommunicated.

But if a man is penurious, selfish, hard in dealings with his dependents; or if a man is proud, ambitious, and unscrupulous in his aims, no such discipline can be practiced. If a woman of high position is a gossip and tale-bearer, or one whose veracity no one trusts, no church discipline reaches her. If a man of wealth and influence is unjust and overbearing; if he fails dishonorably, runs down his own paper in the market, and then buys it up himself; if a man lives in wealth and splendor while his debts are unpaid, no church action can touch him. For I have heard you say from the pulpit that it is impossible to bring the business matters of the mercantile world into church investigations.

And so it is that children, and servants, and the humbler classes hear church members discussed as exhibiting all these disgraceful traits and actions, and yet ministers and church officers are vouchers that they are "the regenerate." And when the failings of church members are discovered, it is very common to say that we must judge charitably, and hope, in spite of all this, that they are still of those who are born again, and this, too, when no repentance, confession, and reformation are perceived.

All this directly tends not only to perplex and confuse, but to lower the Christian standard; nay, more, it tends to direct immorality, especially in the weak and unreflecting. "If Christians can do such things and be fit to go to heaven, where is the great harm in others doing the same things? It may be, some time, God will regenerate us also, and then it will be as easy to repent of a good many sins as of a few." I have repeatedly been told by my friends that those often were the early reasonings of childhood.

These things being so, is it strange that we find in the *Independent* a respected Calvinistic minister say that, in his observation, the majority of young children who undertake to live a religious life make a failure? So Dr. A. Alexander, of Princeton, says: "I can not remember one solitary instance of decided piety in childhood, when the child lived to adult age, to prove the genuineness of the change."

I present these considerations to you, not to induce you to find refuge, as I have done, in the Episcopal Church—not but that I think you would find more true religious liberty in that church than in any other—not that I do not believe you would find it easier and pleasanter to work in that communion—but there is a harder service opening before you; one that, I trust, will tax your highest mental powers and wisest practical skill.

The system of slavery is drawing to a close in our nation, and you have been one of the foremost champions in working its overthrow. And now there is another more fatal slavery to be assailed—entwined in the consciences of good men, and upheld by the chief religious organizations of the Christian world.

It was to escape this slavery that the noble John Robinson led his flock to Holland, and then sent them forth to lay the first foundations of this nation. And this is recorded as his parting counsel:

"He charged us before God and his blessed angels to follow him no farther than he followed Christ; for he was very confident the Lord had more light and truth to break forth from his holy Word."

Thus he instructed every man *to interpret the Bible for himself*, and not be held in bondage by minister or creeds. Furthermore,

"He bewailed the state and condition of the Reformed Churches, who would go no farther than the instruments of their reformation. As, for example, the Lutherans could not be drawn to go beyond what Luther saw; for, whatever part of God's will He had farther imparted to Calvin, they will rather die than embrace it. So also the Calvinists, they stick where he left them."—"For it is not possible that the Christian world should come so lately out of such thick anti-Christian darkness, and that full perfection of knowledge should break forth at once."

This slavery, which our fathers came to this land to escape, is now upon us. The 2000 non-conformist ministers driven from their homes and pulpits in Old England were no more enslaved by king and bishops than are the clergy of this nation by creeds and confessions of faith. What minister, professor, president of a college, or editor of a religious periodical would not be instantly ejected from his home and profession should he openly interpret the Bible contrary to the creed of the sect to which he belongs?

In our theological seminaries, if a young man attempts freedom of discussion, he is marked as dangerous, advised to desist or to leave; and if he does leave, it is with a mark of suspicion impeding license and settlement.

Albert Barnes sat silenced under his pulpit a whole year, till he could prove to a majority that he agreed with the Westminster Confession of Faith. My father was tried three times, at the peril of reputation, profession, and livelihood, till he could satisfy an ecclesiastical majority that he agreed with that creed.

One of my brothers was forced to resign a Western college, founded and flourishing under his presidency, because he held that infants sinned *before* Adam instead of *in* Adam.

Another brother, for the same shade of deviation, was tortured and tried, till his "parish," resenting the persecution of a faithful and successful pastor, took the case from "the Church" into their own hands, making salary and profession safe in spite of clerical interferences.

And my editorial brother is saved from the same experience only by the conviction that his parish could and would sustain him by the same method.

You, like these my brothers, are surrounded by an intelligent and liberty-loving parish, and to you and them, and especially to your people, I desire to present these inquiries:

Is it not the first principle of Congregationalism,

as established by our Puritan ancestors, that it is *the people* who are to be the interpreters of the Bible, each man for himself, responsible to none but God and his own conscience?

Was it not the grand aim of the first Pilgrim fathers to establish churches in which *the people*, aided by their minister, should study the true meaning of the Bible as their *only* creed, and not be conscience-bound by the interpretations of any man or body of men whatever?

Were not all the children of the Pilgrim fathers, at whatever age, regarded as in the church with their parents?

Has not the attempt to divide congregations of believers in the Christian religion into two separate organizations, as "regenerate and unregenerate," proved a failure, so that "the churches" thus organized out of parishes are confessedly made up of both "chaff and wheat" as really as those parishes where no such organization exists?

In the Episcopal Church, and originally in the Presbyterian Church, there has been no such separate organizations. The church and the congregation are the same, all entitled to have their children baptized, and the children entitled to church privileges after a given age and amount of instruction, provided there is no "evil living." On this plan, every person in the parish is responsible to no one but God and his own conscience as to interpreting the Bible, and as to obedience to its teachings. Can there be perfect religious liberty on any other plan than this?

Is the "professing religion" and "confessing Christ before men" at the present day at all what it was originally? To confess that Christ was Lord in the primitive times involved shame and the loss of all things, but now to believe in Christ is honorable, and to be an infidel is a disgrace; and yet men are led to suppose that joining a Puritan church is "professing Christ" as the early Christians were required to do.

Instead of this, history teaches that the grand point of contest between the Roman government and the Christians was *assembling to worship*. It was not being a Christian in private that subjected to bonds, imprisonment, and death, but it was the joining a Christian congregation as a worshiper.

Suppose your whole congregation were to meet you once a week to discuss this topic, and also the solemn questions proposed in Chapter xvii. of this volume, each one searching the Scriptures for himself, and then all discussing all with their minister as guide and moderator, would not this method come nearer to accomplishing the great ends for which our Pilgrim fathers established this nation than any of the religious meetings now maintained?

Were you and the young ministers in your vicinity to take this course with your congregations, and publish the results, would it not be the opening of a new era in religious liberty?

The Christian world, as it seems to me, are now at a dead stand, very much like a ship under full sail suddenly becalmed.

Two generations ago, President Edwards attacked the dead torpidity induced by the doctrine of man's depravity of nature so "total" that there is no power of *any* kind to turn to God and work righteousness, or even "to prepare himself thereto." With his theory of "*moral* ability" by which man *can* (though, owing to his depraved nature, he *never will*) turn to God, a new mode of preaching obligation and danger arose, attended by revivals, by the first enthusiasm of foreign missions, and by faith in the near advent of the Millennium, to be secured by increasing revivals in heathen as well as Christian lands.

But that glow of hope and enthusiasm has gone. Revivals do not increase as was predicted, and missions do not succeed so as even to meet the increase of heathen population; and the "doctrinal preaching" which prevailed in my father's day has ceased because the people will not hear it; and our young ministers, though they go through theological seminaries, are obliged to reject the systems taught there as what they can not use with their people, while they are all afloat as to any other.

It seems to me this emergency is to be met by

a return to faith in *the Bible as our only creed*, and faith in *the people* as its authorized interpreters.

Moreover, there have been claims made for the Bible that can not be sustained, and there are better and stronger claims for its authority yet to be developed that will give this blessed Word new power and dignity.*

And the people, aided by their ministers, are to learn to study the true claims of the Bible, and to interpret it for themselves, in bondage neither to creed, minister, or ecclesiastical authority of any kind.

That the world is advancing in intellectual and moral development; that all sects are to cast off the shackles of past errors; that infallibility belongs to no man or body of men; that one generation is to learn wisdom by the mistakes of their predecessors; that every man is in error and ignorance *somewhere*, and is to learn wisdom by past mistakes, and that we are to forsake and protest against error and wrong—these are current and commonplace truisms.

And yet practically to recognize these truths in our own individual case is a difficult matter, and often involves the heaviest sacrifices. Luther felt this when he faced the powers and wisdom of the

* A work soon to be issued, entitled "*The Bible: what it is, and how to use it; by Prof. C. E. Stowe*," will more fully illustrate the views of the writer on this point.

whole Christian world. John Robinson and John Wesley felt it when they set themselves against the Church in which they were born, and most of the wisest and best men of their age.

A similar career is open before you, and with advantages such as none of those noble confessors enjoyed. You have a wealthy, intelligent congregation, who will sustain you in all your righteous aims. You have the spirit of the age to sustain you. You have the opening day of our new-born national career, when, delivered from the chains of a hateful system of wrong, our country is to illustrate to all the people of the earth that "*righteousness* exalteth a nation."

In what way you are to work out the grand problem before you can be foreshown only by Him who is leading us all by paths we can not understand.

The terrible earthquake that has shaken our nation has evolved benevolent energies that, when peace comes, are to seek new fields of moral conquest. A *revival of religion* is before us on a glorious scale; not in mysterious interpositions to new-create minds ruined in Adam, but to secure self-sacrificing *educators*, to train myriads of the ignorant and neglected "little ones" scattered all over the earth, whom the Great Shepherd is seeking, by the instrumentality of his followers, to gather into his heavenly fold.

NOTES.

Note A, page 49.

This example exhibits the difficulty that meets every educator who assumes that young children, taught to believe in Christ as Lord, and in a course of training to understand and obey his teachings, are *young Christians*. If the writer, in this case, had told the child she was already a Christian, the parents would have felt that there was an improper intrusion upon their family religious training. It was necessary, therefore, to accommodate to the circumstances, and teach the child how to *begin* to be a Christian.

Had the child been trained in the family of such as Dr. Arnold, of the English Church, she could have been addressed as a young and very imperfect Christian, and urged to higher aims and a more perfect imitation of her Savior.

Note B, page 345.

The author of the *Conflict of Ages* claims that he does not hold to a *mystical* union with God; nor to a "grace" without which, even in its normal state, the mind is incomplete and dead; nor to the outflow of holy emotions and desires from the constitution independently of the will and main purpose; nor to the nature of holy love as a mere emotion; nor to regeneration as produced by an operation on the faculties and not by the truth.

These statements are not disputed.

The writer, in her *Appeal to the People*, claims that the common people have a clear and complete system of mental philosophy of their own, expressed in common language, and easy to be understood. It is claimed also that this system is recognized and adopted in the Bible, and that it is coincident with reason and common sense. This system takes the mind of man *as it is* in this life.

But theologians teach that God created all minds on another pattern, which they call the normal and perfect pattern. This they attempt to describe, while, at the same time, they are obliged to adopt the common system of mental philosophy also. This is one of the causes of the fact illustrated in the thirty-second chapter of the *Appeal to the People*, where, by quotations, it is shown that on this subject even the most acute and honest theologians *contradict themselves.*

It is owing to this fact that it is impossible to state the views of theologians to their satisfaction. For, if we take some of their statements, they deny the depravity of infant minds, and, if we take others, they affirm it.

Therefore, on this subject, the writer does not claim that she gives the views of Augustine, or of her brother, or of any theologian *correctly.* All that she claims is to give the impression made on her own mind by the language used by a writer, at the same time allowing that it is probable that a directly opposite opinion can be found in the same work. So, also, in stating the views of a *class* of theologians, there are always individual exceptions in certain details.

But the main question is one of *facts,* and not of systems of mental philosophy, which all depend on facts, *which must be proved by proper evidence.*

The question of mental philosophy, therefore, should be waived till the *facts* on which all depends are settled, viz.:

1. Were the minds of the first created angels diverse from those of infants, and on the normal and perfect pattern?

2. Are infant minds diverse from what God created them, and diverse from the normal pattern?

The opinions of Augustine, as stated in this work, were taken from standard Church histories almost verbatim.

The author designed to append in a note extracts from the decrees of the Council of Trent. But she has no hope of satisfying any Catholic friend that she or any Protestant understands and interprets them aright, or does justice to the Catholic system of theology. The most she can hope is that she may have the credit of having honestly and fairly tried to do so.

It is very certain that it is not in the power of human language to form a creed which will not be interpreted in exactly contradictory senses. Thus we see the Thirty-nine Articles to be Calvinistic in form, as approved by Calvin himself, and yet held with an Arminian interpretation. So the deorees of the Council of Trent, though Augustinian in form, are Pelagian in interpretation.

☞ "*The Author's standing address is Hartford, Conn.*"

THE END.

Dr. Spring's Sermons.

PULPIT MINISTRATIONS;

OR,

SABBATH READINGS.

A SERIES OF DISCOURSES ON CHRISTIAN DOCTRINE AND DUTY.

BY REV. GARDINER SPRING, D.D.,

Pastor of the Brick Presbyterian Church in the City of New York.

WITH PORTRAIT.

2 vols. 8vo, Cloth, $6 00.

From the NEW YORK OBSERVER, *June* 16*th*, 1864.

The venerable Dr. Spring has given to the press (Harper & Brothers) two octavo volumes, including his choicest, richest, most spiritual, edifying, and permanently valuable sermons, those masterly, devotional, and instructive discourses, which have made his church a house of worship and religious improvement through two generations in this great, restless, changing city. Their peculiar excellence consists in a happy unfolding of the deep things of divine truth, bringing out the marrow of the Word of God, with an amount of that undefinable virtue in preaching called *unction*, which brings the speaker and hearer into holy sympathy. This virtue does not lie in the tones or manner of the preacher. It is in the words his heart prompts him to speak. Dr. Spring always had this grace, and it has rendered his ministry a blessing to successive congregations.

In these volumes, entitled Pulpit Ministrations, or Sabbath Readings, the author has arranged those productions which his own judgment has approved as the most edifying and best fitted to be popular in the family, conveying his maturest thoughts and most finished illustrations of divine truth. There must be many who have sat under his pulpit, and many whose fathers and mothers sat under it, who will receive these books as a precious legacy from one whose words of holy counsel they have been accustomed to receive with reverent affection. And we anticipate from these sermons extensive and permanent usefulness; for they are not ephemeral, but exhibit truths that will be as dear to God's people and useful to the Church in the Millennium as they are now.

PUBLISHED BY HARPER & BROTHERS, FRANKLIN SQUARE, NEW YORK.

☞ Sent by Mail, postage pre-paid, on receipt of $6 00.

It is a work of real historical value, the result of accurate criticism, written in a liberal spirit, and from first to last deeply interesting.—*Athenæum.*

The style is excellent, clear, vivid, eloquent; and the industry with which original sources have been investigated, and through which new light has been shed over perplexed incidents and characters, entitles Mr. Motley to a high rank in the literature of an age peculiarly rich in history.—*North British Review.*

It abounds in new information, and, as a first work, commands a very cordial recognition, not merely of the promise it gives, but of the extent and importance of the labor actually performed on it.—*London Examiner.*

Mr. Motley's "History" is a work of which any country might be proud.—*Press* (London).

Mr. Motley's History will be a standard book of reference in historical literature.—*London Literary Gazette.*

Mr. Motley has searched the whole range of historical documents necessary to the composition of his work.—*London Leader.*

This is really a great work. It belongs to the class of books in which we range our Grotes, Milmans, Merivales, and Macaulays, as the glories of English literature in the department of history. * * * Mr. Motley's gifts as a historical writer are among the highest and rarest.—*Nonconformist* (London).

Mr. Motley's volumes will well repay perusal. * * * For his learning, his liberal tone, and his generous enthusiasm, we heartily commend him, and bid him good speed for the remainer of his interesting and heroic narrative.—*Saturday Review.*

The story is a noble one, and is worthily treated. * * * Mr. Motley has had the patience to unravel, with unfailing perseverance, the thousand intricate plots of the adversaries of the Prince of Orange; but the details and the literal extracts which he has derived from original documents, and transferred to his pages, give a truthful color and a picturesque effect, which are especially charming.—*London Daily News.*

M. Lothrop Motley dans son magnifique tableau de la formation de notre République.—G. GROEN VAN PRINSTERER.

Our accomplished countryman, Mr. J. Lothrop Motley, who, during the last five years, for the better prosecution of his labors, has established his residence in the neighborhood of the scenes of his narrative. No one acquainted with the fine powers of mind possessed by this scholar, and the earnestness with which he has devoted himself to the task, can doubt that he will do full justice to his important but difficult subject.—W. H. PRESCOTT.

The production of such a work as this astonishes, while it gratifies the pride of the American reader.—*N. Y. Observer.*

The "Rise of the Dutch Republic" at once, and by acclamation, takes its place by the "Decline and Fall of the Roman Empire," as a work which, whether for research, substance, or style, will never be superseded.—*N. Y. Albion.*

A work upon which all who read the English language may congratulate themselves.—*New Yorker Handels Zeitung.*

Mr. Motley's place is now (alluding to this book) with Hallam and Lord Mahon, Alison and Macaulay in the Old Country, and with Washington Irving, Prescott, and Bancroft in this.—*N. Y. Times.*

THE authority, in the English tongue, for the history of the period and people to which it refers.—*N. Y. Courier and Enquirer.*

This work at once places the author on the list of American historians which has been so signally illustrated by the names of Irving, Prescott, Bancroft, and Hildreth.—*Boston Times.*

The work is a noble one, and a most desirable acquisition to our historical literature.—*Mobile Advertiser.*

Such a work is an honor to its author, to his country, and to the age in which it was written.—*Ohio Farmer.*

Published by HARPER & BROTHERS,
Franklin Square, New York.

HARPER & BROTHERS will send the above Work by Mail (postage paid (for any distance in the United States under 3000 miles), on receipt of the Money.

Harper's Catalogue.

A Descriptive Catalogue and Trade List of Harper & Brothers' Publications may be obtained gratuitously on application to the Publishers personally, or by letter inclosing Five Cents. The attention of gentlemen, in town or country, designing to form Libraries or enrich their literary collections, is respectfully invited to this Catalogue, which will be found to comprise a large proportion of the standard and most esteemed works in English literature—comprehending nearly three thousand volumes—which are offered in most instances at less than one quarter the cost of similar productions in England. To Librarians and others connected with Colleges, Schools, &c., who may not have access to a trustworthy guide in the selection of literary productions, it is believed the Catalogue will prove especially valuable as a manual of reference.

To prevent disappointment, it is suggested that, whenever books can not be obtained through any bookseller or local agent, applications, with remittance, should be addressed direct to the publishers, which will meet with prompt attention.

Harper & Brothers will send their books by mail, postage pre-paid, to any part of the United States, on receipt of the Catalogue price.